Reinventing Democr

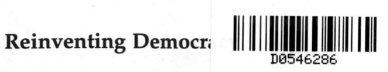

Reinventing Democracy

Edited by

Paul Hirst and Sunil Khilnani

Blackwell Publishers

Copyright © The Political Quarterly Publishing Co. Ltd.

ISBN 0–631–20263–1

First published 1996

Blackwell Publishers
108 Cowley Road, Oxford, OX1 1JF, UK.

and

238 Main Street,
Cambridge, MA. 02142, USA.

British Library Cataloguing in Publication Data
Cataloguing in Publication data applied for

Library of Congress Cataloging in Publication Data
Cataloging in Publication data applied for.

Typeset by Joshua Associates Ltd., Oxford
Printed in Great Britain by BPC-AUP Aberdeen Ltd.

CONTENTS

Introduction 1
PAUL HIRST and SUNIL KHILNANI

Reinventing Democracy? 7
TONY WRIGHT

From Strong Government and Quasi-Government to Strong Democracy 20
STUART WEIR

Democracy and Local Government 39
JOHN STEWART

Dilemmas of Accountability: The Limits of Accounting 57
PETER MILLER

The Implications for Democracy of Computerisation in Government 70
HELEN MARGETTS

Towards Economic Democracy in Britain 85
ROBIN ARCHER

Democracy and Civil Society 97
PAUL HIRST

The Limits of Democracy 117
ANDREW GAMBLE

Democracy and the European Union 132
IAN HARDEN

Three Challenges to Reinventing Democracy 144
BENJAMIN R. BARBER

The Creation of Democracy? 157
ANTHONY BARNETT

Index 177

Introduction

THE idea of democracy is everywhere triumphant today, and yet it stands curiously unguarded and vulnerable. Over the past fifty years, Western supporters of democracy have generally fallen into two broad camps: on the one hand, liberal and conservative advocates of the virtues of representative democracy, who during the Cold War could defend its extant forms in the West against the palpably less attractive systems of the socialist world; and on the other hand, radical critics of representative democracy, yearning for direct democracy in some unrealisable form or other. The end of the Cold War has revealed the severe limitations of each of these positions as a defence of democracy, and it has contributed to making a good deal of post-war democratic theorising (the bulk of it cast in the idioms of representative or radical democracy) appear redundant. The belief that the existing institutions and practices of representative democracy can simply be swept away and replaced by something marvellously better has been shown up for the illusion that it always was. But it is at least equally clear that representative democracy as it exists in Western Europe has grave weaknesses in ensuring the accountability and responsiveness of government to the people. It can hardly be said to represent the highest possible form of human political association. This book is designed to identify some of the most glaring defects of existing forms of representative democracy, and to suggest practical remedies rather than utopian alternatives.

Western democratic theory today can no longer content itself merely with vaunting its ideological prowess against its undemocratic competitors. Government and society are changing, and democracy needs to change too. In recent decades, new forms and practices of government have emerged in the established democracies, and these new developments present real challenges to the democratic idea. Democratic theory must directly face these new developments, just as it must also recognise the ramifying complexity of government today, and consequently it must accept that it cannot only focus on already recognised and studied problems and solutions (for example, electoral reform). Reinventing democracy requires the identification of new areas of public activity that need to be opened up to the democratic idea, as well as the invention of new ways of instituting this idea—as Tony Wright suggests in the opening essay of this volume.

The need for a new agenda of democratic politics, as well as for new vigour in prosecuting it, is very clear in the British case. One of the striking convergences of political opinion in Britain today concerns the ills of democracy in Britain. From intellectuals of the libertarian and liberal Right such as Simon Jenkins and Ferdinand Mount, via Andrew Marr, and on to those on the Left such as Will Hutton and organisations like Charter 88, a consensus

© The Political Quarterly Publishing Co. Ltd. 1996
Published by Blackwell Publishers, 108 Cowley Road, Oxford OX4 1JF, UK and 238 Main Street, Cambridge, MA 02142, USA

has emerged that British democracy is in dire need of reinvigoration and renewal. Until recently these differently accented arguments did not amount to much more than disconnected criticisms. But now one can see a coherent diagnosis emerging. The current collection is designed both to further this diagnosis, and to suggest practical remedies to the problems that are specific to the United Kingdom.

That this critical consensus should appear in the twilight years of a period of Conservative rule ostensibly dedicated to decentralisation and greater popular accountability is perhaps ironic. Indeed, many of the problems identified are the creation of recent policies; but some are long-standing and historically deeply rooted. The concerted drive toward centralisation is one such long-term trend, evident in many modern societies. But it has received spectacular acceleration in Britain over the past twenty years. Arguably the true significance of the period of Conservative government under Mrs Thatcher and her immediate successors lies here. In the name of greater economic efficiency and respect for individual rights, Conservative governments since 1979 have accumulated unprecedented powers for the central government. They have done so by two main means. They have wielded the doctrine of parliamentary sovereignty with dangerous abandon, while simultaneously observing a studied neglect of the constraints imposed upon such powers by the unwritten constitution. Indeed, the Conservatives have treated the unwritten constitution as if it were written in a legalistic spirit: what is not absolutely and expressly forbidden is permitted. They have thus cast away the assumptions of moderation and compromise in policy that are essential if such unwritten conventions are to function. As John Stewart demonstrates in his contribution, the novel powers thus generated have been used to dismantle local government and democracy, and to suck up these powers to central government, leaving a hollow shell of local government.

This destruction of local government is part of a wider corrosion of a range of intermediate institutions which could stand between the individual and political authority. The enormous centralisation and strengthening of the powers of central government which has resulted is not merely open to the charge that it is democratically illegitimate. It is also ineffective. The actual political and economic processes which nation states must try to govern have become vastly more complex and unamenable to control from one central 'brain'. The relevant causalities are no longer controlled by centrally operated levers, and the consequences of such processes affect territories and regions differentially, in ways which central power is unable adequately to respond to or even register.

Faced with this dual process—a centralised state which has cut itself off from society, and actual processes of increasing complexity, which cut across the conventional boundaries of 'state' and 'society'—the standard agencies of political change, political parties, appear increasingly aimless and ineffective. At one level, given high levels of public spending to GDP and a tax-resistant electorate, opposition parties are less able to promise much variation from the patterns of existing policy set by incumbent governments. But perhaps even more significantly in the long run, political parties are themselves drifting away from the society they were designed to represent. They are losing their bases of support in specific and well-defined social constituencies, and this has placed in question their wider representative function and capacity. Classically, political parties were related to elements in their societies by means of a model of social interests. This link today stands all but eroded: the end, for all practical purposes, of the Trade Union and labour movement as the social foundation of the Labour Party, and the inability of the Conservative Party to recruit younger individual members are telling indications of this. The effect of this is that elections confer less legitimacy. Electoral majorities are artefacts, snapshots of public opinion, that rapidly disintegrate under the pressure of unpopular government actions and negative economic performance. Representative government is thus weakened, because its foundations in the wider society are shallower and less stable than they were.

Weaker electoral legitimacy and shallower social roots convert politicians into yet narrower professionals, and reduce their autonomy *vis-à-vis* the machinery of government. This drift by government and political parties away from society has provided an opportunity to the civil service and Whitehall to enhance its own powers. Under the guise of 'administrative modernism', and of claims to greater efficiency and accountability, subjects which fell properly within the domain of political control and public scrutiny have been entrusted to 'experts' supposedly more competent to make decisions. As Stuart Weir's article in this volume makes clear, the past two decades have witnessed the rise of a new form of 'quasi-government', composed of unelected and weakly accountable bodies who have been granted considerable powers.

These developments are symptomatic of a larger shift, which has led to a greater intimacy between government and management. Politicians are now the apex of a managerial class that, whether in the public or the private corporate sector, enjoys greater capacities for top-down control and less countervailing power from organised interests like trade unions than ever before. As Peter Miller shows, control is increasingly exercised through performance indicators. Public accountability is expressed in managerial terms. In this redefinition of accountability, accountancy has become the key profession, which provides the generic skill whereby activities can be measured and evaluated. As Miller points out, the faith that complex activities can be expressed in simple numbers has grown among politicians and managers in the public sector even as the more critical and intellectually aware accountancy academics and professionals are raising the most fundamental doubts about the valid scope of their discipline. If costs cannot be accurately assigned to specific aspects of even moderately complex joint activities in manufacturing, the prospect of doing so in open-ended multivalent public service activities like nursing or teaching will be hopeless.

Without the ability to assign costs and compare them, an entire edifice of control ceases to have real rationality or legitimacy. Politicians are governing blindly through numbers, acting contrary to everyday experience, as with the closure of London hospitals and wards because apparently London had too many beds relative to population.

Helen Margetts' analysis of the government's attempt to embrace and utilise new information technologies is equally critical and challenging. If governing by simple numbers is ineffective, the potential of new technologies is vast. Government *could* be made more consistent, more transparent, and more directly responsive to the citizen. Yet it is unlikely to do so without radical change in ideas, practices, and institutions. To benefit from an open information system, governments will have to surrender a great deal of exclusive control over data and permit far more open access to such data by citizens.

Both the Left and the Right have generally chosen to set democracy and the market in opposition to one another, and have drawn different conclusions about the degree of interference which ought to be allowed between the two. Yet this stark opposition, Andrew Gamble argues, cannot continue to be sustained. In particular, the Left must learn to tame some of its fears about the market, and in doing so, Gamble suggests, it may come to see the market as an institutional order which can be used to sustain democratic government. If the market and democracy can no longer be simply set in opposition to one another, neither he argues can the classical image of inherent economic conflict between labour and capital be sustained. This has ceased to be a valid description of economies such as Britain's. A clear distinction between the two, and the claim that their interests necessarily and invariably conflict, is no longer plausible.

To take only one example, pension funds are an obvious case where the interests of labour and of managers of capital could converge. Capital is increasingly generated from the financial assets of citizens and managed by professionals in financial institutions. Nor is the simple division between public and private sectors now of much help in thinking about the governance of the economy. The activities of firms cut across such divisions, and it follows that ways of trying to make firms accountable have to be specifically tailored to this new situation. The activities of firms have a range of consequences which extend beyond the economic (and which include social, environmental, technological effects), and these in turn affect a broad range of interests. Management structures have accordingly to be designed in ways that recognise this range of interests, and which give them voice at least in decisions which can plausibly be held to directly affect the interests in question. This is also one of the arguments put forward by Robin Archer's paper on economic democracy. The notion of a stakeholder society, if it is not to be mere rhetoric, depends on institutional changes in corporate governance and financial markets that can make both of them more directly accountable to the citizen as worker, consumer, and resident.

4

The boundaries of political, economic, and social processes are shifting, as are the channels of intervention and governance. Politicians almost universally accept the necessity of markets as the main mechanism of economic allocation. However, they continue to think of them in classical nineteenth century terms, when in fact we have an economic system dominated by corporate organisations, not autonomous individual traders, and one in which the divide between public and private sectors has all but dissolved. We are today in what Paul Hirst in his contribution calls a 'post-liberal society', one where the inherited conceptions of institutional frameworks and of the relationships between state and society have ceased to hold. In seeking to devise new instruments of democratic governance, it is perhaps best to move away from the idea of an opposition between state and civil society, where the latter is conceived of as a realm of spontaneous order and natural democratic legitimacy. Issues of governance apply to both sides of this divide. Civil society must itself be ordered, and enabled to constitute itself, and this requires among other things the presence of legal powers of association as well as the creation of mechanisms which enable regulation of such associations by their members.

Underlying the extensive re-drawing of domestic boundaries is, of course, a shift in the scope, both domestic and international, over which the state can claim sovereign power. It is far too premature to declare the 'end of the nation state': nation states are bound to continue to hold important functions, particularly in regard to the regulation of physical movement of human populations. Yet equally clearly, supranational forms of governance are appearing, especially at the European level. These new forms of government have real powers (such as those of taxation), but they are only very tenuously democratic. In its political structure, supranational forms of government such as those associated with the European Union cannot hope to be scaled-up versions of nation states: if nothing else, this hope forgets at its peril the question of identity, and therefore legitimacy. Many people in Europe feel national governments are remote enough, and are quite rationally afraid of effectively unaccountable technocratic institutions of European-wide governance. Ian Harden demonstrates the urgent need for new forms of accountability, and argues that greater flexibility must be allowed to the membership of regional blocs, in particular in allowing member states greater scope to decide for themselves exactly to what they wish to commit their domestic populations.

If the idea of democracy still retains an unsettlingly simple coherence to it, modern democratic theory, on the other hand, can no longer claim to have a single focus or thrust. It is forced to respond to new developments across a range of activities, it must speak to a widening range of issues. In addressing new problems, and in offering specific and practical solutions, it needs to constantly reflect back on its own premises and prejudices, to confront them and justify them anew. This collection ends with such a questioning, in the form of a debate between Benjamin Barber and Anthony Barnett.

Western democratic theory has passed beyond a period of great simplicities, when the ideal of democratic rule could be opposed to autocratic or dictatorial government. What the essays in this collection show is that there is no longer a single form of democracy, nor a single site of democracy (the modern *pnyx*), nor a fixed range of activities to be governed by democratic means. The reinvention of democracy is thus a daunting task; but it is not an impossible one. The goals of democracy remain, as Lincoln stated them, to make government accountable to the people, answerable to the people, and in the interests of the people. If the 'people' has become a more complex category, and if there is no single *demos* (that for European institutions is obviously quite different from that for corporate governance), the undesirability of guardianship, of rule by self-interested and unchallengeable experts, remains as real and simple as ever. Despite all the complexities, democracy still has that simple, essential and critical meaning. And that remains a constant goad to us to reinvent new forms of control and accountability.

Paul Hirst
Sunil Khilnani

Biographical Notes

Sunil Khilnani teaches politics at Birkbeck College, University of London. He is the author of *Arguing Revolution: The Intellectual Left in Postwar France* (Yale, 1993). Member of the *Political Quarterly* editorial board.

Paul Hirst is Professor of Social Theory, Birkbeck College, University of London. Author of *Representative Democracy and its Limits* (1990), *Associative Democracy* (1994) and *The Pluralist Theory of the State—Selected Writings of J. N. Figgis, G. D. H. Cole and H. J. Laski*. Member of *The Political Quarterly* editorial board; deputy chair of Executive of Charter 88.

Reinventing Democracy?

TONY WRIGHT

THE conference from which this volume was spawned was held at Wye. That alone perhaps justifies the question mark in my title. One wag suggested that our next conference should be at Ware. Unlike the Webbs' on the Soviet Union, it is unlikely that this question mark will one day disappear. The desire to 'reinvent' democracy is restless and endless, rooted in the visionary ambition of the idea of self-government, of people ruling themselves; that is at the heart of what democracy is.

A certain modesty of approach is therefore appropriate. Each generation in each place will come to the question afresh, trailing its own historical and ideological baggage. We may all be democrats now, but we may well not talk in the same way or even mean the same thing. It is always useful to recall the cross-national survey conducted by UNESCO after the Second World War that found both universal affirmation of the democratic ideal and widespread uncertainty about the meaning of what was being affirmed. Confusions and ambiguities abound. Democracy is both an achievement of the past and a project for the future. It needs defending, but also extending. These false opposites have been the source of much confusion in the past, not least on the left. It is important to follow the democratic argument where it leads, but this does not remove the need to have a reliable map. It is an argument about power and provides a popular answer to Aristotle's old question about 'who rules'. But to be operative it also has to be disaggregated. We need to know what kinds of power are relevant to it (and which are not); and in terms of what criteria (for example, accountability, participation, representation, and openness) it is being assessed. This process does not dissolve the central self-governing vision of democracy, but it does force us to define the kind of democracy that we want to be visionary about.

So much for the preliminaries. The discussion here now returns closer to home. The modest aim is to make some connections between these wider considerations and aspects of current arguments about democracy in Britain, with an eye on the larger world beyond. I want to identify some issues, get some bearings, ask some questions—and perhaps fly a few kites and even tread on a few toes. There is a real sense in which the democratic argument in Britain now is too easy for those of us on the political left-centre. The purpose here is to try to make it a bit more difficult.

The Clever State

Why is it too easy? Let me suggest two reasons. First, there is a nicely available symmetry in being able to trump the fashionable argument about

© The Political Quarterly Publishing Co. Ltd. 1996
Published by Blackwell Publishers, 108 Cowley Road, Oxford OX4 1JF, UK and 238 Main Street, Cambridge, MA 02142, USA

the 'reinvention' of government (set text from the United States by Osborne and Gaebler, but with the Conservatives in Britain claiming their public service programme as its leading practical edge) with an argument about the real need being to reinvent democracy. Where this latter argument becomes too easy is in its implied suggestion that a reinvented democracy is an alternative to a reinvented government rather than a necessary complement to it. It becomes easier still if what is meant by reinvention is really only a traditional restoration. We need to reinvent *both* the way in which government works *and* the way in which democracy functions—and to do this together as part of the same process.

An instant balance sheet of the Conservative public service programme might conclude, on the positive side, that it has moved the emphasis from those who provide services to those who consume them and that it has opened up new models of service delivery; but also that, on the negative side, it has been transfixed with quasi-market models, has eschewed all collective means of user empowerment and has eroded public accountability to a point where nobody seems to be responsible for anything anymore. Yet the appropriate response from the left is surely not to want simply to return to the world before 1979. Rather it should want to develop its own version of reinvented government. There is a general point of some importance here. It might be expected that those who most believe in using the state to achieve public purposes would also be those who are most active in ensuring that the state achieves such purposes as effectively and efficiently as possible. That was certainly the promise contained in that old Fabian slogan of Measurement and Publicity, a commitment to innovation, evaluation and emulation.

Yet this is not what has happened. Labour has not in the past been much interested in exploring new forms of public service delivery (or new forms of democracy). Its concern with what went in to services in terms of resources was not matched by an equal concern with what came out of services in terms of performance. No doubt there are good and bad reasons for this. But producer capture is not an invention of the right; nor is the recognition that the state (and those who run it) is a powerful special interest group in its own right. If the left's critique of the market is indispensable, then so too is the right's critique of the state. The argument here is that the left needs to know this, precisely because it is most committed to an effectively performing state. So too with the organisation of democracy. The right has identified the blunt infirmities of traditional electoral representation as the rationale for its substitution in a range of areas by an individualised consumer democracy. In its proper dissatisfaction with the latter, the left is too prone to succumb to an uncritical embrace of the former.

What the left should embrace is what I want to call the clever state. The clever state will display a restless ingenuity in devising new forms of government to enable it to perform better; and equal ingenuity in devising new forms of democracy to give practical expression to the promise of self-government. These are not different enterprises, but part of the same project and inherently interconnected. New forms of democracy, in which citizens come to exercise more direct control over the activities of the state, will do more than anything else to ensure that the state serves their interests rather than its own. This may be unsettling to, and resisted by, those interest groups clustered around the state, but this is necessary and unavoidable. Of course the neo-liberal right will insist that the clever state is a chimera: only markets are clever, whereas the state is inherently bureaucratic, unresponsive, self-regarding and self-aggrandising. The left has to prove this wrong, not least because people's willingness to pay taxes for public provision of services will increasingly depend upon their belief in the effectiveness of such provision and in their sense of ownership in relation to its character. The clever state is one which reconnects citizens to it, but this needs to be done in new ways.

One example makes the point. When elected parent governors arrived in schools in the 1980s, they met the hostility of the teacher unions, resentment from many local party machines (especially Labour ones) and suspicion from much of the local educational establishment both inside and outside schools. Yet this citizens' army carried with it the potential to transform the school system for the better, putting parental issues on the agenda and giving parents a greater sense of ownership of schools themselves. It is not surprising (though it seems to have surprised the Conservatives) that governors have emerged as vociferous and informed defenders of their schools against those who would undermine their effectiveness. In the clever state, democracy and efficacy are mutually enhanced.

There is not a single model. Indeed, one of the hallmarks of the clever state is that there is a hugely variegated landscape of organisational forms. The trouble is that the traditional left was not much interested in exploring this landscape, with the result that opportunities were missed and high political prices eventually had to be paid. When A. H. Halsey told the North of England Education Conference in 1977 that schools should become self-managing, old municipal socialism preferred not to listen. The unpopularity of the former nationalised utilities could have been transformed (and their journey into privatisation prevented) if the form of public ownership had been translated into the reality of popular ownership, for example through their conversion into consumer cooperatives. Current issues present similar challenges. The quango state invites an imaginative response that involves something more than either a swap of appointees or a return to traditional forms of public service organisation. The distinction between a commissioning (or contracting) function and a providing function is an important one in thinking about public services and the confusion of these functions has often contributed to a lack of effectiveness. This is true of education, where it would be sensible to divide the role of local education authorities into a contracting authority (for which new forms of democratic representation should be considered, including direct election) and a provider association for schools (with their own form of representation on this body). Again, both democracy and effectiveness would be enhanced. On another front, the current attempts to rethink the welfare state should have as one of their central purposes the construction of welfare institutions that plausibly carry with them some sense of citizen ownership. This is one of the real merits (if not the current reality) of the national insurance principle, which is also why it is worth exploring hypothecated forms of taxation; but it is also a merit of state-sponsored compulsory mutual schemes of the kind advocated in some quarters. The clever state will range widely in its search for appropriate models.

What it will not do is to be content with the traditional position of the left, which preferred to rehearse the familiar antinomies of state and market rather than to explore ways in which the state might be redesigned to improve government and reinvigorate democracy. There was a brief period, in the early part of this century, when there was vigorous and imaginative debate on the British left about alternative forms of democracy that would be required in the developing collectivist state. Between them G. D. H. Cole and R. H. Tawney defined the problem of combining community purpose with self-governing institutions that remains at the centre of the democratic socialist project. Yet for too long this issue was not actively pursued and explored, allowing the right to associate the left with an unreconstructed statism. It is time to renew that earlier debate, not in simplistic, naive or utopian ways but as an essential part of the contemporary task of inventing a clever state.

Terrain, Traditions and Techniques

I turn now, more briefly, to a second reason why the democratic argument is perhaps too easy in Britain at present. It is too easy to convert it simply into the familiar agenda of constitutional reform. That agenda is indispensable. The democratic deficit is so yawning, the need to constitutionalise British government so long overdue, that the running together in the circumstances of Britain now of the wider democratic argument with the narrower focus on the reform of the constitution is almost inevitable. I yield to no one in my enthusiasm to reform the British political system from top to bottom. Its unreformed condition, the product of a particular history and culture, mocks the requirements of a mature democracy and impedes our ability to tackle a range of problems. Yet the fact remains that, so obvious, urgent and available is the reform agenda in this area, that it too easily allows us to make it the universal answer to almost every democratic discontent. And that is, at bottom, an evasion.

Might it not even be a substitute for other agendas that we find more difficult and intractable? Does the new certainty on the left about the centrality of political reform really serve to hide its new uncertainty about so much else? Are we sure that the real issue is not the purpose of government rather than its process? Is there not also an irony in the embrace by the left of an old-fashioned liberal constitutionalism concerned with setting a limiting framework around democratic government? There is enough force in such questions to make it important not simply to duck them. They require hard answers, not easy evasions. Then there remains the toughest question of all: if and when a serious programme of constitutional reform is enacted in Britain, would not the wider problems of a 'reinvented' democracy still remain? The short answer is that they would, for they are general problems of the kind identified earlier. The political reform agenda is local and domestic. Its necessity invites us to make it identical with the larger task of democratic reinvention. That invitation has, sadly, to be rejected.

On this wider front, the prospects can seem thoroughly gloomy. We do not need to buy all the currently fashionable rhetoric of globalism to know that the contemporary world looks an unpromising place if the purpose is to refashion the instruments of collective self-government. If old arguments in support of direct democracy seemed to have been trumped by the problem of size in the big state, then arguments in support of almost any kind of effective democracy can easily seem to have been trumped by the problems of both size and power in the big world. It is a world of big states and big corporations, but it is also a fragmenting world, a post-enlightenment world, a world out of control, a world stalked by forces that threaten much and promise little. Or so it can easily appear. It is a world that invites us to take refuge in an ideology of personal survivalism, or to surf off into a cyberspace of virtual and personal democracy. As we lock our doors we hang out the 'gone surfing' sign. Technological panaceas are not the only responses that fail to convince. We are told that the role of pension funds and insurance companies means that we are now all the owners of the modern economy, but we sense that this is really an invitation to exchange the aspiration to self-government for its chimerical form. Faced with transnational power, we respond by imagining schemes of global governance; but know that this could all too easily be a kind of politics with the people left out. Nearer home, Europe exemplifies the problem. If we want to be cheerful, we have a duty to be gloomy as well.

Let us get some bearings by returning briefly to that core democratic idea of self-government, of people ruling themselves in the classical sense of ruling and being ruled at the same time. This vision was transmuted (and abbreviated) in modern times into the struggle for electoral democracy. Different political traditions responded in different ways to this development. The conservative tradition was hostile, fearful that the untutored masses would subvert order, authority and property, but also coming to understand that a conservative statecraft could find something to its advantage in the new democratic environment (thus Lord Salisbury in 1892: 'The French are always defending their worst proceedings by saying their Chamber won't stand for this and won't stand that. It may be an advantage that we too should be able to flourish an inexorable Chamber in their faces'). Liberals were anxious democrats, happier when democracy had been firmly disciplined as representative democracy (as it was by J. S. Mill) and embedded in a secure framework of constitutionalism. The liberal triumphalism that marked the end of the cold war and collapse of communism felt like a huge historical sigh of relief, a final emancipation from anxiety. Modern neo-liberal conservatism gives a new twist to the story of course, in which democracy is again seen as a problem—the carrier of inflationary expectations and a standing invitation to monetary indiscipline and a bloated state—requiring robust management. If some liberal conservatives have wanted to circumscribe such proclivities constitutionally (Hayek, for example), others have been content to manage them politically.

All this is shorthand, of course; but the broad lines of the picture are clear enough. And what of socialism? The short answer is that socialists have both embraced political democracy and wanted to go 'beyond' it into the more expansive realms of social and economic democracy. A Fabian might believe that political democracy would be the inevitable instrument of a wider democracy, a Marxist might believe that political democracy was a sham without a wider democracy, but all kinds of socialist were interested in that wider democracy of social and economic power. If this was what conservatives and liberals feared, it was what socialists wanted and (at least for a long time) expected. This had a number of consequences, one of which only will be mentioned here. It meant that socialists were not much inclined to explore political democracy itself, preferring to move it on to other things. In Britain this had a further consequence of some significance. As Sam Beer argued a generation ago in his *Modern British Politics*, the combination of a socialist tradition that saw democracy as the instrument of state collectivism and a conservative tradition that domesticated democracy in terms of its own Tory paternalism left little space for other and more active versions of democratic self-government. It was a powerful and suffocating combination. Its effects are writ large across the face of British politics and British society. Democracy became the name for the condition of being governed.

It is against this background, both general and local, that any process of democratic reinvention has to be conducted. Unless we are content to watch the further erosion of democracy's role as the legitimating basis of government in the West (and the evidence suggests that such erosion is marked and accelerating), we would do well to devote some thought and energy to how this role can be reinvigorated. In this sense the reassertion of an active understanding of self-government is not merely an exercise in political theory but an urgent and practical task for the times. What matters is not to argue for one reading of democracy against others but to nourish a reading that can speak to the times. If people come to feel that they are able to exercise ever less power over the forces that control their lives, no amount of democratic rhetoric will be able to fill the gap of credibility and legitimacy that is opened up. At best this will produce a sullen and cynical indifference, at worst something much nastier.

So what is to be done? There is no blueprint available. Different political traditions have their insights to offer. It is right to see democracy as the means of majoritarian action, but it is also right to see it as needing a framework of constitutional limitations in the interests of pluralistic liberty (which Bobbio refers to as 'this constant dialectical interplay between liberalism and democracy'). It is right to see electoral and political democracy as fundamental, but it is also right to want to apply the democratic principle to other centres of power. The emphasis of the democratic enterprise will also necessarily be shaped by the circumstances of time and place. Thus the main emphasis here is on Britain, although the connections go much wider. In seeking to reinvent democracy, we need to focus both on the *terrain* and *techniques* of democracy. The question to be asked is whether we can extend its terrain and improve on its techniques. The rest of this chapter offers some brief reflections on both of these fronts.

The Responsible Society

In wanting to open up new democratic terrain, the core justificatory principle is that major arenas of social, economic and political power—power over people's lives and power that shapes the life of society itself—should be harnessed to a doctrine of democratic responsibility. This is a responsibility that acknowledges a framework of obligations and accountabilities, recognises a range of legitimate stakeholders and seeks ways in which these stakeholders can have an effective voice. An approach of this kind will not be impressed by attempts to construct iron walls between 'public' and 'private' centres of power (for such walls turn out to be remarkably flimsy when closely examined) but will instead want to apply the doctrine of responsibility to both.

There are two clear implications for current political argument in Britain. The first is that the case for political reform should properly be understood (and presented) as one part of a wider argument about the nature of a responsible society. This does not in any way diminish its centrality or urgency, but it does anchor it in a wider democratic argument to which it properly belongs. The need to constitutionalise the British polity is part of a larger need to constitutionalise other terrain too. Irresponsible political power sits alongside irresponsible social and economic power on the reform agenda. Political insecurity connects with social and economic insecurity as the contemporary challenge to be engaged with. The attempt to construct a new politics of rights and responsibilities involves the political system but also includes much else. There is an integrated and interconnecting argument here and its durable strength will come from the extent to which it can be assembled in this way. This meets the second implication of approaching matters from this direction. For what it identifies and throws into sharp relief is the central ideological divide in contemporary British politics. This is between what is essentially a doctrine of irresponsibility on the political right, in which the power of global markets is gleefully mixed with domestic ideological proclivities to sustain a politics which strips away securities, mocks social solidarities and erodes communities. In this new world of market liberalism, the very notion of responsibility is dissolved since it speaks to a relationship between human beings in their social setting that is

13

rejected. They simply have to roll over and take what is coming to them, from forces and powers over which there can be and should be no control. Indeed when they are told that they have to become Asians, they are being told that they have to cease even to be themselves. In advancing a politics of democratic responsibility, the left is able to meet this argument head on and clarify the central political choice of our times.

But where else does it lead? What new democratic terrain does it open up? What are the 'sites' of responsibility and self-government? There is no single or simple answer, nor should there be, but there are several promising directions of advance. There is the pivotal choice to be made between the kinds of capitalism on offer in the world, a choice that is at the centre of the contemporary political battle. The argument for a 'stakeholder' capitalism is important precisely because it is the carrier and expression of a doctrine of responsibility in relation to the organisation of economic power. It stands in stark opposition to a doctrine of market irresponsibility. Arguments about the 'private' governance of corporations should not be divorced from arguments about the 'public' governance of states. One of the unintended effects of the privatisation programme in Britain has been to reveal how inadequate is the public/private distinction in relation to the privatised utilities and how unbalanced is any conception of the shareholder as the only legitimate stakeholder. If the policy task in relation to these industries is to develop a conception of the public interest company in the private sector, or to convert them into mutual or cooperative enterprises, the implications of doing this go much wider. Issues of corporate governance are here to stay.

For a long time the old socialist belief in 'economic' democracy was out of fashion, and in some of its versions no doubt deserved to be. Modern exponents of varieties of market and associational socialism build on these older traditions, but even without such visionary excursions there is promising work again to be done. We have learned enough from successful enterprises around the world to know that rigid hierarchies are as bad for companies as they are for states. Teamwork and partnership pay. But they are also right: the world of work should not be an arena of unfreedom in a responsible democracy. It is extraordinary that there are still those who believe that such modest developments as works councils should be regarded as a threat to market prerogatives rather than an opportunity for constructive partnerships. In these matters the state should properly seek to promote democratic virtue, just as it should actively promote and sponsor a variety of forms of ownership including cooperative and self-managing models.

Yet the world of work, so central to traditional socialist thinking on the application of democracy, is only one site (and for many not the most important) where a politics of democratic responsibility and self-government now becomes a serious project. The rich and dense fabric of associational life out of which the labour movement was born—the world of co-operatives, trade unions, mutual and friendly societies, clubs and chapels—has to be reinvented in modern form. If this sounds like compulsory voluntarism then perhaps it is. We desperately need some new little platoons, just as we need some new forms of civic collectivism. A world in which the individual stands alone in the face of the big state and the big corporation, at the mercy of bureaucrats and markets, is not a world in which the civic virtues will flourish.

The trends may not seem promising. The movement from voluntarism into state provision is familiar, but it is supplemented by another movement from mutualism to markets (as with the building societies). Yet on all sides the need to find new ways to reconnect people to civic life is compelling. There is no shortage of sites or opportunities, if we are prepared to devote some energy and imagination to the task. Nor is there an absence of examples of what may be possible, if we are willing to learn from them and build upon them. New forms of neighbourhood and community organisation, animated by dynamic social entrepreneurs, are showing what can be achieved in some of the most desperate inner urban areas. Forging new tools for community self-govern-ment is likely to prove an indispensable part of any durable regeneration strategy in such places. Neighbourhoods, estates, schools, workplaces: this is just the beginning of a list of the sites in which a new politics of democratic responsibility can and should be developed. In framing and re-framing a whole range of institutions and services, the opportunity should always be taken to explore the self-governing options (as with the self-governing pensions corporation in Australia). An empowering state will forever be searching for new ways in which citizens can exercise responsibility for their common life.

A flourishing and active democracy will be immensely variegated both vertically and horizontally, a civic arena of many levels and a rich variety of channels. The desire for uniformity (sometimes misdescribed as a desire for equity) should not be allowed to snuff out democratic diversity. If the terrain of democracy is understood as multi-tiered, then it makes sense to think in terms of the democratic organisation of power at the most appropriate level. Instead of operating with a political equivalent of the 'lump of labour' argument, democracy should properly expand to enable it to follow power where it goes. It needs to flow upwards and outwards, beyond the nation state to Europe and beyond; but it also needs to flow downwards and sideways, into a rich micro-democracy of associational life. The preference should always be for doing things at the lowest level that is efficiently possible. Understood in this way, sovereignty ceases to be a fixed and formal lump to be lost and becomes instead an array of democratic oppor-tunities to be gained.

If we turn from terrain to techniques, there is also an abundance of democratic possibilities waiting to be explored. There is a good deal of intellectual vitality on this front currently, aimed at enhancing those demo-cratic components of representation, accountability, participation and open-ness. A quick trawl would include on-line information flows, the postal voting experiment in Oregon, the development of deliberative polling techniques, the establishment of citizens' juries to consider public policy issues and (as in New Zealand) new opportunities for citizen-initiated referendums. It is not necessary to embrace all such techniques with indiscriminate enthusiasm to acknowledge that traditional forms of representative democracy may not be the last word in democratic development.

Indeed what is remarkable is how undeveloped democratic forms have remained in the face of the enormous growth in both public and private concentrations of power during the twentieth century. It is almost as though we have been operating with a settled mental assumption that democracy had been 'achieved' at that moment in the past when mass enfranchisement had been secured. Yet democracy is properly seen as a continuous process not merely as an occasional event. If its bottom line is the ability of people to kick their rulers out, it should also include ample opportunities for kicking them while they are in. One study comparing elected and non-elected members of assorted public bodies threw up the alarming conclusion that, while those who were not elected worried away at being representative and accountable, the elected members simply assumed that the fact of election had absolved them from any need to worry about such matters. Yet it clearly does not. Walt Whitman's phrase about the 'never-ending audacity of elected persons' remains a text for our times.

Doing Democracy Differently

An equal audacity is now needed in devising new and supplementary democratic techniques. It is not possible here to do more than fire off a few suggestions, in the British context, about possible lines of advance. One indispensable task is to ensure that our central democratic institutions work better than they do now. These institutions are basic and vital, whatever we may wish to supplement them with, and they need to be in good working order. Yet they are conspicuously not. Parliament is nothing short of a scandal in this respect, its unreformed condition making a mockery of the functions of representation and accountability it is supposed to perform. It needs a fundamental procedural revolution to make it less a poodle of the executive and more a robust democratic creature in its own right. The key reforms that are needed are well understood and much rehearsed—above all in relation to the legislative process—but this simply serves to highlight Parliament's blind refusal to take reform seriously. Yet the fact is that any wider process of democratic reform will count for nothing unless our central representative assembly is itself reformed.

A similar argument can be made about local government. It is crucial to restore and renew the role of our key local representative institutions, for they express our common civic life and are the carriers of our public purposes. They have been grievously eroded by the recent onslaught on them and it is therefore a proper task to restore their constitutional integrity on a more secure basis. However, what is improper is to make an unquestioned coupling of 'local government' with 'local democracy', for the need and opportunity for new democratic techniques is even greater at the local level than at the national. This is true of electoral reform, that pivotal innovation in democratic technique as far as Britain is concerned, for it is in local government that one-party states are able to stay in power (at least in normal times) courtesy of an electoral system that guarantees their permanence. However, local electoral reform needs to be seen alongside a range of other reforms to the workings of local government (of the kind identified recently in the report of the Commission for Local Democracy). On electoral reform in general, three points may be added. First, as Labour's Plant Committee argued impress-ively, it is ludicrous to get hooked on a particular voting system. It is horses for courses. Second, notwithstanding the above, those systems which enhance civic participation and promote citizen choice should be preferred to those which do not. And, third, it may be necessary to move to the kind of pluralist politics that would be delivered by electoral reform before it is possible to secure the radical institutional reforms described earlier.

But improvements in democratic technique do not stop at such alterations to the way in which our major democratic institutions work. A wide and exciting range of mechanisms are available, some at least of which are being actively explored in different contexts, whereby citizens may contribute to the democratic process in ways which enhance and supplement the traditional forms of representative democracy. Some of these are discussed elsewhere in this volume. There is no single model, nor should there be; but there is a repertoire of techniques available for exploration and development.

A quick list, in the context of Britain, might include the following. New forms of both territorial and functional representation (with a reconstituted House of Lords as an ideal place to start). An escape from the belief that election and appointment in their traditional forms exhaust the range of representative possibilities. The reform of the quango state provides an opportunity to develop new forms of representation and accountability appropriate to particular services and functions. It may even be possible, and desirable, to explore contexts in which lot or random selection (some-times described as statistical representation) would cease to be merely a classical democratic memory and become an innovative democratic presence. The putative public service consumerism of the citizen's charter programme would become less a charter for managers (a description conceded by William Waldegrave when he was its guardian) and more a real charter for citizen consumers, with secure and enforceable individual rights (with means of redress) in combination with new collective mechanisms of user empower-ment. User councils could be developed for all public services, not just for those without an elective basis (the rationale for Community Health Councils in relation to the NHS) and constituted in a variety of innovative ways. New forms of partnership between lay and professional voices in service provision and evaluation should be developed (as in advocacy schemes and locality planning). User groups will be strengthened, and unrealistic expectations about continuous citizen participation avoided, if they are serviced wherever possible by a nucleus of professional support. The technique of citizens' juries (as with deliberative polling) should be developed as a regular and expected part of the decision making and planning process wherever it has a role to play. Not the least of its merits, which may commend it even to those whose main priority is not to extend democracy, is that it may serve to prevent the planning process being dominated by special interest groups claiming to speak for the public.

Then there is the referendum, the potential of which has yet to be explored seriously in Britain, where the act of decision clarifies and disciplines choices in a way that ersatz devices do not. We should start worrying a lot less about whether referendums are compatible with the sovereignty of Parliament and begin thinking seriously about what they may add to democratic legitimacy. This is as true at the European level (why not a pan-European referendum on further integration?) as it is at the national (why not a referendum on the current proposal that British Summer Time should be extended for example?), while the scope for local referendum is even greater. Local people in local areas could decide whether they wanted a comprehensive or selective system of schooling for example, while the ceaseless struggle between the centre and local authorities over spending levels could be decided by means of local referendums if councils wished to spend (and tax) above a standard level. There will no doubt be argument over the particular examples, but what is not in doubt is the availability of an array of techniques—of which the referendum is only one—capable of nourishing the democratic process in innovative ways.

One final point of a more general kind. We live in an age of deep uncertainties. Old structures and paradigms (not least ideological ones) disintegrate in front of our eyes. Democratic politics is the means whereby we have to define new common purposes and translate them into collective choices, but it has to be a kind of democratic politics that engages openly and honestly with this new world. This has radical implications for the practice of politics, especially so in Britain. The kind of politics that merely trades in false certainties, closed cultures and rival dogmatisms is wholly inappropriate in a world charged with the task of thinking and acting its way through the challenges it now faces. Politics is a struggle of powers, interests and ideas; but it also needs to be a process of mutual learning. Pluralism is a kind of politics that diffuses power and shares political territory; but also has to signify a vigorous and deliberate plurality of ideas and opinions from which political learning can take place. This means a new approach to both the structures and culture of politics. Reinventing democracy now means reinventing politics too.

Biographical Note

Tony Wright is Member of Parliament for Cannock and Burntwood and joint editor of *The Political Quarterly*. Author of several books including *Citizens and Subjects* (Routledge, 1993) and *Socialisms: Old and New* (Routledge, 1996).

From Strong Government and Quasi-Government to Strong Democracy[1]

STUART WEIR

SOME matters are too important to be left to the ordinary run of cabinet ministers and MPs. Trace this intellectual view back to its origins and Plato will surely loom large. Robert Dahl's *Controlling Nuclear Weapons*[2] points out that Plato's idea that the best possible form of government is rule by an insulated 'guardian' class has by no means withered away in liberal democracies. Moreover, decisions in certain major policy areas—decisions with immense consequences for the lives of everyone in these societies—have been created, kept or left as what Dahl terms 'guardianship enclaves'. In these enclaves normal arrangements for democratic accountability are deemed null and void. Instead, decision-making is entrusted to groups of specialists, technicians or professionals, acting largely in secret and constrained only by the most general constraints of remote scrutiny by directly elected political figures. Historically, defence, the military and civil nuclear industry and the intelligence services have been the most extreme instances of guardianship enclaves in Britain and the United States.

Dahl argues that these enclaves will constantly recur in new forms in liberal democracies. They are unlikely to be special features of a particular period (such as the Cold War, the dominance of the new right, or a Labour government). Each period or circumstance will typically call forth a new example of how the lure of guardianship can override or severely circumscribe 'normal' representative politics. The temptation lies deeper than the particular concerns of any one period. Plato's *Republic* captured a key set of solutions to problems of making collective decisions, which recurs in different forms under liberal democracy.

In contemporary Britain, there is a chronic temptation for government to resort to 'guardianship' solutions to problems. Quasi-governments, those agencies which have been described in a wide variety of unsatisfactory terms: 'semi-autonomous agencies' (a 1970s term), quangos, non-departmental public bodies (NDPBs), quasigovernmental agencies, extra-governmental organisations (EGOs)[3] form a classic example of partial or near-full guardianship in a host of areas of government advice, policy and action.

I do not have room to sort out here the variety of traditions and arguments which have led to the creation of this realm of quasi-government, which has come about almost entirely unremarked until very recently. Clearly, the tradition of the 'strong' executive and the 19th century ethos of 'guardianship'

 Published by Blackwell Publishers, 108 Cowley Road, Oxford OX4 1JF, UK and 238 Main Street, Cambridge, MA 02142, USA

in the new meritocratic civil service play a significant part in creating the culture of this parallel 'state'. So, too, does the culture of 'informality' in both government and administration. Ministers possess wide discretionary powers through the royal prerogative, to which they can readily add at will through statute and statutory instruments; statutory instruments now issue forth at a rate of more than 3,000 a year, passing almost entirely unchecked through Parliament, some conferring powers which 'very often (ministers) do not know themselves quite what use they intend to make of them',[4] other powers which will later be used for other purposes. The practice continues of reserving important issues to convention, codes, etc., which supposedly, for example, govern the behaviour of ministers, but are yet elastic enough to give ministers considerable discretionary latitude and are liable to be changed or abolished at a Prime Minister's discretion.[5] All of these factors have combined to create a 'quango state' which has 'just growed', rather 'too far', as Lord Howe once confessed to me.

There is a curious intellectual defence of quasi-governments which draws deeply on these wells of British pragmatism, the legacy of an uncodified constitution, and the complacency of traditional British attitudes of effortless superiority in leading a civilised political life. British public administration theorists have been prominent and influential in fostering this stance. In a counter-intuitive 1995 paper, for example, Brian Hogwood denies that there has been any growth of quasi-governments, and portrays a broadly steady-state situation in which this form of government appears as an expedient device for implementing the legitimate governing aims of successive majority parties, raising no serious questions for the structure of constitutional democratic government.[6] His argument rests heavily on the familiar difficulties in even defining quasi-government agencies and organisations in terms of any single official criterion. After considering these problems at considerable length Hogwood concludes:

We may have to accept that an agreed, workable, inclusive and exclusive definition of type of body may not be possible to achieve and that we should be concerned primarily with the extent to which a range of bodies exhibit varying combinations of characteristics with which we may be concerned, and what the implications of these are for policy delivery and accountability. (p. 210)

Alongside this 'intellectual fatalism' there run several modern arguments to justify the growth of quasi-governments: one of them being from modernity itself, another from New Right ideas of the limits of politics. 'Administrative modernism' has always been a philosophy of the big battalions, stressing the newness and uniqueness of the extended state, the breadth of its concerns, the alleged 'complexity' of its decisions, the specialist expertise of its staffs and, above all, the large scale of its operations. Set against the strength of these functional imperatives, adherence to the old or formal codes of representative government may seem obsolete and inefficient, even irrational. Such ideas were drawn up by philosophers in the pre-welfare state era and are poorly adapted to contemporary realities. Instead, electoral controls are seen as important strategic elements in the operations of the state apparatus, but only affecting the higher reaches of public decision-making and the overall climate in which government institutions must work. Elections have no place in directly influencing the detail of what the extended state accomplishes.

The political theorist Giovanni Sartori summed up the intellectual justification for guardianship in a form which stressed the importance of scale in changing the nature of political control:

Micro-democracies can still be conceived in *input*, that is as a demo-power. But macro-democracies are best conceived and furthered in *output*, that is, in terms of a demo-distribution. What can still be mightily improved is not the power end of the problem—more power to the people—but its end-result—more equal benefits or less unequal privations to the people . . .[7]

You can find such ideas re-stated in the New Right and public choice literature. In *Arguments from the limits of politics*, for example, Mitchell and Simmons proclaim something of the same theme:

Voting is a painfully limited way to express one's values and preferences. It accomplishes its results only indirectly; the vote does not immediately call forth that which is voted for. In fact, if we vote for something but are in a minority we do not get it at all . . [8]

Compare such arguments with the views of the then minister responsible for the Office of Public Services, William Waldegrave, on 5 July 1993, explaining why a general vote every four or five years cannot possibly give enough information effectively to control policy makers:

The key point is not whether those who run our public services are elected, but whether they are producer-responsive or consumer-responsive. Services are not necessarily made to respond to the public by giving our citizens a democratic voice, and *a distinct and diffuse one at that*, in their make-up. [My italics]

So for government ministers, the quasi-markets of the 'reinvented' public sector constitute a realm of efficient and responsive services for consumers, while orthodox public service delivery systems (especially local government) are dominated by political bias and manipulation. Public services, Waldegrave said, '*can* be made responsive [only] by giving the public choices, or by instituting mechanisms which build in publicly-approved standards and redress when they are not attained'.

In reply to complaints of a 'democratic deficit' in the new quasi-government arrangements for the health service, schools, social housing and many other fields, Waldegrave claimed that the government had in fact created a 'democratic gain' in the management of public services:

We have not in any way altered or undermined the basic structure of public service accountability to Parliament, and hence to individual citizens. But we have made it usable. We have strengthened these formal lines of accountability by making our public services directly accountable to their customers.

And reiterating Sartori, he stressed that public services are there to serve: 'it is the output, the end product, not the internal whys and wherefores, that are of crucial concern' [to citizens]. An elegant epitaph for the idea of elected local government in the United Kingdom—schools, public housing, further education, and much more besides, all are too important to be left to local councillors.

The significance of definition

In a rousing speech to the Labour Party conference in October 1995 Tony Blair declared that 'it is time to sweep away the quango state'. Since he did not define his terms, the declaration is meaningless; if it means what it seems to mean, then it is plain daft—impossibilism no less. It is symptomatic of the mood and understanding of the Party that the pledge won a big cheer.

Definition is a radical art—it is not for nothing that Benjamin Disraeli wrote, 'I hate definitions'. To 'sweep away', abolish or reform the 'quango state', one must first define it. By its very nature, quasi-government in the UK defies definition. The loose terms which we use to describe the variety of quasi-governments which exist demonstrates the absence of any stable statutory and constitutional underpinning for the whole ramshackle apparatus. Government bodies float in and out of 'quangodom', change shape or size, die and sometimes resurrect themselves, sometimes in multiple form.

Just as definition is the key to reform, partisan definition and exaggerated displays of the difficulties of definition can be deployed to deflect or obstruct understanding. Government ministers stick closely to Sir Leo Pliatzky's narrower class of public bodies, NDPBs,[9] which have been reduced in number, to claim that they have shrunk the quango state even while it is expanding (see, for example, HC Deb, 24 February 1994, c464). Brian Hogwood, who delights in the complexities of quasi-government, exaggerates the definitional difficulties to offer his own highly idiosyncratic explanation of why quangos have not grown, which rests heavily on the fact that the nationalised industries and public corporations have shrunk significantly in terms of workers and scale of operations, due to privatisation. The continuing role of public bodies in regulating public utility industries mysteriously fails to be mentioned in his account—as if the post-privatisation blues, the 'fat cats' scandals, water shortages and the vigorous politics of regulation of electricity, water, phone and gas industries had somehow escaped his official categories.

The *relative* importance of quasi-governments *vis-à-vis* democratically controlled administrations is also an issue which escapes Hogwood's attention. The binding of local government, the transfer of functions to non-elected bodies, the politicisation of appointments, the hierarchies of central control of local services, and the proliferation of central powers to command the whole apparatus in the last decade—all these are passed by for a detailed examination of exactly the same single-category data sets that Hogwood's definitional problematising has already declared unreliable or misleading.

The climax of the fatalist view is simply to shrug knowingly, and agree that *plus ça change, plus c'est la même chose*:

Despite the lack of systematic explanations, agreed definitions or long-run data on trends, we can nevertheless safely predict that regardless of any change of government:

There will continue to be a substantial role for non-departmental public bodies, but the bodies which exist at any given time will not necessarily be the same bodies as in previous time periods even if net total do not change much.

Some bodies will be terminated and some new ones set up.

Many existing bodies will be merged or split.

Pamphleteers and academics will intermittently write about the alleged growth of the phenomenon, but will still not be able to define a quango (pp. 224–5).

Thus, the guardianship tendency as manifested in its growing quasi-governmental forms is just a fact of life—no use beefing about it if you're a real political scientist!

Accountability problems and quasi-governments

It never seems to have occurred to Hogwood that it would be possible to depart from official categories, or to combine several possible grounds for classifying bodies, still less to combine both analysis of quantitative data with a qualitative assessment of the political and democratic significance of changes within a principled taxonomy of public bodies of all kinds. Happily, this work is now being undertaken in the course of a project on quangos at the Political Economy Research Centre at Sheffield.

Even the apparently all-embracing official term, 'public bodies', does not provide a universal hold-all for all those organisations which may qualify as quasigovernments. There are no clear criteria for classifying public bodies, and those criteria which do exist reflect the bureaucratic pre-occupations and purposes of Whitehall rather than any intention to render public account. In *EGO TRIP*,[10] we took a controversially wide range of bodies at national and local level and analysed the arrangements for their accountability and openness to the public. Yet, to make the exercise possible, we accepted limitations which a reforming government should not. For example, we excluded utility regulatory bodies, executive agencies, tribunals and public corporations and public bodies of varying status, such as the BBC, ITC, Radio Authority, the Forestry Commission, the Post Office, the Bank of England, the Monopolies and Mergers Commission, etc. Yet their relations with government and accountability to the public raise profound issues for democratic society. Government excludes the BBC and similar bodies, on the grounds that they must be seen to be independent of government, a misleadingly innocent explanation, given the intensity of government interference in both the BBC and ITC in recent years.[11] There is therefore a need for a universal taxonomy of quasi-government of all types, based on an inclusive principle of public service or functions, after which it would be necessary to devise criteria for categorising and classifying bodies to establish a stable and coherent framework for quasi-governments. These criteria would encompass the legal and constitutional status of these bodies, the need for various forms of public accountability and openness and the terms of their relations with central government. The *EGO TRIP* analysis excluded detailed examination of issues of accountability which a reforming government should again take into account in drawing up criteria. For example, there is no general duty in English law that public bodies should give reasons for their decisions, unlike the position in most mature democracies.

The overall point is that to reform the 'quango state', you must also reform the state. The opacity and informality in the British system and the absence of legal rules facilitates and fudges the arrogance of the executive, gives ministers wide and virtually unchecked discretionary power, removes whole areas of policy from political and public debate and scrutiny, encourages patronage and sleaze, and allows the wholesale appropriation of local spending and policy decisions by the centre. Quasi-governments reflect and play a major role in the abuses of power of the extended state.

Accountability and openness in practice

To get a better grip on what the accretion of quasi-governments implies for the democratic quality of the UK's political system, it is worth looking in more detail at a specific aspect of the problem: accountability and openness. There should be a fair measure of agreement, even among those of the Waldegrave persuasion, that numerous quasi-governments could pose difficulties of democratic control if they were incapable of being kept under surveillance by concerned citizens. Even the Major Government has made some significant genuflections towards this idea, for example, declaring that: 'We expect all [public] agencies that serve the public direct to publish a charter or charter standard statement, and to report on performance against it over time' (HC Deb, 6 December 1993, c15). However, agencies which do not serve the public directly (such as the Cabinet Office) are excused from such requirements.

The pyramiding of quasi-governments one on top of another, and the semi-privatised or 'commercial' nature of others, combine to mean that many of them also escape these requirements. Nonetheless, the idea that citizens can only possibly control those bodies about which they have some information is one which the New Right cannot intellectually resist, because information underlies markets as much as it does representative politics. The league tables for schools and hospitals, and (raking back in history) even Margaret Thatcher's first piece of legislation on opening up local government meetings and papers, both testify to the importance of this area, and the extent to which there exists a basis for political agreement on it.

Table 1 presents information for all the recognised and 'unrecognised' national and local executive agencies operating as quasi-governments, together with advisory NDPBs which often possess or influence executive decision-making powers. However we choose to define our focus, and whatever the difficulties involved (*pace* Hogwood), the Table offers substantial insights which are robust and highly unlikely to vary with alternative definitions.

There are three main groups of accountability criteria. The first and most applied one includes requirements for bodies to publish annual reports and annual accounts, and to be audited by the National Audit Office. The first column comprises executive agencies which sit squarely in Hogwood territory—they are recognised NDPBs. Just over half of them meet these criteria.

Table 1 The Openness and Accountability of Quasi-Governments in the UK (1993 & 1994)

	Executive NDPBs	Advisory NDPBs	NHS Bodies	Unrecognised EGOs
1 Required to publish annual reports	201 (56%)	163 (20%)	248 (39%)	1866 (41%)
2 Required to publish annual accounts	191 (53%)	n/a	248 (39%)	4534 (100%)
3 Subject to full audit by the National Audit Office or the Audit Commission	191 (53%)	n/a	629 (100%)	1025 (22%)
4 Under the jurisdiction of the Ombudsman	124 (35%)	n/a	629 (100%)	0
5 Required to observe the Open Government Code of Practice	124 (35%)	0	0	0
6 Public right to inspect a register of members' interests	6 (2%)	0	0	2668 (59%)
7 Public right to attend board or committee meetings	6 (2%)	0	289 (46%)	1701 (38%)
8 Public right to inspect minutes of board meetings	5 (1%)	0	289 (46%)	0
9 Required to hold public meetings	2 (0.5%)	12 (1.5%)	314 ((50%)	105 (2%)
10 Public right to see policy papers or documents for board meetings	0	0	0	0

Note: These figures are derived from the two Democratic Audit reports, *EGO TRIP* and *Behind Closed Doors*. The data for executive bodies are from 1993, and for advisory bodies from 1994.

NHS bodies are all subject to government audit, but less than two in five are required to publish annual reports or accounts. All the 'unrecognised' executive bodies publish annual accounts, but less than half publish annual reports and less than a quarter are subject to government audit. Advisory NDPBs are low-spending appendages of government departments, and so the question of auditing and accounts is not relevant. But while government ministers carelessly assume that they all publish annual reports, only one in five actually do so. Overall, the low level of requirements for bodies merely to publish annual reports and accounts is surprising and disturbing. When I presented these figures to senior civil servants at a public administration conference at Sunningdale, they were at first so surprised and disturbed, that they wanted to dispute the figures.[12]

Recourse to the Ombudsman services and the limited provision of information under the government's Code of Practice for 'open government' are potentially valuable instruments in the hands of interested citizens. Only about a third of executive NDPBs come under the jurisdiction of the Ombudsman or are required to provide official information to citizens. Neither touches any of the other bodies, with the exception of NHS agencies, all of which are subject to the NHS Ombudsman (but not yet to the 'open government' code).

The third group of criteria involve ordinary citizens' ability to find out what the board members' interests are, to ascertain what went on at meetings, what was decided or what arguments were put forward for and against particular courses of action. Virtually no executive NDPBs provide for any such access whatsoever, in stark contrast to the post-Widdicombe rules on local government. Somewhere near half of NHS bodies do give public access, but citizens are not allowed to know anything about the interests of board members. A handful of advisory bodies do in practice voluntarily provide information on members' interests, on their decisions, and so on, but the great majority do not. The comparatively good showing of 'unrecognised' executive bodies on members' interests (60 per cent) is largely thanks to the provision of a register at the Housing Corporation which I found to be out-of-date and incomplete when I tested it personally. The standard quasi-government assumptions are generally that the public has no rights of admittance, consultation or elementary information. Almost no quasi-governments must even hold a single public meeting by law from one year's end to another.

Who wants an accountable quango anyway?

The official response to such figures is to assure us all both that all the 'most important' bodies are fully controlled; and that the topics they are dealing with are all matters such that no ordinary citizen is likely to have any reason to want to find out what they are doing beyond the confines of their annual reports. The government confines its defence to NDPBs and further argues that they are a remarkably diverse set of bodies, and standard measures of

Table 2 Ten Major Bodies' Accountability and Openness Criteria (as listed in Table 1)

	1	2	3	4	5	6	7	8	9	10
Audit Commission	y	y	y	y	y	n	n	n	n	n
Equal Opportunities Commission	y	y	y	y	y	n	n	n	n	n
Funding Agency for Schools	n	n	y	n	n	n	n	n	n	n
Higher Education Funding Council	n	n	y	n	n	n	n	n	n	n
Horticultural Development Council	y	y	y	n	n	n	n	n	n	n
Housing Corporation	y	y	n	y	y	n	n	n	n	n
NHS Supplies Authority	n	n	y	y	y	n	n	n	n	n
National Radiological Protection Board	n	n	y	n	n	n	n	n	n	n
Scottish Enterprise	y	y	y	y	y	n	n	n	n	n
Welsh Development Agency	y	y	y	n	n	n	n	n	n	n

Source: Weir and Hall, *op. cit.* The order of criteria is rearranged from the original here.

accountability and openness are not really appropriate in most cases, like, say, the Imperial War Museum or the Horticultural Development Council. To assist in evaluating the first claim, Table 2 lists how all the criteria in Table 1 apply to ten major executive agencies. Bodies not required to publish annual reports or accounts are FAS, HEFC, the NHS Supplies Authority and the NRPB, while the Housing Corporation is not subject to full NAO scrutiny. Six of the bodies escape the jurisdiction of the Ombudsman and are not subject to the open government code. None of them provide for basic public access in any form.

But why might an ordinary citizen want to know about, say, the Housing Corporation—a body which funnels social housing money to housing associations, but delivers no services directly to citizens, has no Citizen Charter and so on? Quasi-governments inherently make policy issues technical and the Housing Corporation is no exception. Its distribution rules start with a highly complex set of decisions which partition its total budget (covering around £1,200 million in 1994 for the whole of England) between different priorities or needs. Next the partitioned total is distributed across housing associations in different local authority areas by reference to technically-derived 'housing needs indicators', based on a complex regression formula similar to those used for distributing local authority grant. But Housing Corporation staff also have the capability to vary the allocations to particular areas up or down by as much as 20 per cent, so that two neighbouring local authority areas might differ by as much as 40 per cent of the local housing needs indicator basic allocation in the sums that they receive.

Now suppose that our concerned citizen is black, and wishes to explore the impact of Housing Corporation practices on the black community. The Corporation operates a national policy of allocating 13 per cent of its funds to ethnic housing associations. Is this too little? Does it carry through into action at the local level? Does the discretionary implementation of Corporation policies at the regional office level produce any kind of fit between the ethnic make-up of those in housing need and the distribution of funds? Our concerned citizen will simply have no basis for finding out this information, no status in seeking it, and no practicable chance of ever being able to mobilise people around her chosen issue. And that is exactly what most current UK quasi-governmental arrangements are designed to ensure.

Suppose, too, that our concerned citizen is interested in several different issues. Take the Imperial War Museum: surely a body which can safely be left to its own devices? But perhaps she is distressed when visiting the museum by the scarcity of reference to the role of black British Empire troops in fighting fascism during the Second World War. All right then; but what of the innocuous Horticultural Development Council? Perhaps she has a small-holding on which she grows ornamental shrubs for a living. She may very well be required by law to pay an annual levy to the HDC, a body which is not accountable to her or her fellow growers, but to the Agricultural Secretary; she cannot vote for its board members, who are appointed by the minister in consultation with the NFU and other elite organisations (though she does possess a token vote for panel members in her sector of horticulture); and she has no say in the five-yearly review of the HDC's performance and future.[13]

She may believe that her children have been discriminated against in being refused admittance to her local grant maintained school. She may apply to her housing association for a transfer after being abused by one of its staff. Her daughter may have suffered disfiguring effects, or even have died, from using a drug prescribed by her doctor. She may worry about emission standards for Britain's nuclear power plants. In each of these areas—all governed by quasi-governments—she must battle alone, against overwhelming complex and inaccessible bodies, to represent her views, as must every other citizen. To exercise voice options deprived of all the building-up and simplifying institutions of representative government is overwhelmingly complex, creating an inherent bias for inaction and passivity. In public choice terms, the collective action problems which supposedly the New Right set out to cure, are extraordinarily magnified. A completely quangoid state would indeed by a polity where in every sphere of social life specialist elites would have freedom to exploit the ignorance and rational inactivity of citizens.

And it is a stunning deceit for ministers to suggest that a general vote—'a distant and diffuse one at that' (to quote Waldegrave again)—every four or five years can give government ministers and their officials the democratic authority to decide highly specific issues in all significant public services in every part of the country; and that a national Parliament is the proper agent and arena for making government accountable for this local universe of decision-making. Even if the public found such a highly centralised system of accountability desirable, it is anyway a practical impossibility. The charts of seven major departments of state discussed in our earlier work (Weir and Hall, *op. cit.*), and the host of agencies and advisory bodies attached to them, amply demonstrate a vast and complex range of responsibilities that ministers simply cannot begin to oversee and correct.

The myths of parliamentary politics

One of the pleasures of Sunningdale was to hear civil servants crooning the soothing myths of parliamentary democracy in the UK: 'Parliament, in its wisdom, decided . . .', 'Parliament took the view that . . .', and so on. Parliament of course rarely decides anything of importance. For the two founding myths of current arrangements—parliamentary sovereignty and ministerial responsibility to Parliament—substitute (1) executive sovereignty; and (2) mechanisms for ministers and civil servants to evade democratic responsibility. Both hold good, except in the most severe political crises. Yet Waldegrave justifies the vast expansion of quasigovernments on the basis that both myths represent reality.

I am not going to rehearse the tale of parliamentary weakness here.[14] Nor that of the parallel weakness of the courts to intervene, except largely on matters of procedure, by way of judicial review.[15] I would, however, like to spell out the importance of quasi-governments to big governments of this democratic and judicial vacuum, and the unruly state in which the executive operates.

Accentuating the negative

I am now about to 'accentuate the negative'—but I ought also to stress that there is a *positive* aspect to quasi-governments. The complaint ought not to be about their existence, but about the environment in which they operate and, above all, the unmediated power of government to do with them more or less what it will. Government ministers of any political persuasion can invent, or abolish, contract or expand quangos at will. They may even press external bodies, such as housing associations, into HMG's service. They can direct these quasi-governments to carry out their wishes in every locality, through the panoply of discretionary powers of direction and patronage at ministers'—or, more accurately, their departments'—disposal. If all this becomes too much like hard work, they can create bigger strategic quangos to boss smaller quangos, and stuff their boards with people who share their convictions. The smaller, more amenable quangos then replace unpredictable local councils with their counter-claims of local mandates and community ties.

Government has to deal with a wide variety of unpredictable issues: the safety of food and drugs, the risks of pesticides, nuclear power and other hazardous substances, the siting of nuclear waste dumps, and so on. But ministers have at hand a regime of advisory quasi-governments, such as the Committee on Safety of Medicine, or on the Microbiological Safety of Food, to take the flak, test out opinion and, above all, apparently to remove such 'expert' decisions from 'hands-on' government while surreptitiously doing no such thing. A key set of these bodies plays a significant quasi-judicial and mediating role on government's behalf, acting as tribunals on life-and-death decisions which affect us all. But they are safely insulated from public opinion or debate by their professional and specialist nature, though not from the major industries, like the pharmaceutical and processed food industries, which are affected by their decisions. They have influential representatives on the boards as well as access to the civil servants who matter.

These advisory quangos have other uses. There are a host of trade bodies, like the British Overseas Trade Board, on which representatives of big business and big government combine in secret to promote British industrial and trade interests abroad, or major public investment projects at home. These quasi-governments live in the shadows of the state. They are not open to the public gaze or peer review. Formally, behind the parade of independent judgment, they are part of the ministerial advice-giving processes of Whitehall. And advice to ministers is of course so confidential that, if need be, innocent people may be gaoled to protect it. It is a lot for any government, however well-meaning, to give up.

Public views about accountability

What citizens think about quasi-governments is too rarely investigated for there to be any reliable indicators of how public attitudes have evolved over time. However, in the last two years polls have covered people's views, including the two reported here.[16] The 1995 State of the Nation survey for the Joseph Rowntree Reform Trust included a battery of questions on 'quangos', in the general context provided by the Nolan committee's first report. There proved to be a high level of public consensus about the arrangements which should cover local quangos. Our question ran:

'Many important services are now run by "quangos"—boards of people appointed by the Government. I am going to read out a number of statements about how services might be run in future, and for each one could you tell me to what extent you agree or disagree.'

Table 3 shows how people responded. By large majorities, they agreed that quango boards should meet in public, and that legal rules to require balanced composition were needed. There was only fractionally less support for statements requiring parliamentary scrutiny and a general public say in appointments to quasi-government agencies. People seem overwhelmingly to endorse exactly the kind of arrangements which Tables 1 and 2 show are almost completely absent from existing quasi-government agencies' practices. Even on the last question on ministerial powers of patronage, there is a two-to-one majority (50 to 26 per cent) against allowing ministers to 'appoint whoever they think is most suitable'. This is the only question on which there was a substantial minority which accepts the status quo (and which

Table 3 Public attitudes to how 'Quangos' should be run

	Percentage			
	Agree	Disagree	Neither	Net agree
'Quangos should hold their board meetings in public and make all their board papers available to the public, subject to protection of commercial confidentiality and people's privacy'	81	3	17	+78
'There should be clear legal rules to ensure that all quango boards are balanced in their membership'	80	2	17	+78
'All appointments to quangos should be subject to scrutiny by parliamentary committees'	72	7	21	+65
'The general public should have a say in appointing some people to each quango'	71	10	20	+61
'Government ministers should have the right to appoint whoever they think is most suitable to run quangos'	26	50	25	−24

Source: Rowntree/MORI, 'State of the Nation 1995' survey. Details of the question preamble are given in the text.

divided respondents on partisan lines). Overall, current arrangements are clearly out of line with public expectations. These responses should be assessed with the perspective of poll results revealing strong public support for a Freedom of Information Act and a written constitution (both endorsed by four-fifths of respondents, with negligible numbers of opponents).

Another insight into some of the complexities of public opinion about quasi-governments can be gained from a 1994 Channel Four poll on democratic attitudes. We asked one question to test public support for local government rather than the local quango agencies which have become key public service providers, 'Please look at the card and tell me which kind of organisation should run . . .', and then specified six different services. Table 4 shows the results.

Several features stand out. First, the public do not want more quasi-government. Even in policing—a special case—where the principle of appointed bodies received its highest vote (37 per cent), marginally more people favoured 'elective' control (39 per cent). Secondly, the only service for which a convincing majority of respondents opted for local councils to provide was rented housing—given the traditional role of local authorities in public housing, this ought again to be considered a special case. Yet for

Table 4 Who should run certain public services?

SERVICES	Local Councils	Locally elected committee	Committees partially elected & partly appointed	Government appointed committees	Self-appointing committees
Rented houses	65	13	6	5	4
Schools	38	26	13	8	8
Further education	35	18	15	18	7
Health authorities	30	20	18	20	6
Hospitals	27	23	18	16	8
Employing training	30	19	11	24	5
Police forces	24	15	13	37	3

Source: Channel 4 Poll of Democracy, March 1994.

schools, local authorities attracted less than two fifths support. Overall, more than half of respondents favoured elected control by councils or other locally elected bodies for all services, except the police. Yet there is clearly no simple, across-the-board public preference for local authority control. Some people want them to play an all-round role, but others favour specialist elected committees and mixed bodies in sensitive functional areas (like health or policing) where professional independence is valued. The simple idea, common in Labour Party circles, that local services should be 'returned' to local authorities not only fails to deal adequately with the diversity of local quasi-government, but does not measure up to public appreciation of that diversity and their experience of 'remote' local government, out of touch with local people, that previous ICM polls have revealed.[17]

These findings again need to be set in a context provided by other poll responses. When we asked: 'Is Britain a democratic country?' people split 61 per cent 'Yes' and 30 per cent 'No' (compared with a 68/20 split in 1969). And when we asked: 'Is Britain getting more or less democratic', 12 per cent answered 'more', 39 per cent answered 'less', and the vast bulk of the remainder saw no change.

Reforming the 'quango state'

Nearly forty years ago, Mackenzie and Grove could end their discussion of independent public bodies with a comforting quote from Bagehot:

We love independent 'local authorities', little centres of outlying authority. When the metropolitan executive most wishes to act, it cannot effectually because these lesser bodies hesitate, deliberate or even disobey. (p. 446)[18]

More than a century later the little centres are outposts of the extended state, spending billions of pounds of public money with little citizen surveillance, under the tightly-knit control of central departments, their boards and committees hand-picked by ministers to accomplish their purposes without hesitation. We need to face up to the growth of quangoid guardianship, increasing in its absolute and relative importance within the British state. We now know that the system of accountability for quasi-governments has long since become inadequate, fatalist assurances to the contrary, and that the erosion of elected controls and representative politics (at local and national levels) is serious. And we know that the public favour a radical, necessarily a constitutional, overhaul. Above all, the public wants government, ministers and MPs to obey the rules—and to create the rules where they are missing.[19]

There are two basic facts which ought to govern reform. The first is that we need quasi-governments and always will. The second is that even a reformed Parliament is incapable of rendering them all accountable on its own. All governments require agencies to fulfil the multiplicity of functions which have devolved upon the modern state. Britain is not unique in possessing a wide range of quasi-governments; but we are unique in the near total absence of legal structure and rules, administrative coherence and public accountability and openness of quasi-governments. It is also important to recognise that, in certain important respects, it may very well be better to have major functions of government, like the financing and shaping of public housing, done out in the open by a body like a reformed Housing Corporation, rather than in the bowels of the Department of the Environment.

'Abolition' simply wouldn't work, it would peter out fairly shortly after the first sacrificial victims had been despatched—the Funding Agency for Schools, the Polar Medals Advisory Committee—and the shambles would remain, unreformed and unaccountable as ever. Very soon, reform-minded ministers would discover that it is jolly useful to have a handful of new quasi-governments to take the strain at their bidding and extend their powers (for benign purposes, to be sure). From their new offices in Whitehall, Fabian cronies would be drawing up lists of the Great and the Good to run these quangos on behalf of Britain's new masters.

The third basic fact is that radical reform of the state entails reform of the quango state. Freedom of information, a Bill of Rights, devolution, electoral reform, new parliamentary powers, reinvigorated local government with constitutional protection, a written constitution—all the standard reforms would instantly transform relations between both government and quasi-governments and Parliament, the regions, localities and citizens. It is also necessary to abandon the pretence that even a stronger Parliament could adequately oversee the universes of decision-making that take place within the extended state. The changes above would provide new foci for oversight too. But few democratic legal systems are as handicapped by the absence of an active public law as the UK. For quasi-governments and the administration of the state in general, a new regime of public law is urgently required.

To a great extent, this means giving the public what they want: rules of conduct for quasi-governments and public access on the US model to their documents, meetings and decisions. Changes of this kind would revolutionise government in the UK overnight. Given the multiplicity of quasi-governments, however, it is likely that reformers would have to instal at least a two-tier system of public accountability: first, the public law basics and other requirements, such as perhaps a duty to demonstrate exactly how each body has consulted the public or ascertained their views each year, should be put in place for all quasi-governments (with, if necessary, statutory rules for any exceptions). Secondly, the diversity of public bodies demands additional arrangements to satisfy the public interest in the particular roles of many quasi-governments.

The emphasis should be on instituting 'strong democracy'. For example, where quasi-governments operate in a particular area of interest, why not enfranchise or involve the people affected? Thus, horticultural growers could elect the board of the Horticultural Development Council and decide, every five years, whether they want to continue its levy-paid existence. Consumer councils for the utilities could also be elected—ballot forms could be issues with bills—or attached to new national parliaments or regional assemblies, or both, with direct rights of representation to the regulators. Ethnic minorities could be more directly involved in the work of the Commission for Racial Equality. Why not create annual regional conferences for the ethnic minorities, with voting rights for some places on the CRE and statutory 'report back' on issues raised? Indeed, the BBC has a Royal Charter which is intended to signify its 'independence'. As the 1980s made clear, however, determined Prime Ministers and their governments are not necessarily respecters of the convention of independence and the renewal of the Royal Charter became one of the instruments of the government's campaign to curb the BBC's investigative journalism. The survival and renewal of the licence fee was another. The BBC's future was secured in essence by public trust in its ethos and conduct and the institution's own faith in its purpose and culture, accompanied by a fair amount of 'ducking and weaving'.

There is no reason why the basic measures of accountability to the *public* should not apply to institutions like the BBC. But government stewardship has to be confined to financial management and probity, and exercised through non-governmental bodies, like the National Audit Office. To this extent, too, the BBC and other 'arm's length' bodies could be subject to parliamentary scrutiny through select committees. But it is not appropriate for such bodies to be answerable to the overweening executive and a Parliament in its partisan image, nor for them to be vulnerable to the bullying strategies employed by the government in the 1980s. Reform of the patronage system to allow for a truly independent means of appointing governors to such bodies would be one answer. But clearly new means would have to be devised. Bodies like the Royal Fine Art Commission and the Arts Council would have to establish a popular standing and ought not to become merely the personal fiefdoms of their chairpersons. (The RFAC needs also to be un-royalled.)

Local quasi-governments are the subject of another article in this book. But clearly the views of the public have to be taken into account. Local quasi-governments cannot be plunged en masse into local government, even if it is reformed. There is a case for new elected public bodies, probably with 'mixed' boards on which professionals and users have a (carefully defined) place. The professional and user members could themselves be elected representatives. Such boards could be obliged to hold annual open meetings and citizens and users could be given rights of petition. If a given number of either, for example, petition a part-elected, part-cooptive health authority on a particular matter, the authority would be obliged to consider the petition and explain its decision publicly to the petitioners.

If public housing policies and investment became the responsibility of a revamped Housing Corporation, the decision-making could be shared between the central body, regional authorities and its regional offices, and at local level, between the Corporation, local authorities and housing associations. Consultative committees could be established in every local authority area; and tenants' representatives could be elected onto council housing committees and housing association boards. Local authorities and housing associations could be obliged to draw up five-year local housing plans in partnership, to be debated in the consultative committee and negotiated with the Housing Corporation. Again, citizens and users would be given rights of petition.

Britain's host of advisory quasi-government would also benefit from legal rules of disclosure and public access and the release of people-friendly information of all kinds. However, it is not necessary for such bodies to be wholly composed of experts, business representatives and the odd token 'consumer' who owes her or his place to ministerial patronage and is expected neither to act as a 'representative' of any consumer group nor even to make waves. Advisory quasi-governments, above all, require new legal rules to ensure that their composition is balanced and give them independence from sponsoring ministers and departments. Their role should be openly to advise the public, not secretly to advise departments. Further, Denmark has shown that ordinary groups of citizens can decide the most specialist and controversial issues with the aid of advisers, and generally produce conclusions which demonstrate a wider social concern than those produced by experts alone. There can be no argument against expert quangos, reconstituted according to legal rules of 'balance', playing a monitoring role, with special issues being subjected to a citizens' committee.

It is not hard to devise means of democratising the state. The last few paragraphs were the easiest to write (and perhaps it shows). What seems to be hard is for reformers to abandon the critiques of what is wrong and to get down to hard discussion of what needs to be done, not merely to raise Britain's essentially pre-democratic state apparatus to modern standards of liberal democracy, but to transcend those standards and begin to establish a strong participatory democracy in Britain. There is no place for facile optimism here. On democratic practice, we are even further behind Scandinavia, western Europe and countries like Costa Rica than our stale club and national sides are in world football.

Biographical Note

Stuart Weir is Senior Research Fellow at the Human Rights Centre, University of Essex, and Director of the Democratic Audit of the United Kingdom. With Wendy Hall, he is author of EGO-TRIP, a study of executive quangos; Behind Closed Doors on advisory quangos (also a Channel 4 documentary); and a Briefing Paper on National Quangos specially commissioned for the Nolan Committee. The Democratic Audit report on political freedoms in the UK, The Three Pillars of Liberty (Francesca Klug, Keir Starmer and Stuart Weir; Routledge) is published in September, 1996.

Notes

1 This article draws heavily on work already published elsewhere, and I should like to acknowledge several debts: to Anthony Barker, Reader in Government, Essex University, and inventor of the term 'quango'; to Professor John Stewart, University of Birmingham; Wendy Hall, co-author of the Democratic Audit papers, who undertook the arduous task of systematically scrutinising the arrangements for making quasi-governmental agencies and organisations accountable; and to Professor Patrick Dunleavy, London School of Economics.
2 R. Dahl, Controlling Nuclear Weapons, Syracuse, Syracuse University Press, 1985.
3 My own description of the large and fairly diffuse set of executive agencies as 'extra-government organisations', or EGOs, failed to supplant 'quangos' in the media and offended many outside that world. When I came to study advisory NDPBs, I decided not to proceed with my initial nomenclature, 'government advisory bodies', or GABs for short.
4 Henry Knorpel, Speaker's Council, in Minutes of Evidence submitted to the Select Committee on Procedure, HC,350, 1986–7, p. 9.
5 See Sir Robin Butler's comments on Professor Peter Hennessy's inaugural lecture, 'Searching for the Great Ghost', 1 February 1994.
6 Brian Hogwood, 'The "growth" of quangos: evidence and explanations', in E. Ridley and D. Wilson, The Quango Debate, Oxford, OUP, 1995.
7 G. Sartori, 'Will democracy kill democracy? Decision-making by majorities and by committees', Government and Opposition, vol. 10, 1975.
8 W. C. Mitchell and R. T. Simmons, Beyond Politics: markets, welfare and the failure of bureaucracy, Colorado, Westview Press, 1994.
9 L. Pliatzky, Report on Non-Departmental Bodies, Cmnd 7797, HMSO, 1980.
10 S. Weir and W. Hall, EGO TRIP: extra-governmental organisations in the UK and their accountability, Essex University, Charter 88 Trust/Human Rights Centre, 1994.
11 S. Barnett and A. Curry, The Battle for the BBC, London, Autumn Press, 1994; and S. Weir, Bad Timing: political constraints on BBC journalism, Violations Paper No. 23, Charter 88, 1994.

12 The occasion was the Public Administration Committee's 25th Annual Conference, September 1995. The paper was a previous version of this article, 'The State, Quasi-governments and Accountability'.

13 The Democratic Audit acted in an advisory role to a group of small growers, who named themselves the HDC Reform Group. See *Horticulture*, Agriculture Committee, 4th Report 1994–5, 61–II; a joint HDC Reform Group/Democratic Audit report, *Stitchup* is in preparation.

14 See for example, I. Harden and N. Lewis, *The Noble Lie: the British constitution and the rule of law*, London, Hutchinson, 1985; and A. Wright, *Citizens and Subjects*, London, Routledge, 1993.

15 See M. Sunkin, L. Bridges and G. Meszaros, *Judicial Review in Perspective*, London, Public Law Project, 1993.

16 The majority of the questions asked in the Rowntree/MORI poll were devised by Patrick Dunleavy and myself, in consultation with Professor Trevor Smith, chair of the Trust, and Bob Worcester and Simon Braunholtz of MORI. The survey was carried out in April–May 1995 by MORI who interviewed a representative quota sample of 1,758 adults across Great Britain. See *British Public Opinion*, vol. 18, No. 4, 1995, pp. 3–9. Questions for the Channel 4 poll were devised by Dunleavy and Weir in association with Nick Sparrow of ICM. ICM interviewed a sample of 1,427 adults across Great Britain in March 1994.

17 P. Dunleavy and S. Weir, 'Democracy in doubt', *Local Government Chronicle*, 29 April 1994.

18 W. J. M. Mackenzie and J. W. Grove, *Central Administration in Britain*, Longman, 1957.

19 P. Dunleavy and S. Weir, 'Public want the law set on MPs', *Observer*, 14 May 1995.

Democracy and Local Government

JOHN STEWART

The Democratic Potential of Local Government

THERE IS a growing recognition that after over fifteen years in which the role of local government has been systematically reduced, there is a need to reverse that tendency. Strengthening local government is advocated as a necessary step in overcoming the problems of an over-centralised state. The case for strengthening local government rests not only upon the problems to be overcome, but on the positive contribution that local authorities can make to the quality of democracy. It has long been recognised that local authorities enable far more people to participate in government. This was the main argument put forward by John Stuart Mill:

But in the case of local bodies, besides the function of electing, many citizens in turn have the chance of being elected, and many, either by selection or by rotation, fill one or other of the numerous local executive offices.

For Mill, one of the main consequences was political education particularly for what he regarded as the lower classes: 'It may be added that these local functions, not being in general sought by the higher ranks, carry down the important political education which they are the means of conferring to a much lower grade in society.'[1]

Other writers have seen the potential of participation in wider terms than membership of the council, important though that is in involving citizens in the process of government. Those writers would see the existence of local authorities as extending the scope for choice by local people through elections, not just about the services they receive but about the condition of the locality. 'Local Government is not just a matter of delivering services to the public, it is about making choices for a locality.'[2]

But local government has the potential for participation not merely in elections or through membership of a council, but through the active involvement of citizens. It has been widely recognised by writers committed to the development of public participation that the scope for participation in national affairs is more limited than in local affairs, but that participation at local level is within the compass of citizens.

The larger scale of decisions need not lead inevitably to a widening sense of power-lessness, provided citizens can exercise significant control over decisions on the smaller scale of matters important in their daily lives: education, public health, town and country planning, the supply and quality of the local public sector; from streets and lighting to parks and playgrounds and the like.[3]

© The Political Quarterly Publishing Co. Ltd. 1996
Published by Blackwell Publishers, 108 Cowley Road, Oxford OX4 1JF, UK and 238 Main Street, Cambridge, MA 02142, USA

Even sceptics about public participation have recognised its greater possibility at local level. Schumpeter who argued that any hope of active citizen participation in national affairs was both unrealistic and undesirable, because the citizen

. . . is a member of an unworkable committee, the committee of the whole nation, and that is why he expends less discipline on mastering a political problem than he expends on a game of bridge.

nevertheless saw that

In the realm of public affairs there are sectors that are more within the reach of the citizen's mind than others. This is true, first, of local affairs. Even there we find a reduced power of discerning facts, a reduced preparedness to act upon them, a reduced sense of responsibilities . . . Still, especially in communities not too big for personal contacts, local patriotism may be a very important factor in making democracy work.[4]

The greater potential for citizen participation at local level is seen both by advocates of participation as the basis of democracy and those who define the role of democracy in a more limited way. That potential is reflected in the greater participation at local level shown by research. The study of *Public Participation in Britain* by Parry, Moyser and Day, 1992, showed that the main target for action over issues which were the subject of public participation was local government in 44.2 per cent of cases as opposed to only 15.1 per cent when the main target was central government. Equally, 20.7 per cent of the public had contacted a councillor in the past five years, but only 9.7 per cent an MP.[5]

The Weakness of Local Democracy

While the case for strengthening local government can be made, it should not be assumed that all is well with local democracy. Whereas it is possible to make the case for local government through its potential for greater public participation, it does not mean that potential is being realised. One simple measure can be used to show the weakness of local democracy. Table 1 compares the turnout in local elections in Great Britain with the turnout in other EC countries.

Electoral turnout is only an indicator. It can, however, be regarded as a symptom of the weakness of local democracy in this country. If only 40 per cent of the electorate take part in local elections it can hardly be argued that local authorities are based on a vibrant local democracy.

What distinguishes local government is not its role as an agency for the delivery of services but its base in local democracy. If that basis is weak, then the case for local government is itself weakened. Thus it is not sufficient to argue for strengthening local government, without also facing up to the need to strengthen its democratic base. This paper argues that the weakness lies in:

Table 1 Indicative Turnout in recent Sub-National Elections in EC Countries

EC Country	Mean %
Luxembourg	93
Italy	85
Belgium	80
Denmark	80
Germany	72
France	68
Spain	64
Ireland	62
Portugal	60
Netherlands	54
Great Britain	40

Source: European sub-national database Plymouth (Commission for Local Democracy, *Taking Charge: The Rebirth of Local Democracy, op. cit.*, p. 10).

a limited conception of local government
a limited representative base
a limited conception of representative democracy
the limited approach to democratic practice

A Limited Conception of Local Government

In Great Britain local government has been seen as an agency for the delivery of a series of services. Its internal organisation reflects that conception, emphasising as it does in its committees and departments a series of separate services. Seen in that way, rather than as a political institution, the need for and the role of local democracy is more limited. In so far as there is scope for local choice and local voice, the case remains but it is a weaker case, leading to a weaker approach to local democracy. A different conception of local government is possible as the community governing itself—which is a stronger concept of local government.

A different concept of local government is found in many European countries. Local government is not, as it is too readily seen in this country, a creature of statute, with a specific range of powers. Local government, although not its specific form, is written into the constitutions of most European countries. The right of local communities to govern their own affairs is therefore a constitutional right. Local government is not seen as created solely to secure the provision of a series of services, but as a political institution through which communities govern themselves.

The difference is reflected in the prevalence of the power of general competence in other European countries. That power means that local authorities as communities governing themselves have the right to take action on behalf of their communities except where it is barred by law. It is the reverse of the position in this country, where local authorities can only take action within specific powers. The importance of the power of general competence is the concept it represents, rather than in the range of functions it makes possible.

It bolsters the conception of the municipality as a general political authority which acts in its own right to foster the welfare of its inhabitants and confronts whatever problems may arise in the local community. It encourages the citizen to see in the local authority not one agency among many carrying out administrative tasks, but the corporate manifestation of the local community (collectivité locale) which is the first resort in case of local difficulty.[6]

It may well be that the low turnout in local authorities in the United Kingdom in part reflects the limited concept of local government. A limited concept of local government reflects a limited emphasis on local democracy. Local democracy is apparently limited to choice about the level and nature of a series of statutory services, and not about wider issues facing local communities.

In local government there is today an aspiration to a wider role. Indeed perhaps there has always been. The Bains report saw the role of local government as:

. . . not, in our view, limited to the narrow provision of a series of services to the local community, though we do not in any way [mean] to suggest that these services are not important. It has within its purview the overall economic, cultural and physical well-being of that community and for this reason its decisions impinge with increasing frequency upon the lives of its citizens.[7]

Yet in reality the local authorities have never gained recognition in the role of, as quoted above, as '. . . a general political authority which acts in its own right to foster the welfare of its inhabitants and confront whatever problems arise in the community'. Nor have local authorities organised themselves to play that role. Their committee and departmental structures reflect a more limited role as agencies for the delivery of a series of services. While local authorities have always been ready to speak out on behalf of local communities, it has been almost peripheral to their main work.

There are signs of a recognition of the need for a reconsideration of the role of local government. The Labour Party in its recent policy statement *Renewing Democracy, Rebuilding Communities* (1995) contains a number of commitments reflecting a wider role for local government. A new duty will be place on local government:

We propose that Parliament places on councils a duty to promote the overall social, economic and environmental well-being of the communities they serve. This would enhance both their status and their capacity to respond to the needs of local people.

In parallel, councils could be given a new power of community initiative giving them greater freedom to respond to local needs, providing what they did was not unlawful and did not wholly duplicate the duties of other statutory bodies.

The status of local government would be recognised:

As part of our new constitutional settlement. Labour's proposed Bill of Rights, besides giving rights to individual citizens, could also give rights to communities by defining the rights and responsibilities of each tier of government.

If a Labour government were to implement these changes it could mean a movement towards a recognition of the role of local government as the community governing itself. The Conservative Government itself has given some indication of a readiness to see a wider role for local government, although it does not go anything like so far. In a speech in the House of Commons David Curry, the Minister of State for Local Government spelt out the roles of local government.

I believe that local authorities now have three essential roles. The first is that of regulator and there is no point in ignoring it . . . It is clear that that role will remain.

The second role is that of service commissioner—I use the term deliberately—because local government organises the delivery of a range of services, whether the individual services are delivered directly or through the competitive process . . .

Local government's third role is that of a regenerator. I realise that the term is not appropriate to all authorities. It is one that will be more relevant in urban areas than in some rural areas. Local government has a role to work more and more with other agencies, with the private sector, with organisations such as training and enterprise councils, chambers of commerce and educational establishments so as to bring the resources of the community to tackle specific problems . . . I think these three functions that I have outlined will be at the heart of the local government as it is now developing (House of Commons, 1994, *Parliamentary Debates*, pp. 618–19).

This statement reflects a limited movement towards a role of local government as community government at least in respect of regeneration. So far it has only been given limited expression in practice, in such initiatives as the Single Regeneration Budget, on which the local authority is expected to play a lead role along with the Training and Enterprise Council. The statement does however represent a recognition of the role of local government that is more positive than previous statements from the Government.

The Labour Party's policy statement goes much further and recognises the potential of local government as a political institution with wide-ranging concerns. Such a conception may be a stimulus to local democracy. Certainly it requires and is only justified by a viable local democracy.

The Weakness of the Representative Base

Local government is based on representative democracy. Yet there are weaknesses in the representative base of local government in Great Britain. The low turnout in local elections has been highlighted. What is perhaps equally serious is how little attention has been paid to this issue either by central government or by local government. While the problems of low turnout reflects wider issues, there are a number of steps that could be considered to make voting easier in local elections. These include: voting at weekends; universal postal voting; arrangements for pre-voting; publicity; siting of poll-stations; maps of polling stations issued with poll cards. While some of these measures would only have a limited effect on turnout, it is significant that they have not been considered in any systematic way.

If the base in turnout is weak, so is the extent of representation. There are only 25,000 councillors in this country. The number of councillors will fall further as a result of local government reorganisation. If the figures put forward by Weir and Hall for the number of members of appointed boards is correct at 57,000–63,000, then there are over twice as many appointments as there are councillors.[8]

One of the qualities of local government is that it makes possible a density of representation that is impracticable at national level. Not only can this involve far more people directly in the process of government, it can mean that far more people are in contact with an elected representative. That potential is not realised in this country where the number of people per councillor is over 2,000. This compares with an average in most other European countries of 1 councillor to between 250 and 450 residents. In France nearly 1 per cent of the population are councillors. These differences are largely due to the size of the local tier of British local authorities which are on average ten times the equivalent size in Europe (these figures do not include parish councils, which are not like the commune, local authorities with substantive powers). Whatever the reason it means that local government lacks the density of representation that could be its strength. It means that it cannot achieve a form of representative democracy based on closeness of contact, markedly different from that necessitated by Parliament's remoteness. Too often in the past commentators have suggested the need for a reduction in the number of councillors focusing on the size of councils, disregarding the implications for the state of our democracy. The Local Government Commission proposed '. . that the ratio of councillors to local residents in a unitary structure should generally be around 1 to 4,000'.

On the other hand the independent Commission for Local Democracy stressed the representative role of the council and recommended that 'Councils would consist of approximately twice as many members as is currently the case in local authorities'.

A major increase in the number of councillors would be a transformative force in the nature of representative democracy, bringing the representative closer to the represented. This could be achieved by an increase in the size of councils. In an ideal world it could also be achieved by reducing the size of local authorities, replacing the many artificial district councils by authorities based on the communities within a tiered system, rather than by the pursuit of unitary authorities with its inevitable tendency, within an administrative culture based on unproven assumptions about economy of scale, towards creating even larger authorities. The creation of smaller authorities within a tiered structure would bring our local authorities closer to the European model. The structure of local government there has been based on perceived communities, rather than on alleged efficiencies of administration, reflecting the different concept of local government already discussed. Few would wish a further trauma of reorganisation upon local authorities already undermined and distracted by the flawed process recently undergone. So the immediate aim should be an increase in the number of councillors, especially in urban areas where there are no parish councils. This could be achieved by increasing the size of councils and by the creation of elected urban parish councils or neighbourhood councils.

There is another weakness in the representative base due to the electoral system, which can mean that the council's composition does not reflect the balance of political views. This is an argument for the adoption of some method of proportional representation. The arguments for and against systems of proportional representation at national level were rehearsed in the Plant Commission (1993). Unfortunately the Plant Commission was not able to extend its investigations to local government, where the balance of arguments can be different. Certain factors make the arguments for proportional representation even stronger in local government. One of the main arguments against proportional representation is that it produces a hung situation. Such a situation is already commonplace in local government and it has not been found to create major problems. Indeed it could be argued that it has helped to transform the nature of discussions in committees. The committee system gains a new value in the hung situation, involving as it does all parties in day-to-day decision-making, unlike the operation of central government. In a few authorities the hung situation has led to instability largely because the party groups refused to accept the new political reality. Research has shown that most authorities achieve stability:

Past experience of majority control comes to be seen as a misleading guide for both councillors and officers.

And:

If hung authorities are seen as a learning experience what one finds is what one would expect. Initially difficulties may be encountered because authorities have no experience to draw upon except that of majority control. Over time they learn from new experiences, modifying initial approaches.[9]

Such adjustment is the more likely if hung authorities become the norm as a result of proportional representation.

The absence of proportional representation can have the dangerous effect of virtually eliminating the opposition on certain councils or reducing it to trivial numbers. Two factors are at work here. The first is the relative social homogeneity of certain authorities, meaning that results in different electoral districts provide no geographical space for opposition. In Newham in 1986 Labour held every seat although they polled only 56.6 per cent of the vote. Similar situations, although not in that acute form, are found in many authorities. The second is for local elections to reflect at least, in part, national swings (and it is only in part, although media comment ignores the very real differences from authority to authority), with the result that the first-past-the-post system exaggerates the effect of the swing as was seen in the defeat of far larger numbers of Conservatives in May 1995 than represented by the fall in votes. It happened the other way round in 1977, when for example Labour and Liberals in Buckinghamshire who had held 22 seats were reduced to only 1 seat between them, giving the Conservatives a virtual monopoly of the council. At the same election the Labour Party in the West Midlands fell from 73 out of a council of 104 to 18, because of a fall in their vote from 48 per cent to 31 per cent. Whatever the views held on proportional representation at national level, there is a stronger case for it at local level.

The Commission for Local Democracy recommended that the council should be elected for multi-member wards by a system of proportional representation. Proposals were also put forward by the Commission for Local Democracy for a directly elected Leader or Mayor to be introduced throughout the system of local government. Such a proposal separates the role of the elected mayor as the head of the executive from that of the council as in effect the 'legislature' or representative body. Similar proposals had been put forward by the Government in a consultation paper (Department of the Environment, 1991) and later investigated by a Working Party on the Internal Management of Local Authorities (Working Party, 1993). These reports, however, considered a number of alternative forms and recommended experiments rather than the universal adoption recommended by the Commission on Local Democracy.

What also distinguishes the Commission's approach is their recommendation of this proposal as a means of strengthening democracy. We are not concerned here with the organisational issues involved, but with the Commission's view that this was the way to strengthen democracy. There have even been suggestions in the Commission's presentations that the introduction of direct elections for mayors would nearly double electoral turnout, although that is not confirmed by American experience. In Phoenix, to give one example, in the direct election of the Mayor in 1991 only 17 per cent voted and turnouts in America are generally lower than in Britain, especially after the low level of registration is taken into account.[10]

It is not as simple as the Commission made out. The weaknesses in local democracy go deeper and are not likely to be resolved by such institutional changes. Nor are the arguments clear cut. The system of committees exercising executive powers has weaknesses but also has strengths involving as it does elected representatives in the work of the council in a way which contrasts with the lack of involvement of MPs in the work of central government. Nor are the arguments for a directly elected mayor one-sided.

True it focuses public attention, but that could lead to an undue concentration of power. There is a danger too of personalisation. Buhlman and Page,[11] contrasting the different systems in Germany, concluded that while '. . . the presidential systems of the South seemed to offer clearer lines of account-ability . . .' other systems '. . . seem to be able to adapt more quickly to social and economic change and offer citizens clearer choices at election time'. They concluded that 'There is a danger that if current moves to "personalise" local politics through direct elections for key officials are pushed forward . . .' those advantages may be lost. 'And such moves may reflect a desire to stifle the lively political debate about basic issues of economic, social and environment policy taking place at the local level rather than any real commitment to improve the quality of local self-government.'

The position is clearly more complicated than envisaged by the Commission for Local Democracy. The proposition that the creation of a system based on directly elected mayors will strengthen local democracy must be regarded as unproven. There is a case for innovation and experiment in the council's organisational form, but they should not be restricted to this form. There are other alternatives. Oslo provides one example.

In 1986 Oslo introduced a city cabinet elected by the council with the right to control the administration. It took over in effect the functions previously carried out by the chief officers. It consisted of full-time members paid on a salary basis. However, at the same time, the council introduced strengthened neighbourhood committees with responsibility for the day-to-day running of certain services in the area. A centralisation of political control was coupled with a capacity for responsiveness to neighbourhood concerns.

The creation of a political executive did not mean the abolition of commit-tees. Scrutiny committees were set up not only to appraise performance, but also to consider proposals put forward by the cabinet to the council. The changes in Oslo involved therefore not merely the creation of a cabinet, but also change in the working of the council and political decentralisation.

This is but one possible model. It would be wrong to approach the directly elected mayor as if it were the only alternative model to the committee system. Such models may be more important for their impact on the internal workings of local authorities than for their impact on local democracy. The problems of local democracy lie much deeper.

The Limited Concept of Representative Democracy

The key problem of local democracy is the attenuated conception of representative democracy on which it is based, which allows little or no place for that participatory democracy which is the potential strength of local democracy. Representative democracy in local government is seen too often not merely as being dependent on the local election, but as consisting of the local election and of little more. The act of being a representative is sufficient, removing any need for a continuing process of representation. The

Schumpeter conception of the democratic mode has tended to dominate the working of local authorities.

Such an approach allows therefore little place for citizens other than their involvement in elections. Beyond that the citizen is reduced to the politics of protest, and that for many is their only active experience of local democracy. Yet as has already been argued, local government has through the scale at which it operates a potential for citizen involvement that may for practical reasons be denied to central government. Because of the restricted concept of local representative democracy that is dominant in the workings of local authority, participatory democracy is often seen as opposed to representative democracy. If it were possible to see all decisions taken by direct democracy, that could be seen as an alternative to representative democracy. The Athenian City State has a powerful hold on thinking. Citizen assemblies and town meetings are still found in Switzerland and the United States. They were also found in this country under private bill procedures until 1974 and parish meetings are still a feature of many areas. In practice however in areas with large populations they are likely to be meetings for the few rather than the many. There are necessary limits to direct democracy.

Participatory democracy, which involves citizens in the process of local government, can take many forms which, far from challenging representative democracy, can strengthen it. Citizen participation may well require representative democracy. Citizens do not speak with one voice. They place different and often conflicting demands. The communities in which people live are marked by lines of competition as well as co-operation. Within any community of place there are many communities of interest or of background. It is the role of elected representatives to seek to reconcile, to balance and in the end to determine the different demands made upon them. Citizen participation informs but does not determine the process of representative government, although where it takes the form of direct democracy it can reduce the burdens placed upon representative government.

Such an approach to public participation reflects an active process of representation as opposed to the passive act of being a representative. The elected representative 'represents' or rather re-presents the views of citizens. To re-present is not to follow blindly the views of citizens, but it is to be aware of them, to understand them, to discuss them and to put them in to the context of other views and other demands. Representation seen in this way is dependent on a continuing relationship between representative and those represented. If the relationship is seen as a relationship of stewardship then it is true that from time to time the steward is held to account through elections, but the process of accounting—both giving the account and listening to reactions—is continuous.

This conception of representative democracy involves a rediscovery of the importance of deliberation in representative democracy amongst the citizens, between citizens and representatives and amongst the representatives. As Miller states:

The deliberative ideal also starts from the premise that political preferences will conflict and that the purpose of democratic institutions must be to resolve this conflict. But it envisages this occurring through an open and uncoerced discussion of the issue at stake with the aim of arriving at an agreed judgement. The process of reaching a decision will also be a process whereby initial preferences are transformed to take account of the views of others. That is, the need to reach an agreement forces each participant to put forward proposals under the rubric of general principles or policy considerations that others could accept.[12]

James Fishkin has argued that deliberation is a necessary condition for a fully realised democracy:

Without deliberation, democratic choices are not exercised in a meaningful way. If the preferences that determine the results of democratic procedures are unflective or ignorant they lose their claim to political authority over us. Deliberation is necessary if the claims of democracy are not to be delegitimated.[13]

The argument is for a concept of representative democracy based not on the vote alone, but also on deliberation. That raises issues about our representative institutions in which the quality of deliberation is constrained by excesses of party discipline. If a council is a place for taking counsel, that role is denied through a routine requirement of the party whip. Party discipline has an important role in giving cohesion to political direction and in giving meaning to the electoral process. It can, however, be extended to vote through detailed officer recommendations without real discussion. The deliberative assembly is denied by unthinking application of the whip and decisions made by party groups prior to discussion in committees. If party groups have to impose decisions, perhaps views should be formed after discussion in council and committee, not before!

But it is through the deliberation based on citizen participation that representative democracy at local level can realise its full potential. It will, of course, be argued that to expect widespread citizen participation is unrealistic. The failure of various initiatives to rouse public interest will be quoted. The dominance of the articulate will be feared. Past failures of initiatives may be due to the form given to them by the local authority. Too often initiatives for public participation have been designed by the local authority to meet organisational requirements rather than to work with the grain of how people behave. To invite the public to speak in council or committee can be an important symbol of the openness of the council, but it is unlikely to lead to a widespread response. To invite the public to discuss the objectives of the authority is unlikely to secure a response, whereas a discussion of the problems on an estate is more likely to secure attendance, and in the end lead to more meaningful objectives. There is a need for innovation in democratic practice, but innovation that works with the grain. That innovation should be grounded in recognition of the need to balance the voice of the articulate with the voices that are rarely heard within the workings of local authorities.

Innovation in Democratic Practice

There have been very significant changes in management in local government and in the policies governing it, but little innovation in democratic practice. This point has already been made about electoral turnout, but it is much wider in its impact. Public meetings convened by local authorities often follow the tired pattern of platform presentation followed by questions from the floor—a format more likely to lead to protest through public frustration than to encourage deliberation.

It is not the case that the public are unwilling to be involved. The public vote and while the low turnouts in election can be deplored, it still represents 40 per cent of the electorate. There are indications that the percentage voting on issues that are of concern to people can be greater, particularly if the method of voting is made easier, as it is in opting out ballots or ballots about the transfer of council house estates, where voting is by post. In such cases voting is higher than in local elections. In the Strathclyde referendum on water reorganisation in Scotland—also held by post—78 per cent of the electorate voted. A high percentage of the population take part in surveys for market research. It would be interesting to build on that model, formally treating it as citizen consultation and reporting back on the results of such surveys.

Some of the lines for innovation in democratic practice are set out below. It is not argued that any one of these approaches will meet all requirements, but rather that there should be an array of approaches which in various combinations can be used to develop citizen participation, not as a challenge to representative democracy but to strengthen it.

The Informed Citizen

The local authority will hear the voices of the interested parties on any of its proposals, or at least of those who know of the proposals and are articulate in expressing their views. It can find through the use of surveys the immediate views of ordinary citizens. It will not normally have access to the informed views of ordinary citizens about an issue, who have had the opportunity to reflect upon it. A number of approaches have been developed to reach out to such views. These approaches have in common three features. They require that those so selected hear evidence before forming their views. They provide an opportunity for deliberation and reflection. They are based on random selection or on a representative sample. They build on the principle of selection by lot established in Athens and argued for by John Burnheim: 'Elections, I shall argue, breed oligarchies. Democracy is possible only if the decision-makers are *a representative sample* of the people concerned.'[14]

Citizens' Juries (or planning cells as they are called in Germany) were developed by Ned Crosby of the Jefferson Centre in America and Peter Dienel at the University of Wuppertal in Germany. They bring together for up to a week a group of citizens, selected to be representative of the general public, to consider a policy area or a specific issue, hearing evidence and discussing the issue amongst themselves. In Germany planning cells (often multiple cells) have been commissioned by local authorities, the lander or the Federal Government. They undertake to take seriously the views of the jury and to give a considered response. Citizens' juries could have been used in this country to appraise town centre developments or could be used to examine the problems of urban transport.[15]

Deliberative opinion polls have been developed by James Fishkin . They differ from opinion polls in that, while constituted from a representative sample, opinions are only recorded after hearing evidence and discussion. Both citizens' juries and deliberative opinion polls have safeguards to avoid bias in the selection of those to take part, in the presentation of information and in the choice of witnesses.

Another possibility is that a local authority might appoint a representative panel to meet regularly to discuss the council's policies and be used as a sounding board. Ten per cent of such a panel could change, securing a turnover of members. It would be possible if all these approaches were developed in an authority for many citizens over time to have the opportunity to serve on this capacity, building up a habit of citizenship. Such developments are not seen as replacing decisions by elected representatives, but a means by which they can test our views.

Recognising the Communities Within

A number of local authorities are developing forums to give expression to the diversity of communities within their area. Local authorities recognise most readily communities of place, constituted as they are on the basis of area. Some councils have set up area committees of councillors to support their representative role. Such committees may have substantive powers or be constituted to monitor services and to raise local issues; they can be linked neighbourhood panels, open to members of the public, as in Bradford.

Other councils such as Middlesbrough or Islington have set up neighbourhood forums. These can be constituted by direct election, or by community groups, and be open to the public generally. Normally these will be consultative bodies, but their long-term vitality depends upon the local authority being ready to respond to their concerns.

There is a danger in the authority that only recognises communities of place. In any given area there will be minority interests and concerns. Across many areas are wider communities of interest and concern. Authorities are creating forums in which such interests can be expressed. Nottingham has an elderly persons forum. Arun, as well as creating forums for parishes, has created a series of forums for coastal interests, for amenity groups and others. Where it is identified that certain voices are not being heard, then special focus groups can be constituted for consultation.

The development of community forums informs the representative process. The role of the elected representative gains in importance in the balancing and reconciling of interests. Of course it is possible to go further and give substantive powers to community forums whether of place or of interest, as for example in the development of tenants' management boards or giving neighbourhood forums certain decision-making powers, although legal provisions may limit that possibility.

Advocates of associative democracy would go further in giving decision-making powers to communities of place or of interest: '. . . that voluntary self-governing associations gradually and progressively become the primary means of democratic governance of economic and social affairs.' This is seen as a necessary step to reduce '. . . both the scale and the scope of the affairs of society that are administered by state agencies overseen by representative institutions'.[16] The argument is that an over-burdened government undermines representative democracy.

New Forms of Public Meeting

Innovation is needed in the form of public meetings if the constraints of traditional meetings are to be avoided. The place of meeting, the layout of the meeting, and the arrangement of business should be designed to meet the purpose of the meeting. The giving of information may require a different format from the meetings to encourage participation. Meetings for some groups may be held in houses to enable involvement of those reluctant to go to larger meetings. The larger meeting can be divided into discussion groups. People who are reluctant to speak could be encouraged to write comments. Planning for real techniques developed by the Neighbourhood Initiatives Association enable people to work with physical models.

Citizen participation can be encouraged by informal settings but there are occasions when a local authority may seek a more formal process, possibly with a series of public hearings. Montreal City Council has set up a Bureau of Consultation on an independent basis to hold public hearings by a panel on proposals or on policy issues.

Mediation Groups

It is normal for groups in conflict over proposals for development or other issues to put pressure on authorities to support their points of view. In America and in Germany local authorities have set up mediation groups to bring the parties together for discussion (deliberation) to see to what extent agreement is possible. Such processes can focus on agreeing what is disagreed about and understanding which issues are important to the different parties, identifying the extent of disagreement on facts and whether it can be resolved.

Even where all issues are not resolved through this process, they will have been clarified for the elected representatives to determine.

Citizen Monitors

Citizens can be involved in monitoring services as in Lewisham, where citizens are invited to undertake this role. They can be involved in exercises in environmental appraisal or village appraisal or be appointed to quality panels. In this way they are extending and deepening the councillor's representative role in reviewing performance through the insights of many citizens.

Referenda

While national referenda are rare in this country, there has been a long established tradition of local polls. In parishes any ten citizens can call a local poll. In the nineteenth century polls were held to establish whether a local authority should become a library authority. Until 1974 there was provision for electors to call for a poll on councils' proposal for a Private Bill. There used to be provision for polls on Sunday opening of cinemas, and there still are in Wales on Sunday opening of pubs. Polls are required by legislation on opting out for grant maintained status or for the transfer of housing stock.

Over the years local authorities have themselves organised referendums. In the 1970s referendums were held in Buckinghamshire on comprehensive education. In 1981 a referendum was held in Coventry on the level of rates. Strathclyde Regional Council held a referendum on water reorganisation. Recently Ross and Cromarty District Council held a referendum in two areas on a subject of great local controversy, the Sunday opening of leisure centres. In Switzerland and in parts of the United States there is provision for the citizens' initiative, or the calling of a referendum by a specified number or percentage of electors. In the United States there can also be provision for the right of recall by similar percentages, requiring a new election for the council or councillors.

Referendums do not necessarily challenge representative democracy. The referendum can be seen as an instrument to be used by a council to test opinion. Provided that the number of such referendums is not excessive and the subject arouses interest, it can be seen as encouraging deliberation and an active citizenship. The use of the citizens' initiative if binding can be seen as replacing representative democracy. The extent of that use is likely to be limited and in that context it is better seen as complementing representative democracy. Thomas Cronin summarising American research says:

Although experts still argue about the consequences, most would say that direct democracy has not weakened our regular legislative process . . . Americans over-whelmingly endorse leaving the job of making laws to their elected representatives and view direct democracy devices almost entirely as a last alternative to the legislative process . . . On balance then direct democracy has developed as a supplement and not an undermining force in American Government.[17]

Teledemocracy

The development of communication technology has shaped the development of democracy and of political processes over time from the printed word onward. Inevitably new forms of information technology will influence democratic practice enabling innovation. Two developments are important. The first is the use of a variety of modes to ease access to information, itself a precondition of effective citizenship. Amsterdam digital city effectively puts Amsterdam City Council on-line.

The second is the use of interactive technology to create in effect the 'electronic town meeting'. That can extend beyond the immediate neighbourhood:

Thus for the first time we have an opportunity to create artificial town meetings among populations that could not otherwise communicate. There is little doubt that the electronic town meeting sacrifices intimacy, diminishes the sense of face to face confrontation, and increases the dangers of elite manipulation. Yet it would be foolish to allow these dangers to stop us from exploring television as a civic medium.[18]

There are many problems in the use of new forms of communication. At present there is limited access. However, it is often groups who rarely participate in public affairs—the young—who most readily respond to the emerging technology. For the future access will grow and local authorities, where for example cable is widespread, should be prepared for its use in innovation in democratic practice.

Choice and Strategy

The local authority can have a wide range of instruments for citizen participation. The need is for commitment to a strategy for their development, not as a means for replacing local representative democracy, but for strengthening it as a condition for a wider role as community government. The Labour Party's Consultation Paper *Renewing Democracy, Rebuilding Communities* (1995) recognises the need for such an approach. It proposes methods of increasing turnout and also many of the innovations discussed here, not as statutory requirements but as a stimulus to local development. The Commission for Local Democracy proposes that local authorities should be placed under a duty to prepare annual plans (Democracy Plans) for the representation of local communities based on a democratic audit.

It is important that each authority be allowed to develop an experimental approach. They should judge themselves both on their ability to increase the involvement of the many and also on their success at reaching out to groups regularly isolated from the democratic process. We are seeking nothing less than a citizenship strategy within localities (p. 33).

It is the strategy that is important rather than an annual plan which could become a burdensome routine.

Conclusion

The case for local government rests upon the vitality of its democratic base, because it is as a political institution based on local institution that it makes its distinctive contribution. As a political institution it has a potential for effective representation and citizen participation that is only imperfectly realised in this country. Strengthening local democracy requires a developed role for local authorities, as community government, a reform of the representative base, an active concept of representative democracy and innovation in democratic practice. These are necessarily linked in overcoming the inherent weakness of local government and of local democracy and hence of democracy in this country.

Biographical Note

John Stewart is Professor of Local Government in the Institute of Local Government Studies, The University of Birmingham. He was appointed to the Institute in 1966 to launch management courses for local government officers and was Director of the Institute from 1976 to 1983. From 1990 to 1992 he was Head of the School of Public Policy which includes the Institute and other departments concerned with the public sector at home and overseas. He has written extensively on the case for local government and on public management.

Notes

1 John Stuart Mill, *Considerations on Representative Government*, London, Routledge, 1904.
2 Commission for Local Democracy, *Taking Charge: the Rebirth of Local Democracy*, 1995, p. 3.
3 Robert A. Dahl, *Democracy and its Critics*, New Haven, Yale University Press, 1989, p. 321.
4 E. Schumpeter, *Capitalism, Socialism and Democracy*, New York, Harper and Row, 1950.
5 Geraint Parry, George Moyser and Neil Day, *Political Participation and Democracy in Britain*, Cambridge, Cambridge University Press, 1992.
6 Philip Blair, 'Trends in Local Autonomy and Democracy: Reflections from a European Perspective', in Richard Batley and Gerry Stoker, *Local Government in Europe*, London, Macmillan, 1991, p. 51.
7 Bains Report, *The New Local Authorities: Management and Structure*, London, HMSO, 1972.

8 Stuart Weir and Wendy Hall, *EGOTRIP: extra-governmental organisations in the U.K. and their accountability*, Charter 88 Trust/Human Rights Centre, University of Essex, 1994.

9 Steve Leach and John Stewart, *The Politics of Hung Authorities*, London, Macmillan, 1992.

10 Robin Hambleton, 'Local Leadership and Decision Making in the U.S.', in Joseph Rowntree Foundation, *Local Leadership and Decision Making: A Study of France, Germany, the United States and Britain*, London, LGC Communications, 1994.

11 Udo Buhlman and Edward Page, 'Executive Leadership in German Local Government', in Joseph Rowntree Foundation, *op. cit.*.

12 David Miller, 'Deliberative Democracy and Social Choice' in David Held (ed.), *Prospects for Democracy*, Cambridge, Polity Press, 1993, p. 75.

13 James S. Fishkin, *Democracy and Deliberation*, New Haven, Yale University Press, 1991, p. 29.

14 John Burnheim, *Is Democracy Possible?*, Cambridge, Polity Press, 1985.

15 John Stewart, Elizabeth Kendall and Anna Coote, *Citizen's Juries*, London, IPPR, 1994.

16 Paul Hirst, *Associative Democracy*, Cambridge, Polity Press, 1994, pp. 20, 21.

17 Thomas Cronin, *Direct Democracy*, Cambridge, Harvard University Press, 1989.

18 Benjamin Barber, *Strong Democracy*, Berkeley, University of California Press, 1984.

Dilemmas of Accountability: The Limits of Accounting

PETER MILLER

How might we assess the performance of others? This apparently simple question has been at the heart of managerial ambitions for much of this century. More recently, it has been one of the most insistent demands that has driven the growth of performance indicators in the 'new public sector'. A creeping distrust pervades such demands, and this distrust helps to conceal the dilemmas of accountability that underlie an apparently simple question. To appreciate these dilemmas, let us consider two very different types of performance indicator, one from the new 'customer-driven' world of health care, one from the old world of the market place. The guides selected are: a National Health Service performance guide, and a restaurant guide.[1]

To begin with, the NHS performance guide. This guide is in the form of a number of tables. These provide information on NHS Trusts, rather than individual hospitals, and are organised by region. The tables tell you, for instance: waiting times for first outpatient appointments; waiting times in outpatient clinics, and in accident and emergency departments; and whether day case surgery is available, permitting patients to go home on the same day as an operation. Performance is indicated by percentage figures, for instance what percentages of patients is seen within 30 minutes of the appointment time. Performance is also indicated by the awarding of between one and five stars. These are only awarded when the Audit Commission is satisfied with the data collection systems in place. Roughly speaking, the more stars the better the performance, although the percentage point at which stars are awarded varies from table to table according to the difficulty of the performance target. Take, for instance, the table detailing the percentage of outpatients receiving an appointment within 13 weeks. Here, one star means a score of less than 70 per cent, two stars mean 70–79 per cent, three mean 80–89 per cent, four mean 90–94 per cent, and five stars mean 95 per cent or more. Compare with this the table detailing the percentage of outpatients receiving an appointment within 26 weeks. Here, one star means a score of less than 90 per cent, two stars mean 90–94 per cent, three mean 95–97 per cent, four mean 98–99 per cent, and five stars mean 100 per cent. In addition, arrows show changes in performance, an upward arrow indicating an improvement of a specified amount on last year's performance, a downward arrow indicating a deterioration. As with stars, arrows are only shown where the Audit Commission's auditors were satisfied with the data collection systems in both years.

Next, the restaurant guide. This ranks restaurants individually on a

© The Political Quarterly Publishing Co. Ltd. 1996
Published by Blackwell Publishers, 108 Cowley Road, Oxford OX4 1JF, UK and 238 Main Street, Cambridge, MA 02142, USA

numerical scale of 1–20, with actual ratings awarded extending from 10 to 19.5. This numerical scale is supplemented from 13 upwards by a symbol (of a chef's hat—a 'toque'). This means that you are entering the realm of 'cuisine'. As restaurants climb the scale, they are awarded one, two, three, or even four of these hats. Colour introduces a further variation: from 13 upwards, the hats may be coloured red to show that the cuisine is 'particularly creative'. A similar differentiation is introduced in the printing of the name of the restaurant. This, too, can appear in red, denoting 'value for money'. Then there is the 'laurel' symbol, to indicate that the cooking has a strong regional emphasis. When all this information has been absorbed, you can then read the verbal description, which may describe the service, the view one obtains from the terrace, the atmosphere, particular dishes, and so forth. Roughly speaking, the more words, the better the restaurant. At 19.5, this verbal description can extend to a brief life history of the chef, and much more besides.

Of course, choosing a restaurant is a more congenial activity than choosing where to have a colostomy performed, so direct comparisons are difficult. To this extent, some translation may be helpful. To express the hospital guide in restaurant terminology, one might say that it tells the 'customer' how far in advance you have to reserve a table (waiting times for first outpatient appointments); how long you have to wait for your table when you arrive at the restaurant (waiting times in outpatient clinics, and in accident and emergency departments); and how long you can keep your table (whether day case surgery is available). Unfortunately, there is no mention of the food (medical outcome indicators).[2] Nor is there any mention of the quality and standard of the service provided. Perhaps even more important, if customer choice is the aim, there is no mention of individual restaurants (entries are for groups of restaurants, named 'Restaurant Trusts', say), so selection of a restaurant has to be on the basis of an aggregated number derived from two or more restaurants. This number might tell you, for instance, that your local Restaurant Trust had been awarded a score of 15. But it would not tell you whether this average score for the two restaurants derived from 2 scores of 15, or one score of 11 and one of 19, or indeed any other permutation.

Selecting a restaurant armed with such a guide would be a meaningless activity. This highlights the disparity between the public rhetoric of the customer, as embedded for instance in the Patient's Charter, and the through-put measures that count as 'performance guides', and yet provide no basis for individual choice or managerial evaluation. The information contained in such guides is too aggregated, concentrates excessively on volume-based measures, and lacks the service-specific information that would enable a patient to assess the quality of health care provided for a specific specialty in an individual hospital. Of course, it is important to reduce hospital waiting lists, to reduce waiting times in outpatient departments, and to limit the cancellation or postponement of operations. But volume-based throughput measures that assess such factors are only a small part of the picture. People attend hospital in the hope that they may be cured, or at least that their symptoms may be treated, the development of their disease arrested, and their pain alleviated. Yet this curative dimension of health care, this qualitative aspect, is strikingly absent from the NHS Performance Guide.

This suggests that 'accountability', whether it be to 'customers', to internal management, or to an external monitoring agency, is a more complex phenomenon than might appear from the clamour of voices unproblematically demanding it. A number of more or less fundamental dilemmas have to be addressed before this seemingly simple demand can be met. Let us consider just three such dilemmas of principle, meaning, and mechanism.

Dilemmas of Accountability

First, the dilemma of principle: should we place our trust in experts? Or should their activity be subject to some external monitoring of performance? Should doctors, social workers, teachers, the police, university lecturers and others be held accountable to a body other than themselves?

It might appear that this question has been settled already by the avalanche of performance indicators, league tables, reviews and other forms of monitoring that make up the audit society.[3] But trust in experts runs deep in British society, even if some experts are trusted more than others.[4] Simply to call people customers incessantly does not transform them into customers. More is required. The transformation of a citizen into a customer is part of much wider institutional transformation.[5] It requires a vast apparatus of information comparable to that available to customers purchasing goods and services that range from cars to computers, from beer to bathroom fittings. The long history by which this transformation has been effected in other spheres has only just begun for public service. Before it progresses any further, it is important to ask what is lost, and what may be gained, by placing public service on the same footing as other forms of customer choice.

Secondly, the dilemma of meaning. Despite the extension of the language of the market in the new public sector over the last decade, it remains unclear what exactly it means to be a 'customer' in areas as diverse as health care, education, and refuse collection. When parents are provided with league tables on school performance, but have no effective choice between schools, it is not clear in what sense parents or pupils are 'customers'. When one's local authority informs you that a new system of 'wheeled bin' refuse collection is to be instituted, and that the contract has been awarded for a period of seven years, the same applies. And when one is 'free' to choose one's GP, but has no information on the quality of medical care provided on which to base such choice, the meaning of customer or patient choice is again unclear.

The dilemma of meaning arises for a similar reason to the dilemma of principle: the fundamental issue that it raises has not been satisfactorily resolved. For the rhetoric of the customer sits uneasily with the rhetoric of accountability. Performance indicators often translate demands for accountability into practices that are more suited to the needs of external monitoring agencies, rather than the information needs of customers. To this extent, performance indicators become allocational mechanisms, rather than sources of information for end-users.

While the market-driven meaning of the new public sector may be clear, there is a tension between this aspiration, and the residual public service ethos that continues to pervade domains such as health care and education. In any event, the distinction between markets and hierarchies, and the attempt to transform the latter into the former, is much less clear-cut than supposed. Markets are not the simple entities that are often imagined. As new 'network' forms of organisation become more pervasive in the private sector, the neat dichotomy of markets and hierarchies becomes less and less accurate as a description of the options faced by organisations. The boundaries of the firm are increasingly difficult to identify in such settings. The difficulties being encountered by the regulatory regimes put in place for the newly privatised industries should alert us to the complexity, and institutional embeddedness, of markets.

Thirdly, the dilemma of mechanism. This can be formulated as follows: can we place our trust in numbers? Even if the first two dilemmas were to be resolved, the matter of *how* exactly to assess performance, *how* to enact accountability, still has to be faced. It might appear that this, too, has been resolved, by giving the job to accountants. But the perverse nature of this choice of a mechanism of accountability is often missed, even when it is criticised. For a distrust of experts is to be countered by a trust in numbers, particularly financial numbers. One particular body of expertise—accountancy—is to be made the expertise of expertises. The single financial number, whether in the form of a ratio, a percentage, a budgetary target, or an absolute amount, is to become the common language into which all other forms of expertise are to be translated. Yet this trust in financial numbers is gaining ground at precisely the time when criticisms of accountancy and financial expertise have been running at their highest level for a decade or more. This is not just a result of the various audit scandals that rock repeatedly the major accounting firms. It is also a matter of the deep-seated criticisms of accounting as a means of controlling shop-floor operations. Ever since the early 1980s, management accounting has been attacked for its abstracted, aggregated, and distant character.[6] These criticisms are more than the routine self-criticism that is part and parcel of the modernisation of all bodies of expertise. They go to the very heart of the aspirations of accounting to know and to regulate people and processes.

These three dilemmas are interrelated. The difficulties inherent in seeking to resolve the dilemmas of principle and meaning are to some extent being avoided by placing trust in a particular mechanism. We need to consider whether this is a satisfactory resolution to the calls for accountability, or whether this particular mechanism is as suited to the task in hand as is often implied. With this in mind, let us turn now to consider the 'limits' of accounting information.

The Limits of Accounting

If accountants are to continue to play an ever-increasing role in managing the new public sector, it is important to identify the limits of their expertise. To do so is not to dismiss the potential of accounting information. It is simply to raise the possibility that accounting information may be more suited to some tasks than others, that it may not have universal validity, and that there may be some important issues that it neglects. It is also to suggest that, if the public sector is to be transformed in important part by the calculative technologies of accounting, then any assessment of such a transformation should take note of the recent criticisms of management accounting information. For, as already noted, over the last decade or so management accounting has been subject to a wide-ranging and potentially damaging critique. The most influential example of this criticism is that expressed by Johnson and Kaplan in their book *Relevance Lost*.[7] In that book they stated bluntly their concern about contemporary management accounting:

Today's management accounting information [. . .] is too late, too aggregated, and too distorted to be relevant for managers' planning and control decisions.

If we are to assess the possible limits of accounting, this bleak judgment on a century or so of management accounting needs to be taken into account. Two of the key areas of management accounting—product costing, and investment appraisal—will allow us to illustrate the type of issues that need consideration.

Costing

A deceptively simple question has caused a huge amount of trouble for accountants over the last century. This question is: how much does something cost?[8] One might expect that, in an era of ever-increasing computer power, this would be a relatively simple question to answer. But across the whole of the twentieth century, this question has proved highly resistant to an accurate answer. Accountants have failed to provide a way to measure accurately the costs of products that are produced in multi-product environments.

Standard costing provided the first attempt on the part of accounting expertise to predetermine systematically the costs of a particular activity, so as to measure outcomes against predictions. Borrowed from the engineers, and developed in conjunction with Taylorism between 1900 and 1930, theories of standard costing and budgeting became a central part of the accounting literature. This profoundly transformed cost accounting, and massively expanded its domain. Henceforth, cost accounting was to be concerned with the future as well as the past. Cost accounting was no longer to be limited to ascertaining only the actual costs of production or activities. Standard costing and budgeting made it possible for accounting routinely to address questions of waste and efficiency in the employment of resources, whether human, financial or material. Standard costing enabled the calculation of variances at the level of the profit of the total firm, at the level of material or labour use in production, or at the level of every accountable person within the firm.

Standard costing was part of a much wider 'efficiency' craze in both North America and British society, and focused principally on labour efficiency. It was central to the attempts to govern in ever greater detail the working lives of employees. But standard costing has been criticised increasingly over the last decade for its inappropriateness to advanced manufacturing environments where standards are less readily available, and where measures of flexibility and response time take precedence over the norms established in an era of large volume runs of standardised products. As more and more companies shift from standardised mass production to modern manufacturing systems, standard costing has been argued to be less and less relevant to current needs.

In the inter-war years, on both sides of the Atlantic, a further development in costing developed. This was the introduction, from economics, of the idea that the *behaviour* of costs was central, their variation in relation to volume of output. The point emphasised here was the avoidability or unavoidability of costs, the additional expense incurred by producing one additional unit of output. All other expenses should be termed the 'fixed cost'. Cost accounting, that is to say, should be based on 'differential' or 'marginal' costs, for it is those costs that vary with output. Cost accountants should, it was argued, ignore expenses that are unchangeable, and not spend their time calculating arbitrary allocations to departmental expenses which fail to address marginal variations in cost and revenue. Cost accounting should address the entrepreneurial problem, which meant a focus on marginal revenue and marginal cost, supplemented by attention to the avoidance of waste.

Activity Based Costing

This idea that cost behaviour should be understood from the perspective of output volume has recently been subject to extensive criticism. The name Activity Based Costing has been given to the idea that it is activities that drive costs, rather than simple volume-based measures.[9] Activity Based Management is the wider rationale for such an approach, the idea that activity based information should focus employee efforts on attempts to improve continuously quality, time, service, cost, flexibility and profitability. For, as one of the principle proponents of Activity Based Costing has argued, people cannot manage costs, but they can manage the activities that cause costs to be incurred.

Much of the point of Activity Based Costing is to address the fundamental changes that have been occurring in manufacturing industry over the past decade and more. Just-In-Time manufacturing, inventory reductions, flexible manufacturing systems and so forth have, it is argued, made irrelevant many of the assumptions that underlay traditional mass manufacture. The allocation of overhead costs according to scale of output, rather than scope of output, it is argued will tend to 'overcost' high volume products and 'undercost' low volume products. Cost information is thus distorted, according to the proponents of Activity Based Costing. Attention should be shifted towards the identification of 'cost drivers', those activities that cause costs to be incurred. Rather than units of output, the cost driver for an activity such as customer liaison might be the number of customers or orders, the type of customer, or the location of the plants with which liaison is required. That is to say, activities such as transactions, set-ups, and the number of quality inspections and so forth come to replace volume of units of output as the basis for allocating or tracing indirect costs.

But just as traditional methods for dealing with indirect costs are necessarily arbitrary to an extent, so too are Activity Based Costs unable to capture 'true' product costs. Some costs, called joint or common costs, cannot be traced to a particular product. For instance, set-up costs that result from switching from one product to another, and back again, are difficult to trace to one product or the other. A flexible manufacturing system may process a range of products in the course of a day, and it would be extremely difficult to identify what portion of total costs for such a system should be borne by which product. As with conventional methods for allocating indirect costs, joint costs cannot be dealt with in their entirety by Activity Based Costing. Equally, the fixed costs associated with activities are difficult to identify accurately. For Activity Based Costing assumes a linear cost function of the same type as is conventionally assumed for direct costs, such as materials and labour. But the conditions under which such an assumption holds are strictly limited. For instance, the level of operations of one activity should not affect the costs of other activities, and there should not exist economics of scope between activities. To the extent that these restricting assumptions do not hold, some arbitrary allocation of costs is necessary under Activity Based Costing. Thus accountants are left at the end of the twentieth century in the awkward position of being unable to determine accurately the costs of producing a particular product in multi-product environments.

Investment Appraisal

Investment appraisal has proved similarly resistant to accurate measurement and management, despite the introduction of concepts drawn from economic theory. Indeed much debate over the last sixty years or so has centred on the appropriateness of such concepts, notably the time value of money and the cost of capital. Three separate points in time during this period will serve to illustrate the shifting views on the Net Present Value approach to investment appraisal: the year 1938; the year 1965; and the decade of the 1980s.[10]

In 1938, it was argued in a series of articles by Ronald Edwards in *The Accountant* that discounting techniques were essential when considering alternative investments. The crucial point here was the insistence that the *timing* of the cash flows was decisive. Only by translating all financial values into present values could the influence of timing be addressed satisfactorily. A series of articles by Ronald Coase in the same journal that were seen to be regarded as seminal reinforced the point, and articulated the idea that the time value of money, and principles of discounting, were essential when seeking to express costs and revenues in money terms.

But the accountants were not happy at this incursion of economic theory into their domain. In response, Stanley Rowland referred to discounting techniques as 'dangerous nonsense' and 'sheer insanity'.[11] Rowland drew up the battle lines between economists and accountants. The arguments of Edwards, he stated, had 'the unanimity which is so characteristic of economists'. Edwards was 'enjoying for its own sake the sport of bludgeoning the heads of accountants with intent that they shall be both bloody and bowed'.[12] According to Rowland, the domain of the accountant was that of the ledger, 'a world in which cool sanity reigns (. . .) the bed rock on which his whole scheme rests'.[13] He continued: 'the accountant should be content to "record the present as it flows into the past" and should leave to others "the risky business of tearing aside the veil which conceals the future".'

By 1965, things had changed fundamentally. In less than thirty years, the calculus of discounting had become part of accounting. A new mentality reigned. An editorial in *The Accountant* in 1965 provides a convenient market. This stated confidently that 'No one would deny the utility of the DCF technique relatively to other less precise methods'.[14] Much had happened since the fierce debate in the pages of *The Accountant* in 1938. In 1954, Joel Dean had published his massively influential article in the *Harvard Business Review*. This appealed to discounting techniques as 'demonstrably superior to existing alternatives in accuracy, realism, relevance, and sensitivity' (p. 129). Dean argued that management relied to a worrying degree on 'intuition and authority', and that it lacked the 'skilled analysis and the scientific control' needed for intricate, vital capital investment decisions. An avalanche of words had reinforced this appeal to discounting techniques, and to economic reason as the basis for managerial decisions. 'Science' and 'objectivity' had become the battle cry for accountants and managers.

Discounting techniques and the concept of the time value of money were disseminated throughout the 1950s and 1960s in disparate locales. They provided a knowledge base for the new business schools in the UK, offering both a calculus and a conceptual foundation that could be taught to managers. Diverse actors, working within the academy, within firms, and often crossing the boundaries of these distinct terrains, extolled the merits of the discounted cash flow technique for making investment decisions. Professional bodies organised talks for those eager to learn this new calculus. Government agencies such as the National Economic Development Council promoted the technique, for the individual investment decisions of managers were seen as linked to macro-level economic growth. Even a television series in the UK showed DCF techniques in action.

In these different settings, and with a different tempo in the US and the UK, accounting was to be transformed at the margins. An economic-financial mentality was to replace the existing accounting mentality. Economic expertise was to supplant intuition and rule of thumb criteria, as the concept of the time value of money was incorporated in investment decisions. Personal judgment would henceforth be based, or so it was hoped, on the claimed neutrality and objectivity of a 'scientific' evaluation of investment opportunities.

But things were to change yet again. Across the 1980s, and into the 1990s, a number of commentators inside and outside accounting criticised the use of discounting techniques for evaluating investment opportunities. They argued that their use 'is seriously shortchanging the futures of corporations'.[15] The notion of the time value of money was somehow seen to reduce the consideration of strategic opportunities presented by technological advance.[16] More generally, the 'entire capital investment system', including shareholders, lenders, investment managers, corporate directors, managers, and employees has been held to have failed.[17] The effect of this alleged failure, according to Michael Porter, is that the most efficient capital markets in the world, coupled with highly sophisticated investors, produces suboptimal investment behaviour.[18]

Other arguments have reinforced this questioning of DCF methods. Most notably, it has been argued that investment in modern manufacturing systems will be optimal only if the firms coordinate their capital spending across diverse but mutually reinforcing sets of assets, so as to maximise the benefits available from 'complementarities'.[19] An historical survey of capital budgeting systems in the US since World War II makes the same point: certain types of investment need to be understood as investments in 'organisational capabilities', combinations of human skills, procedures and routines, physical assets, and systems of information and incentives that enhance performance along a particular dimension.[20] Such capabilities are organisational assets that increase a company's productivity and the value of its opportunities. However, such capabilities often 'fall through the cracks' of formal financial evaluations of investment opportunities. The point here is that without coordinating investments in diverse types of assets, firms may lose the competitive advantage available from a system of manufacture that depends crucially on integrating activities across sub-units in firms, and across the various stages in the design, manufacturing and marketing process. Terms such as 'synergy' and 'fit' capture the same point, which is that investment decisions should no longer be treated as if the firm was purchasing an 'island of technology', but should address integrated systems of manufacture.

It is too early to predict what will be the outcome of these criticisms of existing financial methods for evaluating investment opportunities. One influential textbook advocates greater caution in the use of discounting methods, yet refrains from a more far-reaching criticism.[21] Meanwhile, the number of voices criticising the financial mentality that underlays discounting techniques continues to increase.[22] But once again the current debates highlight the perceived limits of accounting information. Introductory textbooks may extol the advantages of Net Present Value methods for evaluating investment opportunities, and suggest ever more complex methods for calculating the returns. But the wider debates that surround such tools demonstrates that there is far from unanimous agreement on how such techniques should be applied.

Conclusion

These examples of the problems of attributing costs and of investment appraisal show that there are fundamental ambiguities and uncertainties in accounting practice. They demonstrate the limits of accounting in providing ready answers to demands for accountability, and suggest that performance indicators should not be viewed as an easy solution to the more messy problems of democratic accountability. This is important as accountability is once again on the political agenda. This can take a number of forms. One version is managerial accountability, which can easily be reduced to a call for performance assessment and performance related pay. Rather than resolve questions of principle and meaning, a mechanism or technique for calculating appropriating financial rewards is set in motion. Once the machine is up and running, it has to be made to work. Another version is 'democratic accountability', which is more difficult to define and even more difficult to enact. Whichever is chosen, it is important to take note of the long history and immense difficulties of enacting any form of accountability. Ever since Berle and Means spoke in 1932 of 'a new form of absolutism' when describing the rise of the large corporation and the rise of a new executive class, accountability has proved an elusive goal.[23]

To speak of the limits of accounting is to call for a more cautious assessment of what accounting can deliver, and how it might contribute to enacting accountability. For if accountants continue to have difficulty in measuring precisely product costs, or in valuing accurately particular types of investment in the private sector, it is likely that such issues will prove even more difficult to resolve in the world of the public sector where goals are more ambiguous and multiple constituencies have to be served. This amounts to a word of caution to all those who would place accounting techniques and managerial devices at the heart of political debate. For accounting is not the neutral technique that is often supposed. Accounting does not exist in a neutral world, above the fray. Once installed, it becomes fundamentally implicated in ways of organising and ways of regulating economic life.

In the circumstances, it would be reassuring if one could turn to a literature, and a body of evidence, that would allow one to evaluate the appropriateness of a particular technique in a given situation, as well as the wider issues in question. For other professions, ranging from law to architecture, have long-standing traditions of reflecting not only on this or that technique, but on fundamental principles. And these traditions of reflecting on practice are intrinsically linked to the modernisation of the profession itself. But accounting and management lack such a body of reflective knowledge. Their world is one in which 'solutions' are often enthusiastically proffered, but often without sufficient consideration of the diversity of conditions and consequences. Indeed, one of the most influential recent books on the new public sector presents its diagnosis explicitly as a universal 'checklist'.[24]

The desire to proffer solutions is linked to the idea that accounting is nothing other than technique. If one criticises a particular technique, then the cry goes up: what do you propose instead? The apparent validity of the cry only serves to reinforce the conception that accounting and management are neutral techniques. What is missed in making such an appeal is that accounting techniques are used in particular contexts, they are part of a much wider programme for seeking to govern and regulate economic and social life. If we are to go beyond simply recommending the latest technique that has been developed, we need to consider the three dilemmas outlined at the beginning as an ensemble.

Instead of asking which technique should be used, we need to ask how does a particular technique combine with a particular principle and a particular meaning. Rather than taking as self-evident the dictum that an organisation needs to know its costs, we should ask why is this needed, and for what purpose. Instead of asking how we might calculate the performance bonus to be awarded to a manager, we should ask what type of an organisation is desired, what type of goals are to be fostered. Instead of siding enthusiastically with current calls for leaner organisations, flatter hierarchies, process reengineering, and so forth, we should ask whether the technologies of distrust that pervade the new public sector are appropriate to services as diverse as sewage disposal and medical care, refuse collection and school teaching. To answer such questions fully is likely to take us substantially beyond existing diagnoses and remedies.

Biographical Note

Peter Miller is Professor of Management Accounting at the London School of Economics and Political Science. Originally trained as a sociologist, he has published extensively in the fields of accounting, management, and sociology. His most recent book is *Accounting as Social and Institutional Practice* (Cambridge University Press, 1994). He is Associate Editor of *Accounting, Organizations and Society*.

Notes

1 The NHS guide chosen is: Department of Health, *The NHS Performance Guide, 1994–95* (London: Central Office of Information, 1995). The restaurant guide chosen is: Gault Millau, *Guide: France 1994* (Paris: Gault Millau, 1994). These two guides are chosen for illustrative purposes only.

2 As reflected, for instance, in five-year survival rates for different types of cancer.

3 Cf. M. Power, *The Audit Explosion*, London, Demos, 1994. See also A. G. Hopwood and P. Miller (eds), *Accounting as Social and Institutional Practice* (Cambridge: Cambridge University Press, 1994).

4 The medical profession in Britain is no doubt the most trusted of all the recognised professions, with little of the systematic 'opinion shopping' that takes place for instance in the US.

5 Cf. P. Miller and N. Rose, 'Mobilising the Consumer', *Theory Culture and Society*, 1996.

6 Cf. Johnson & Kaplan cited below.

7 H. T. Johnson and R. S. Kaplan, *Relevance Lost: The Rise and Fall of Management Accounting* (Boston, MA: Harvard Business School Press, 1987). On the wider debates that surround these issues, see P. Miller and T. O'Leary, 'Accounting Expertise and the Politics of the Product: Economic Citizenship and Modes of Corporate Governance', *Accounting, Organizations and Society* (1993), pp. 187–206.

8 This 'something' might be a particular product, a service, a department, a hospital operation, or whatever.

9 On Activity Based Costing, see: M. Bromwich and A. Bhimani, *Management Accounting: Pathways to Progress*, London, CIMA, 1994.

10 My discussion here is deliberately brief, as I have discussed the first two of these moments extensively in P. Miller, 'Accounting Innovation Beyond the Enterprise', *Accounting, Organisations and Society*, vol. 16, no.8, pp. 733–63, 1991.

11 *The Accountant*, 1938, pp.609–10.

12 *The Accountant*, 15 October 1938, p. 519.

13 *Ibid.*, p. 522.

14 *The Accountant*, 6 February 1965, pp. 145–6.

15 R. H. Hayes and D. A. Garvin, 'Managing as if Tomorrow Mattered', *Harvard Business Review* (May–June 1982), p. 72.

16 B. Avishai, 'A CEO's Common Sense of CIM; An Interview with J. Tracy O'Rourke', *Harvard Business Review* (January–February 1989), p. 112.

17 M. E. Porter, 'Capital Disadvantage: America's Failing Capital Investment System', *Harvard Business Review* (September–October 1992), p. 65.

18 M. E. Porter, 'Capital Disadvantage: America's Failing Capital Investment System', *Harvard Business Review* (September–October 1992), p.68.

19 P. Milgrom and J. Roberts, 'The economics of modern manufacturing: technology, strategy and organization', *The American Economic Review* (June 1990), pp. 511–528. See also for an illustration of such an approach, P. Miller & T. O'Leary, 'Capital budgeting and the transition to modern manufacture', Working Paper (1996).

20 C. Y. Baldwin and K. B. Clark, 'Capital budgeting systems and capabilities investments in US companies after the Second World War', *Business History Review* 68 (Spring 1994), pp.73–109.

21 Cf. R. Kaplan & A. A. Atkinson, *Advanced Management Accounting*, 2nd edition (Englewood Cliffs, NJ: Prentice-Hall Inc, 1989).

22 For a more extended discussion of these issues in the context of the US, see P. Miller and T. O'Leary, 'Accounting Expertise and the Politics of the Product: Economic Citizenship and Modes of Corporate Governance', *Accounting, Organizations and Society*, vol. 18, nos. 2/3 (1983), pp.187–206. With respect to the UK, Will Hutton proposes a related argument in *The State We're In* (London: Jonathan Cape,

1995). See in particular his comments in chapter six regarding the desire for liquidity that underpins the British financial system.

23 A. A. Berle & G. C. Means, *The Modern Corporation and Private Property* originally published 1932: New York, Harcourt Brace, 1968.

24 D. Osborne and T. Gaebler, *Reinventing Government: How the entrepreneurial spirit is transforming the public sector* (Reading, MA: Addison-Wesley, 1992), p. 311. Of course, in the appendix the authors itemise a number of caveats; but these do not alter fundamentally the universal prescriptions contained in the book.

The Implications for Democracy of Computerisation in Government

HELEN MARGETTS

THE widespread use of computers by government is commonly regarded by both practitioners and academics as having democratic implications. On the one hand, enthusiastic modernists consider that information technology allows the possibility of more accurate fitting of implementation to policy decisions and facilitates new citizen state interactions. Some go further, envisaging a new form of direct democracy through technology, with electronic town halls and a technically created forum for citizen participation in policy decisions. On the other hand, pessimistic commentators regard technology as heralding the 'control state' with equally dramatic but malign consequences for democracy. The first part of this article investigates the claims of both houses by examining the reality of government computing over the last forty years. Having concluded that neither scenario fits accurately with reality, the second part outlines five reasons why government's hold of the technological reins of the new-style state is tenuous. The third section outlines the probable implications for democracy and suggests some remedies for a tendency of the computerised elements of the state to slip out of control.

Computerisation in Government: Electronic Democracy or the Control-State?

The concept of a unified civil service to implement the policy decisions of elected politicians is one of the traditional tenets of a liberal democracy. Since Weber observed the characterising features of administrative organisation and labelled them bureaucracy, some kind of unified administration has formed a recognised part of the state in most liberal democracies. The British civil service was especially noted by Weber to typify his definition of bureaucracy. From the late 1950s, this civil service has undergone a slow and gradual change: a significant proportion of administrative operations are now carried out through the use of computerised systems. Starting with the computerisation of financial systems during the 1950s and 1960s, computers spread throughout government through the 1970s, forming an increasingly important part of each Department. Information technology expenditure in UK central government in the 1990s is around £2 billion annually, one per cent of public expenditure. The three highest spending departments are the Ministry of Defence (£748 million in 1995), the Inland Revenue (£247 million) and the Department of Social Security (£371 million), for which administrative

© The Political Quarterly Publishing Co. Ltd. 1996
Published by Blackwell Publishers, 108 Cowley Road, Oxford OX4 1JF, UK and 238 Main Street, Cambridge, MA 02142, USA

operations now form 12, 11 and 13 per cent of administrative costs respectively.

In the 1990s, the computer systems that have been developed within departments are critical to policy. First, because at the most basic level if they fail to function policy cannot be implemented. Mistakes or failures tend to be more systematic and of a larger scale than with traditional administrative methods, as the London Ambulance Service found when their new computer aided ambulance dispatch system failed comprehensively and disastrously in 1993. Secondly, increasingly policy innovation depends upon technological innovation. For education, the Deputy Prime Minister Michael Heseltine has claimed that information technology will bring the 'nervous system of a new order'[1] with a £10 million project to link schools and colleges to a national network. In the Home Office, initial dramatic impact of a Police National Computer on policing strategies in the 1980s was followed by a batch of innovations in the 1990s including a system to check DNA, collecting the 'genetic fingerprints' of people charged with burglary, serious assault and sexual offences and matching them against blood, mouth cells, hair roots or semen collected from the scenes of crime. The system was described by the Home Secretary as the 'most significant scientific advance in crime-fighting since the introduction of fingerprints'.[2] During the 1990s, smart cards have been under continual discussion by policy makers, offering access to a new range of electronic transactions between citizen and state. If such innovations are not successful, then policy decisions are affected. Curfew orders introduced in the 1991 Criminal Justice Act cannot be implemented, for example, because of the persistent failure of electronic tagging of prisoners.

What are the democratic implications of such changes? At first glance, it might be assumed that computers enable more 'accurate' policy making. First, through the systematisation of administrative operations, which allow more precise implementation of policy decisions. Secondly, through overcoming problems of bounded rationality, so allowing more sophisticated investigation of policy alternatives. In this way, we might expect computer systems to 'out-Weber Weber', as Christopher Hood has elegantly put it, facilitating a greater rationalisation of bureaucracy. And the additional scope for policy innovation, especially the extension of citizen-state interactions through computer networking facilities would also seem to enhance the democratic process. Indeed the most enthusiastic of modernists suggest that information technology can act as a driver in encouraging members of the public to become more engaged in political decisions through a form of direct democracy, with voter juries, extended use of consultative referenda and the engagement of citizens in deliberation of controversial local issues using the combined television and telephone networks built by cable companies in collaboration with local authorities.[3]

More pessimistic observers of the process are fearful of information technology driven change, claiming that malign governments holding the technological reins will drag us into a 'control state'. Beniger[4] for example, claimed that the 'progressive convergence of information-processing and communications technologies in a single infrastructure of control' was sustaining the 'Control Revolution'; 'a concentration of abrupt changes in the technological and economic arrangements by which information is collected, stored and processed and communicated, and through which formal or programmed decisions might effect societal control'. In the United States, David Burnham saw a causal relationship between new technology, state tyranny and the undermining of democracy: 'the spread of computers has enabled the National Security Agency to dominate our society should it ever decide such action is necessary'. Warner and Stone described 'the Onrush of Technology and the Threat to Freedom' through computers and the storage of information by state organisations in Britain and America. Other writers predict that computers are leading us to a 'cyborg world' in which 'infotech systems promote new models of rationality, cognition and intelligence', or a 'military revolution'. Such accounts are derived from military world-views and founded on the pursuit of a logic of total control, both internal and external: 'the military information society involves internalising a self-discipline, technologies of the self, in ways that come to be seen as normal, rational, reasonable'. Such writing belongs to a wider tradition of anti-utopianism that also has its roots in the Weberian tradition. Just as Weber feared that if bureaucracy were not properly controlled and regulated an unbridled bureaucratic domination would result, Kafka in the 1920s and Orwell in the 1940s saw a rule of impersonal officialdom, disastrously strengthened by technological advance. The human 'machine' of Weberian bureaucracy would be dehumanised, first by the systematisation of human procedures, followed by the replacement of humans with automated machines.

A robot, however responsive, is useful only to someone who holds its remote control. So does the Government hold the remote control? Both sides of the argument outlined above rest on the assumption that the core of contemporary government holds the technological reins of the computerised elements of the state. The argument of this article is that the core's hold over the new style government is tenuous, for four reasons. First, because the gradual development of information systems throughout government has been unregulated, unguided and poorly evaluated. Secondly, because the particular style of British government with tightly vertical lines of control and little inter-agency working works against the integration of computer systems upon which innovations depend. Thirdly, the particular nature of information technology creates a new need for organised expertise throughout government, which then engenders new problems of control. Fourthly, because governmental response to the need for organisational expertise has been to rely increasingly on the services of global computer services providers. And finally, because the development has occurred at a particular point in administrative history, the form of such contracts has taken on a particular size and shape that is not conducive to future management or control. All these factors have inhibited the development of a technological infrastructure upon which the latest batch of innovations depend.

Guidance, Evaluation and Control

In the early days of computers in government, their use was quite tightly guided from the centre. Central agencies offered guidance to inexperienced departments, and expenditure on information technology was tightly controlled. During the 1980s, however such controls were relaxed, partly in response to departments' increasing capabilities and partly in line with a more general trend towards administrative decentralisation and the intended 'executive autonomy' of new public management change, notably the Next Steps programme. The CCTA, the Government Centre for Information Systems, has since 1972 been the principal agency with government-wide responsibility for information technology. Until 1984 the Agency played a central controlling role; it 'owned' all the computers in government and from within the Treasury exerted strong control over agencies' information technology budgets. In 1984, however, the agency was criticised for its excessive role in project control and its authority was removed, since when the Agency has existed as a solely advisory body with persistent rumours that it will be either privatised or abolished. In 1995 CCTA seemed set to continue with the public sector when its establishment as an Executive Agency was announced, but the stipulation that the agency must recoup 90 per cent of its costs (already up from 75 per cent) from department and agencies that use its advice ensures that its role is likely to remain reactive rather than proactive and the Agency has no strategic planning role.

Evaluation of information technology investment is also decentralised. Unlike the General Accounting Office in the United States, the National Audit Office (the chief administrative watchdog in the UK) does not look at general government-wide developments, partly because it is idiosyncratically organised within units which are divided by department rather than administrative function. Thus the National Audit Office, unlike the General Accounting Office, does not evaluate information technology at a government-wide level, nor does it identify government-wide information technology issues. Indeed, two recent reports covering similar, hitherto unique information technology control contracts awarded by central government departments (the Inland Revenue and the Department of Transport) did not even refer to each other.

In 1996, one central government actor recognised that there was a problem with central guidance of information technology development. Michael Heseltine set up the CITU, a division of around ten staff largely seconded from the private sector and run along the lines of a company board within the Cabinet Office. The new unit was given the brief of linking Whitehall departments covering benefits, tax, passports, driving licences, student loans and state grants, thereby creating an 'electronic window' into government by allowing citizens to order passports, fill in tax forms and claim benefits over the computer network.[5] Thus in the 1990s, a more pluralistic arrangement for central control and guidance of information technology is developing. But it is difficult to see how, with around ten staff the new CITU will have a significant impact on government-wide information technology as a whole. Indeed, it seems almost perverse that the new agency will operate in isolation from an agency specifically designed to deal with the machinery of government issues, the Office of Public Service (OPS), in which the CCTA currently resides. And the Labour Party expressed justifiable confusion as to who was actually responsible for information technology in government when the Office of Science and Technology was removed from the OPS within the Cabinet Office in 1995. A Labour MP asked in Parliament who was responsible for science and technology in the government—the Deputy Prime Minister or the President of the Board of Trade?[6] Such confusion is exacerbated by the existence of the Private Finance Unit within the Cabinet Office which has a brief to supervise those information technology projects funded under the Private Finance Initiative and whose responsibilities relative to the CITU and the CCTA remains unclear.

Integration and Innovation

As noted earlier, information technology offers the possibility for policy innovation in the 1990s. Early computers were used to automate existing administrative tasks, but during the 1980s considerably more possibilities presented themselves due to the wider availability and lower cost of more technically sophisticated solutions. But many of the latest batch of policy innovations rely on the communication of computer systems across departments, matching between computer systems and the development of a technical infrastructure across government.

The organisation of British government is particularly unconducive to such developments taking place. The civil service has traditionally been organised along vertical lines of control, with strong rivalries existing between departments. Inter-agency projects are difficult to initiate and even harder to fund. Although computer systems are ritually identified as a 'challenge' to 'the traditional vertical integration of government administration where information only meets at the top of the Cabinet level',[7] it is a challenge that has been only patchily met. This tendency is especially ironic with respect to information technology, because many practitioners speak of information technology development offering increased potential to develop 'whole person' and 'citizen-oriented' services, whereby the consumers of government services are no longer cut up into 'social slices' through the necessity of dealing on an individual basis with each department. Such developments depend crucially on the integration of computer systems. The introduction of the Jobseeker's Allowance was delayed by six months because computers used by the Benefits Agency and the former Department of Employment were incompatible. Indeed the CITU was created partly in response to reported alarm from Heseltine when he discovered that each department was allowed to develop its own computer system, with resultant duplication and incompatibility.[8]

Technological Complexity–and Ignorance

Bureaucracy has always been something that government were deemed to 'know about' and 'be good at', while the development of complex technical systems does not fall into this category. In fact, perhaps surprisingly, in the early days of computing government departments were leaders in the field, using computers at the forefront of technological development. But during the 1970s, government use of computers moved gradually away from this position, with the Civil Service Department admitting in 1971 that 'there is some validity in the criticism that departments have moved from their earlier position as national leaders in computer development'.[9] In 1988, looking back on the recent history of government as a user of computer technology, the Trade and Industry Committee reported consultants' evidence that 'some of the Government implementations are without doubt the best practice anywhere in the world . . . but most are not'.

Information technology since the 1970s has presented a challenge to government in that it engenders the need for a particular kind of organised expertise within bureaucracies. Such a challenge has increased over time as the technical possibilities become wider, introducing the same kind of complexity (and equivalent possibilities for high expenditure) into administrative operations as in the defence agencies or the Health Service. As the National Audit Office put it with respect to the Inland Revenue computer systems (once described as the 'Rolls Royce' of government computing after a largely successful project to computerise PAYE in the 1980s), 'those systems, though still providing good service, have become more complex over the years. They cannot now be enhanced to provide the functionality needed to support all the changes the Department wants to make'.[10] Government organisations have been further hampered in meeting this challenge by civil service pay and promotion scales and regulations, which prevented them from recruiting staff, especially at times when there was a shortage of staff in both private and public sectors, described by the Trade Union, MSF, to the Trade and Industry Committee in 1989 as 'the single most important issue affecting the IT industry'.

Thus the machinery of government is less comprehensible than it used to be, further exacerbating traditional problems of accountability in bureaucracy. A second implication of technological tasks forming a core part of administrative operations is a further layer of complexity between policy makers and administration, rendering the understanding of administrative operations, not usually at the forefront of politicians' interests, even more complex and less conducive to understanding. Such problems are particularly acute in the UK, given the extreme capacity of politicians to forget about issues of administration (especially in comparison with the United States), and the closure and secretiveness of British government (again in sharp contrast to the US). Technological complexity also presents a challenge to traditional oversight arrangements, illustrated by the Central Veterinary Laboratory, part of the Ministry of Agriculture, Fisheries and Food, which secretly abandoned a computer system designed to integrate results of tests on animal blood and organs, part of an initiative aimed at improving the laboratory's efficiency at monitoring the spread of diseases including Bovine Spongiform Encephalopathy (BSE) and salmonella. The Treasury had approved the development of a £1.2 million system in 1990; the decision a year later to abandon the project was not made public and the annual accounts of the laboratory made no mention of it.

Contracting Out

To an increasing extent, the response of government departments to the perceived difficulty of information technology has been to contract the task out. This trend was fuelled by the architects of the Market Testing programme introduced by the Conservative government in 1991, under which departments and agencies were mandated to subject certain areas of work to competitive tendering by private sector organisations, with information technology work identified as a promising candidate. In fact William Waldegrave, who implemented the first stages of the market testing initiative, specified information technology as one of the areas 'where the Government could not maintain the investment and expertise necessary to compete effectively with the private sector and from which it was best for the Government to withdraw'.[11] The information technology activity in the Ministry of Agriculture Fisheries and Food, Customs and Excise, MoD, Department for Education and Employment, Foreign Office, Home Office, Inland Revenue, Lord Chancellor's Department, Northern Ireland Office, Office of Public Service and Science, the Department of Trade and Industry, the Department of Transport and the Welsh Office were all earmarked for market testing.

As a consequence, by 1995 UK central government departments contracted out on average around thirty per cent of their information technology operations,[12] a percentage which is higher than the average European private sector company. The shape and size of such contracts has also changed over time. While earlier use of private sector assistance involved the ad-hoc involvement of individual computer consultants, the 1980s and 1990s brought the rise of 'Systems Integrators', companies which offered to take over the management of information technology divisions in their entirety. Such companies have grown in response to a private sector trend away from 'spot contracting' and towards strategic alliances and partnership arrangements, with customers asking for long-term contracts which varied over time with demand. Thus across public and private sectors the size of information

technology contracts has grown; by the 1990s, the average life of an information technology outsourcing contract in the UK and Europe was five to seven
years. Systems integrators often aim to develop expertise in a wider range of
their clients' 'systems' than merely developing information systems, seeing
information systems as intertwined with other service functions: 'a new
outsourcing model is being developed in Europe—a vertical cut of business
process rather than the horizontal cut of information technology'.[13] Such
contracts are described as 'partnerships' with customers rather than service
contracts and are often negotiated on new terms. For example, the Computer
Sciences Corporation entered an eleven year agreement with the retail
company British Home Stores under which it took over the company's
computing and 115 staff but also worked with it to sell the combined expertise
of the two organisations to the retail industry. By the 1990s, Electronic Data
Systems was signing contracts under which it took on system development at
no cost in return for a percentage of the business gains by the customer, with
the company's managing director claiming that this type of contract would
account for 70 per cent of EDS' growth in the next three to five years. Thus
when EDS bids for an information technology deal, the company's long-term
aim will be to gain control of a wider range of functions and some measure of
profit sharing.

The market of computer companies that presents itself to government
departments (as opposed to private sector companies) seeking technical
expertise has developed in a distinctive way. Although the number of vendors
of information technology services in general almost doubled between 1987
and 1990, one survey identified the development of a two-tier market with a
'few very large, increasingly global players offering the whole range of
outsourcing services, and secondly, an increasing number of smaller, niche
vendors'.[14] Computer companies that successfully tender for government
computer projects have tended to fall into the upper tier of this market. In
many cases, government computer systems are unusual by virtue of their size
(the project to computerise the UK Social Security system, for example, was
the largest civilian computing project in the world during the 1980s) and only
the largest companies can cope with the processing load. A further push for
government contracts to attract only the largest of companies is that such
deals are subject to the Transfer of Undertakings (Protection of Employment)
regulations (1981) under which civil service transferred to the successful
bidder are entitled to retain their existing terms and conditions of employment, representing a powerful disincentive to smaller companies.

In the 1990s, a handful of huge global companies have emerged as the key
players in government computing. Electronic Data Systems, the largest
computer company in the world, has been successful at winning UK government contracts for the Ministry of Defence, the Child Support Agency, the
Benefits Agency, the Inland Revenue and the Department of Transport. The
SEMA Group (which made a plan as early as 1989 to earn 60 per cent of
revenues from systems integration) is another key player. SEMA won a

partnership contract with the Home Office information technology division, a systems integration contract for the Royal Navy and are also developing the national unemployment benefit system (Nubs2) for the Department of Social Security, as well as carrying out systems analysis for the Meat Hygiene Service in MAFF.

Computerisation and the Next Steps Programme

The above developments have taken place at a particular point in administrative history. The Next Steps programme, which divides central departments into agencies, with the aim of enhancing executive autonomy, has also shaped the type of computing that has emerged in government, in some instances acting to fuel the shift towards 'systems integration' type contracts. In some departments the information technology divisions have been made into executive agencies. Therefore, under Next Steps guidelines, they must be submitted for a 'Prior Options' review on creation, three years after creation and systematically thereafter. Prior Options involves asking first, whether there is a continuing need for the activity at all and secondly whether the agency should not be privatised en bloc, usually by means of a negotiated transfer of the undertakings involved to a private corporation in return for a contract to provide the department involved with the same services. Only after these options have been rejected can the agency continue to carry out operations, and must still consider specific tranches of work for contracting out.

For the agencies which have been created specifically to carry out the Information Technology operations of the major departments, the second option has been popular. Two such agencies tendered for privatisation have been the DVOIT, the information technology arm of the Department of Transport, and the Information Technology Office of the Inland Revenue. The DVOIT was offered for sale at the price of £5.5 million in 1993, at the same time offering service contracts for information technology services worth £70 million. EDS was the successful bidder for both sale and service contracts. Obviously the agency considered only companies that could handle the massive DVOIT workload, including the database and processing of details of all UK car drivers and owners. The privatisation of the Information Technology Office of the Inland Revenue in 1994 resulted in an even more important contract for EDS. The Inland Revenue spoke initially to companies with more than 20,000 staff worldwide; only a large manufacturer could be expected to meet their conditions and two clear front runners were identified, the Computer Sciences Corporation (in association with IBM) and EDS. Eventually the ten year, £1 billion contract was awarded to EDS, Europe's largest data processing outsourcing deal, public or private sector. The contract was also covered by TUPE and specified the transfer of 2,000 staff for whom terms and conditions would be preserved. The relationship between the Inland Revenue and the EDS has been characterised as a partnership by EDS.

In this way, public management change has combined with computerisation in a particular way. First, information technology operations have been parcelled up in agency form, and secondly handed over to private sector companies. Contracts of this shape produce an additional layer of administrative complexity for elected politicians, as all administrative and policy decisions in the future must pass through the contract management teams of agencies like the DVOIT and the Inland Revenue Information Technology Office. Only the biggest companies can tender for such contracts and EDS emerges as a key player, having been also successful in winning 85 per cent of contracts when the Information Technology Services Agency (which runs all of the information technology operations of the agencies within the Department of Social Security), market tested its information technology processing arm in 1994.

As the companies that successfully tender for government computer contracts get larger, the government organisations attempting to control such contracts are getting smaller, as Departments break into agencies through the continuation of the Next Steps programme. Such fragmentation has created even more difficulties in ensuring standardisation and integration of computer systems across departments. Fragmentation has not cured the problem of rivalry and non-communication between departments, but rather increased the number of rivalries likely to occur through relationships between agencies while reducing the authority of core departments to overcome such rivalries. In the Benefits Agency, for example, an attempt to develop a joint screen with the Contributions Agency failed, as users were unable to agree on a design which would suit both agencies' requirements. Even the involvement of the core department was unable to resolve the dispute. Technology may be used to reinforce existing links between organisations but it cannot be used to forge links where none existed previously.

The Future of the Computerised State

All the above factors combine to ensure that information technology represents a control problem as well as a solution, with implications for accountability and democracy. There is no technological determinist push to this argument; these are merely the facts that have shaped the particular way that information technology has developed within the UK government. Weber's fears of what bureaucracy might do to a democracy if uncontrolled seem equally applicable to the new global players drawn into government via this process. And if policy innovation through systems integration is to take place it seems that these new players will play a most important role in its implementation. If the tax and social security systems were to be merged, for example, in a radical policy innovation mentioned on several occasions by policy makers (yet impossible to undertake without the merging of two massive and complex computer systems currently operating in virtual isolation), it would be Electronic Data Systems that would be the organisation in a position most likely to influence the development of such an innovation. There is no government agency with so great a collective knowledge of computer systems in the relevant departments and agencies. As the state fragments into Next Steps agencies and quasi-governmental agencies, with minimal (or pluralistic) central agency direction, the organisations which develop and control the new nervous system of government are growing larger. Management of the giants drawn into government by the combination of factors outlined above is likely to be a formidable task.

Such a situation may reassure those who feared the development of the 'Control State'. Government computer systems are very far from being able comprehensively to track citizens' movements. Modernist and anti-modernist assumptions that the march of technological progress is inexorable are often contradicted by exactly the type of problems engendered by such arrangements. For example, in 1995 the Home Office started spending money on a national automated fingerprint system which had been under discussion for 10 years and is now due to come on line at the turn of the century. The system was the object of considerable controversy, receiving criticism from local police forces, 27 of which formed an independent consortium with IBM to develop their own fingerprinting systems. This system was operational for two years, radically enhancing the forces' ability to scan fingerprints at the national level. In 1995, however, the consortia became disillusioned with IBM's fulfilment of their contractual obligations and terminated the contract, with legal action ensuing on both sides. Local police stations issued a writ against IBM and reverted to a manual system for matching fingerprints, leaving themselves with a vastly reduced capability to trace fingerprints at a national level.

Although the Control State has not materialised, the fragmentation of contemporary government combined with the overweening power of computer services providers still gives rise to concern over the democratic implications of information technology and threatens to awaken technological utopians from their dreams. Many of the innovations possible through technology, especially citizen-oriented initiatives and 'electronic democracy', depend upon existing technological infrastructure within the government and the integration of existing computer systems which are becoming increasingly difficult to implement.

Would a change in government provide the solution? Certainly, the prospective Labour Government has already shown strong interest in the subject of information technology, although such interest will not necessarily be accompanied by greater administrative understanding. Labour have expressed enthusiasm for electronic government initiatives in the USA, where Clinton's administrative reform effort, the National Performance Review (NPR) planned several information technology developments to overcome what Vice President Al Gore identified as the root problem of contemporary American public administration: 'the persistence of industrial-era bureaucracies in an information age.' In Britain, Chris Smith, the Shadow

Heritage Secretary has emerged as the Labour Party's 'Al Gore' and has visited the US to investigate Gore's initiatives, setting up a policy forum on the Information Superhighway on his return and developing Labour's National Communications Strategy. In 1995, Tony Blair made the development of policy on the information superhighway his central priority for the year, climaxing in October 1995 when British Telecom (BT) agreed with the Labour Party to link all schools, colleges, libraries and hospitals with a superhighway for free in return for a gradual relaxation of restrictions on BT's access to the cable entertainment business.

However, without concerted rationalisation of computer systems within government departments, neither recent Conservative initiatives nor BT's promise to the Labour Party will alone result in an information superhighway that links citizens to government any more than at present. Indeed, the Conservative Government and especially the Labour Party (given their strong interest in American initiatives) might do well to heed the warnings of the US General Accounting Office, who viewed the National Performance Review's heavy reliance on existing information technology within the Federal Government with concern in their public response to the Reform proposals:

Despite heavy investment in computer technology, executive agencies still lack essential information for managing their programs and resources effectively, controlling expenditures and achieving measurable results. Moreover, many agencies are not using information technology strategically to simplify and streamline their organization, management and business processes to improve service to the public and reduce costs. As a result, projects have consistently run into serious trouble—they are developed late, fail to work as planned and cost much more than expected. The results, in missed benefits and misspent money, can be found throughout the government. Dramatic benefits in cost savings, productivity and services rarely materialize. Rather, some improvements are gained at the margins—but often at a high cost.

It is hoped that both parties will consider that such observations might also be true of UK government departments. However, the Labour Party has not announced any information technology policy within the government. Furthermore, a recognition that tackling such problems is expensive is important: as the Minister for the Office of Public Service (OPS) put it in 1995, 'the main determinant of progress is price. If we cannot bring down the price of communicating electronically, progress will falter'. While new technology can be viewed as the 'handmaiden of open government', it also tends to ensure that open government is more expensive government.[15] So the technological utopian's dreams, like the fears of the anti-modernists, are difficult to realise.

How might the problems outlined above be overcome, thereby deriving the maximum democratic benefits from the technological revolution? Such a question might be tackled through consideration of the distinguishing characteristics of UK government technology outlined above. First, evidence from government computing in the last twenty years suggests benefits might be gained from an enhanced role for the CCTA. The current pluralistic arrangements for controlling information technology within government seem unlikely to be sustainable, especially given their reliance on individual ministerial enthusiasm. Many practitioners throughout government speak highly of the accumulated expertise of the CCTA and perhaps if merged with the authority of the CITU the agency might be able to adopt the strategic role that Heseltine envisages. Such an apparent centralising move would be unfashionable. But without rationalisation, integration and matching of computer systems, duplication and incompatibility will continue to inhibit worthwhile development.

Secondly, there needs to be a widespread recognition among policy makers that technological ignorance can be expensive; the computerised elements of the state cannot be regarded as straightforward administrative tools which can be carried out unproblematically by the private sector in isolation from a policy making elite. Otherwise, the government may find itself in the same position as Barings Bank in 1994. Nick Leeson, the rogue trader who brought Barings Bank to its £730 million collapse, described how technological ignorance among senior Barings staff cleared the way for his trading methods. Speaking of the futures and option settlements executive at Barings, he wrote 'If he had been able to operate just one simple checking device, which any auditor should do when they switch the machines on, he'd have seen some figures which would have given him a heart attack'.[16]

Thirdly, it has to be recognised that contract management, especially of contracts with a high technical content, is a highly expensive and time-consuming task, requiring new kinds of skills and expertise. The type of contracts entered into between the Inland Revenue and Electronic Data Systems are long term relationships, with the company accumulating expertise that will make it difficult for another company to tender for the contract in the future. It is virtually inconceivable that the Inland Revenue will ever run its own computer systems again. Contract management is not generally regarded as a prime position for a civil service high flyer, but with contracts assuming such importance the role will need to be professionalised. And the dangers of such contracts must be taken seriously. An otherwise sanguine National Audit Office report on the EDS/Inland Revenue deal outlined 43 risk factors attached to the contract. The most important risk must be the extent to which the governmental representatives will remain in control of policy-related operations. Information technology operations are difficult to separate from organisations' other functions, which is why companies like Electronic Data Systems are keen to enter into contract arrangements where they take a vertical cut of operations, with a possible expansion of their role. Such contracts introduce the same type of relationships into civilian agencies that have long existed in the defence agencies, and the history of defence contracting does not inspire confidence for their future.

Computer technology does open up new possibilities for democratic interactions between citizens and state. But it is up to current and future governments to ensure that such benefits are reaped; they are not an automatic by-product of the information age. Only a historical rather than a futuristic view of computerisation in government will promote an understanding of what possibilities can be realised. Policy makers must drag themselves away from the exciting innovations they faithfully trust the information superhighway will bring, and devote themselves to the more prosaic subject of administrative computing.

Biographical Note

Helen Margetts is a Lecturer in Politics at Birkbeck College. She has researched and published widely within the field of public policy and management, including several articles on the implications of the use of information technology in government and administrative reform in the United States. She is currently working on books on the US Federal State, government information technology in the US and the UK, and a rational choice account of metropolitan policy-making structures in London.

References

1 *Guardian*, 4 November 1995.
2 *Financial Times*, 12 August 1995.
3 See Andrew Adonis and Geoff Mulgan, 'Back to Greece: the scope for direct democracy', in 'Lean Democracy', *Demos Quarterly*, Issue 3, 1994. For examples of pilot experiments see Theodore Becker, 'Electrifying Democracy' in the same issue.
4 See J. Beniger, 'Information Society and Global Science' in C. Dunlop and R. Kling (eds.), *Computerization and Controversy: Value Conflicts and Social Choices*, London, Academic Press, 1991, p. 388; D. Burnham, *The Rise of the Computer State*, 1983, p. 144; M. Warner and M. Stone, *The Databank Society*, London, George Allen and Unwin Ltd, 1970; D. Goure, 'The Military-Technical Revolution', *Washington Quarterly*, vol. 16, no. 4, 1993; Kafka, *The Trial*, London, Pan Books, 1925; G. Orwell, *Nineteen-Eighty-Four*, Middlesex, Penguin, 1954.
5 *Guardian*, 30 January 1996.
6 *Press Association*, 20 October 1995.
7 *Financial Times*, 7 February 1996.
8 *Financial Times*, 8 November 1995.
9 Civil Service Department (CSD), *Computers in Central Government: Ten Years Ahead*, London, HMSO, 1971, p. 10.
10 National Audit Office, *Change Management in the Inland Revenue*, London, HMSO, HC140, February 1996.
11 Treasury and Civil Service Select Committee, *The Role of the Civil Service Fifth Report*, London, HMSO, vol. 1, 1994.
12 See Kable, *Market Profile: Civil Service IS 1994/95*, London, Kable, 1994; Kable, *Market Profile: Civil Service IS 1995/96*, London, Kable, 1995. On the basis of survey evidence, European organisations in the early 1990s outsourced on average between 6–7 per cent of their information technology expenditure: 47 per cent of organisations outsourced some or all of their information technology; see L. Willcocks and G. Fitzgerald, *A Business Guide to Outsourcing IT*, London, Business

Intelligence, 1994, p. 10 which is also the source for the identification of the 'two-tier' computer company market.

13 David Andrews, partner with Andersen Consulting, quoted in the *Financial Times*, 21 October 1992.

14 L. Willcocks & G. Fitzgerald, *A Business Guide to Outsourcing*, London, Business Intelligence, 1994.

15 Robert Hughes in *The Times*, 16 February 1995.

16 *Computing*, 22 February 1996, p. 4.

Towards Economic Democracy in Britain

ROBIN ARCHER

IN this article I want to suggest that one of the key economic institutions in our society is fundamentally illegitimate. This might seem like an odd thing to say at a time when there seems to be an ever-widening consensus about the legitimacy of the core institutions of contemporary capitalism. In Britain, for example, we have recently seen the Labour Party rewrite its constitution precisely in order to acknowledge the legitimacy of private ownership and the market.

Here, however, I do not propose to challenge these features of the emerging consensus. For the illegitimate institution that I have in mind is neither private ownership nor the market, but rather the firm, and, in particular, its decision-making structure. There is a strong moral case for replacing the current system of corporate governance with a system of economic democracy, where, by 'economic democracy' I mean a system in which firms operate in a market economy, but are governed by those who work for them.

This means that my argument is different from that in some of the other articles in this volume. For it is not about how best to implement a principle that is already widely accepted. Rather, it must seek to establish a principle in the first place. An analogy with the development of political democracy may help to illustrate the point I am making. It is now commonly argued that electoral laws need to be reformed in order to ensure that parliament better reflects the will of the people. This is not an argument about the principle of universal suffrage, but rather about how best to implement it. The task facing proponents of economic democracy, however, is less like that of contemporary advocates of electoral reform, and more like that of the nineteenth century advocates of political democracy who sought to establish the principle of universal suffrage in the first place.

As a result the first part of my article may seem somewhat utopian (just as political democracy seemed for much of the nineteenth century). But it is important not to shy away from goals simply because they are utopian. Even if we cannot achieve these goals immediately; indeed, even if we can never fully achieve them, they are still of fundamental importance because they establish the direction in which we should try to move. So long as *some* movement in the direction of the goal is feasible, then the utopia is worth pursuing.

I want to do two things. First, I want to offer a moral argument for why a system of economic democracy ought to be introduced; and secondly, I want to offer a political and economic argument about why a move towards

© The Political Quarterly Publishing Co. Ltd. 1996
Published by Blackwell Publishers, 108 Cowley Road, Oxford OX4 1JF, UK and 238 Main Street, Cambridge, MA 02142, USA   85

greater economic democracy would be a feasible goal for the labour movement.

Utopia

The starting point for my argument is the idea that we should try to maximise every individual's freedom. This aspiration stems from the core values of the Enlightenment and is common to both liberal and socialist traditions, as well as to most versions of contemporary conservatism. Thus, in a country like Britain, there is widespread agreement about its importance.

At the same time, there is, of course, a debate about just what constitutes individual freedom. I do not want to enter into this debate here: rather I will simply point out that most conceptions of freedom agree that an individual is only free if his or her choices govern his or her actions. With this idea of freedom in mind, I give what I taken to be the basic argument for economic democracy. The argument is set out more fully in my book, *Economic Democracy*.[1]

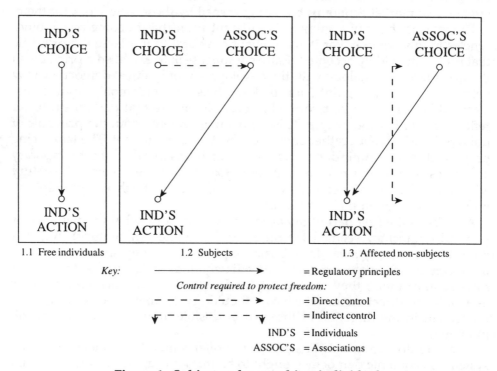

Figure 1. Subject and non-subject individuals

A free individual is an individual whose choices govern his or her actions. This is the situation illustrated in figure 1.1. There are two ways in which an association (whether it is a state or whether it is a shoe factory) can effect that individual's freedom.

One way the individual's freedom might be affected is for the association to exclude and replace the individual's choices (see figure 1.2). That is what happens when an association subjects the individual to its authority. For example, that is what the state does when a policeman says, 'pull over'. The state excludes my choice about where to drive and replaces it with its own.

But there is another way an association might affect me. In this case the association's choices do not replace my own choices, they simply have an additional affect which I must taken into account before I act (see figure 1.3). For example, a firm from which I buy my shoes might makes choices that result in the production of defective shoes. These choices can certainly affect me, but not in a way that makes me subject to the authority of the firm. The firm cannot order me to buy its shoes.

These two ways in which my freedom can be affected correspond to two different methods of protecting my individual freedom.

In the second case (figure 1.2), the way to protect my freedom is simply to remove the additional impact that the association is having. For example in the case of the shoe factory, a competitive market would enable me to do that by enabling me to simply exit from my relationship with that particular shoe factory and go and buy my shoes somewhere else, thereby removing the impact that the original firm might have had. In these circumstances, then— where I am affected by an association without being subject to its authority— what I need in order to ensure that choices which govern my actions (and thereby to ensure that my freedom is protected) is the ability to *exit* from my relationship with the association that is affecting me.

But in the first case (figure 1.2), where I am subject to the authority of the association, then this exit option is no longer open, because of the very nature of the authority relationship. Here the only way to reconnect an individual's choices with his or her actions is to input that individual's choices into the choices of the association. This, for example, is the basic rationale for political democracy. The state's choices (its laws) are only compatible with our individual freedom if we have a voice in making them. In these circumstances, then—where I am subject to the authority of an association—what I need is a *voice* in the decision-making process of the association.

But these are general arguments that apply to all sorts of associations (and not just to states). How do these general arguments affect the specific question of how economic enterprises or firms should be governed?

Workers, shareholders, and consumers are all affected by the decisions of a firm. Do contemporary firms fulfil the requirements of the general argument? We have already considered the case of consumers in the shoe factory. They seem to be satisfactorily dealt with so long as the firm is operating in a competitive market. The problem arises when we look at the shareholders (that is, the capitalists) and the workers. In a conventional Anglo-Saxon firm, both the shareholders and the workers have the ability to exit from their relationship with the firm. Where there is a share market I can take my shares and put them in another firm. And where there is a labour market I can leave the firm and go and work for another. But it is only the shareholders, through Annual General Meetings and their right to elect the management, who have a voice in the firm's government.

If we are trying to maximise individual freedom, this is not morally justifiable. On the contrary, while both the shareholders and the workers should continue to have the right to exit, it is the workers and not the capitalists who should have voice or decision-making control over the firm. The basic reason why this is so is that it is the workers (and only the workers) who are subject to the authority of the firm. And the reason why this is so is that, despite the assumptions of neo-classical economists, labour is a very peculiar sort of commodity. In fact, it is really a fictitious commodity. When a firm acquires a normal commodity, it acquires the exclusive right to decide what to do with it. But when labour is the commodity that is being exchanged, the firm not only acquires the exclusive right to decide what to do with the labour; it also acquires the right to decide what the labourer will do. Because, unlike the normal commodities, labour is 'attached' to the labourer, the firm acquires not only control over the labour, but the authority over the labourer. This is not true of the shareholders. The shareholders can invest their capital in the firm and then go off and do the gardening or play on their yacht.

So the relationship of the worker to the firm is very different from that of the shareholder (or capitalist). In the case of the shareholder, the commodity in question (capital) is a genuine commodity: one which is separate from the commodity's owner. In the case of the worker, it is a fictitious commodity (labour), and because of this—because labour is attached to the labourer—the workers find themselves subject to the authority of the firm. That is why it is the workers, and not the shareholders, who are subject to the authority of the firm. And that is why, in an ideal world, it is the workers who should have voice (or decision-making) control, and not the shareholders.

Britain: Is greater economic democracy feasible?

In *Economic Democracy* I argue that a corporatist system of industrial relations would enable workers to gradually accumulate greater and greater control through a series of trade-offs in which they exchange profit-threatening 'goods' (like excess wage rises or restrictive work practices) for incremental increases in control enterprise decision-making. Corporatism is not, of course, a form of economic democracy itself. It is merely a vehicle for achieving it.

It is clear, however, that there is a good deal of scepticism about the feasibility of corporatist-based strategies in contemporary Britain. In part this is because of the perception that there is a general European-wide trend away from corporatism, and in part it is because of a specifically British argument about the impossibility of grafting institutions of 'social partnership' on to Anglo-Saxon traditions of industrial relations. This scepticism is misplaced. As any survey of recent industrial relations in Europe will show, society-wide political exchange between unions, employers and governments remains an important feature of industrial relations in a wide range of European countries. And the idea that corporatism is incompatible with Anglo-Saxon traditions has been undermined by the successful operation of the 'Accord' between the Australian Labour Party and the Australian unions: a corporatist-style agreement which has helped to keep Labour in government since 1983.

I believe that the argument in *Economic Democracy* can also be applied to Britain. Here, however, in deference to (misplaced) British scepticism, I propose a different argument for the feasibility of a move towards economic democracy.

Works councils

Works councils are representative bodies elected by all of a firm's employees. They have a legally-guaranteed right to make certain decisions and to be informed and consulted about others. Rules governing the composition and powers of works councils differ from country to country; but in one form or another they exist in all European countries except for Britain and Ireland. Moreover, even in Britain and Ireland, large multinational firms will soon have to introduce European works councils as a result of a European Union directive which came into force in 1995.

The German model for works councils is probably the most influential. German works councils are legally distinct and independent of trade unions. Any workplace with five or more non-executive employees can have a works council which is elected by (and from amongst) these employees, whether or not they are union members. However, works councils are not automatically established in every eligible workplace: the initiative must be taken by a union represented in the workplace or by the workers themselves. Where works councils do exist they have a number of legally defined rights to participate in company decision-making. (Note that in the German case these rights specifically forbid bargaining over wage rates which can only take place between unions and employers or their associations.) Works councils are also forbidden to resort to industrial action.

The establishment of works councils would be an important first step towards economic democracy, because it would involve an acknowledgement of the idea that workers should have (at least some) sovereign decision-making rights in the firms which employ them. Of course, works councils would not change the ownership of firms, but economic democracy does not require this. Worker ownership may be an alternative route to economic democracy, but it is *not* a necessary one. It is the government of firms and not their ownership that matters from the point of view of economic democracy.

The Economic Environment

Like other advanced capitalist countries, Britain in the 1990s is experiencing a period of sustained structural adjustment. This process has shifted production away from the 'Fordist' model of mass production of low-cost standardised consumer goods on which post-war prosperity was based. There are at least four developments which have fuelled this structural adjustment. First, the market in the advanced capitalist countries for mass-produced consumer durables became more or less saturated. Secondly, imitators in newly industrialising countries began to compete for customers in the markets that remained, with low wages and poor environmental regulations giving these countries a good chance of success. Thirdly, consumers in the advanced capitalist countries began to demand a greater variety of more customised goods and were increasingly prepared to pay a premium for quality. And fourthly, technological developments enabled producers to respond to these demands without pricing themselves out of the market.

Firms can respond to these developments in one of two ways. Either they can attempt to compete directly with the newly industrialising countries by undertaking a down-market structural adjustment towards a low wage unregulated economy, or they can attempt to satisfy changing consumer tastes by undertaking an up-market response. Firms which opt for an up-market structural adjustment need flexibility not only to produce new goods, but also to produce them in different ways. They must adjust their production process in order to increase the quality of their products, in order to diversity their output to meet the more specialised tastes of their customers and in order to innovate more rapidly as those tastes change. That is, they must adjust from a (Fordist) cost-competitive standardised model of production to a quality competitive customised model.

The Fordist model

In the Fordist model an attempt was made to vest all decision-making authority in the hands of managers. A sharp distinction was drawn between the conception of tasks (which was the prerogative of managers) and their execution (which was the duty of workers). The objective was to minimise costs by specifying precisely what was required of the occupant of each job. But this Fordist distribution of decision-making authority is incompatible with the flexibility requirements of quality-competitive customised production. As we have seen, quality-competitive customised production has three key features. It seeks to improve quality, to increase diversity and to speed up innovation. Contrary to the Fordist model, each of these features requires a blurring of the distinction between conception and execution and at least some degree of discretion for shopfloor workers. Discretion in turn requires the skills, commitment and trust needed to make it work. Let me briefly consider each of the three features in turn.

Where there is a rigid Fordist division of conception and execution, shopfloor workers have no motive to pay special attention to the quality of what they produce. Their job is to follow orders: no more and no less. At the same time, these workers cannot help but observe the production process in which they are engaged, and, as a result, they begin to build up a store of knowledge which could be used to improve it but is unknown to those responsible for conceiving the process. Giving workers greater discretion helps to solve both these problems. It fosters greater commitment which provides workers with a motive to identify and avoid mistakes, and it opens up the possibility of tapping the workers' unused knowledge to improve the production process.

The Up-Market response

The more diversified or customised a firm's products become, the smaller each batch of products will have to be. And the smaller the batch size the more frequent the need to retool, reset, replan, reprogramme and redesign in order to adapt to the different specifications of each batch. But the more frequent this process of adaptation, the more difficult it is for the firm to centrally plan all the actions of each worker while maintaining the continuity of production.

This problem is compounded by the requirement of innovation. Many firms will need to be able to produce not just one diverse set of products, but a continually changing diverse set of products. The more frequently products and processes are changed, the less time there is to translate conceptions into reliable mechanically applicable routines. The more imperfect the routines, of course, the more interpretation and initiative they require from workers at all levels.[2] In short, the requirements of diversity and innovation, like the requirements of quality, force firms to rely, at least to some extent, on the discretion of their workers. To this extent, firms must increase the area in which workers execute their work according to their own conception.

The distinction between conception and execution is the same as the distinction between choice and action. By increasing the area in which workers' own conceptions (that is, their choices) govern the tasks that they execute (that is, their actions), the direct control which those workers exercise over their firm is increased.

Under Fordism, workers must do what they are told by their employer; that is, their actions must be governed by the choices of their employer. Quality-competitive customised production requires greater economic democracy because it requires that, in some cases, workers' actions are governed by their own choices or by the choices of representatives who are accountable to them.

The Actors' Interests

Bearing this background in mind I want to briefly consider how, if Labour comes to power in Britain, the establishment of works councils would affect the interests of each of the main industrial relations actors. Let me start with the government's interests and then move on to the interests of the employers and the workers.

The introduction of works councils would be in the interests of a new Labour government both for a general and for a more specific reason. The general reason stems from the government's core interest in being re-elected. There is a large body of political science literature that argues that in order to be re-elected a government must show that it can successfully manage the national economy. And as we have just seen, in the current economic environment successful national economic management requires the government to facilitate the emergence of quality-competitive customised production. The Conservatives may perhaps be able to sell themselves as the party of competition with south-east Asia through down market structural adjustment, but this is certainly not an option which is open to Labour. But as we have also seen, up-market structural adjustment and the emergence of quality-competitive customised production requires greater economic democracy.

The more specific reason why a Labour government has an interest to introduce works councils has to do with the 'fear factor'. During the last decade, workers have often acquiesced to structural adjustment and wage restraint because of fear. But if unemployment continues to fall and the Conservative Party's unremitting legislative and rhetorical hostility towards organised labour is displaced, then a new Labour government will find itself in a very different situation: a situation in which the government will need to promote the active cooperation of workers and not merely their passive acquiescence in order to achieve ongoing structural adjustment and wage restraint.

A package of policies which links the introduction of works councils with the need for union cooperation in other areas could be a big help to a new Labour government when, inevitably, it will need to demand restraint from its core supporters. This need not just be a short-term fix, for it would also help to put in place the kind of institutional guarantees that would make it rational for workers to cooperate with ongoing structural adjustment in the longer term. Comparisons between Britain and Germany bear this out. German workers—with their strong unions and works councils—have been far readier to cooperate with changes in the organisation of work than their British counterparts.

Let me now turn to consider the interests of employers. As we have already seen, firms pursuing a quality-competitive customised model of production need to redistribute some of their decision-making authority to their workers. In addition to these general considerations the introduction of works councils would have further specific advantages for managers and shareholders. First, a greater upward flow of information would give managers more detailed and reliable access to knowledge which can only be gained from the shop-floor. Secondly, a more credible downward flow of information would make it more likely that workers would accept difficult managerial decisions. And thirdly, works councils would provide shareholders with a better check against managerial opportunism than that which they themselves are able to provide, since it would allow workers who are on the spot to exercise a kind of oversight function.

So it would seem that employers also have an interest in the introduction of works councils, and empirical studies seem to bear this out. The latest authoritative British evidence shows that firms with works councils or works council surrogates have higher levels of productivity than those which do not have these institutions.[3]

It is not surprising then to find that most employers and employer associations are committed in principle to the importance of extending employee involvement and worker participation. They acknowledge that these developments are necessary if their firms are to be as efficient and productive as possible. But in practice things are very different. In the absence of legally-reinforced or union-imposed measures, British employers are failing to initiate any real re-distribution of decision-making authority.[4]

Why is this? One possible explanation is that, while productivity is increased by works councils, profitability is decreased. There is some American evidence for this contention.[5] However, British evidence suggests that works councils do not have any negative effect on profitability.[6] An alternative explanation is that employers are seeking to protect, not their economic interests, but rather their status. If either of these contentions is true then the labour movement can make a strong case that employers' sectional interests should not be allowed to obstruct the general national interest.

Whether or not employers would see the introduction of works councils as being in their interests is an open question; but even if employers do adopt a hostile stance it would be difficult for them to mount opposition to a well-argued case, for not only can the labour movement argue that it is acting in the interests of society as a whole, it can also argue that it is simply trying to ensure that employers follow through on their own rhetoric about the importance of worker participation.

Let me turn now to the workers. First I will consider workers with 'material' interests, then I will consider workers with 'post-material' interests, and finally I will consider the interests of unionists.

Most workers are concerned about their material interests, such as their wages and working conditions. But even workers who are solely concerned with material interests now have an interest in increasing economic democracy. This is because it is becoming harder for workers to insulate the regulation of wages and working conditions from the regulation of a firm's overall strategy. The need to respond rapidly to changing product markets is forcing firms to increase their flexibility by integrating the regulation of wages and conditions into a comprehensive commercial strategy. Thus workers will also be forced to seek some control over this integrated, comprehensive strategy simply in order to maintain some influence over the wages and conditions that are central to their material well-being. Working conditions, for example, are intimately affected by the organisation of work. In a Fordist system, workers would respond to proposed changes in the organisation of work by seeking to renegotiate a detailed schedule of work practices. But as we have seen, this option is no longer available. The negotiation and implementation of such a schedule takes too long, and, once implemented, it hinders a firm's ability to rapidly make further adjustments. Since continual rapid adjustments are now required, there are only two options open to the workers. They can either withdraw from the regulation of their working conditions altogether or they can seek to institutionalise their influence, not by seeking to introduce a rigid code to govern each new issue as it arises, but rather by ensuring that they share some control over the process by which all these issues are decided.

There is good evidence that increasing numbers of people in the advanced industrial countries place a high priority on the achievement of so-called 'post-material' goals such as improving the environment, protecting human rights, *and* increasing self-government at work.[7] Most workers have always inspired to greater control over their firms. What is new is workers are now giving these aspirations a high priority. They can be found especially, but not exclusively, amongst younger people and amongst those brought up in conditions of material security. They include many who are employed in the most dynamic sectors of the economy. For these workers, increasing economic democracy is not just a means to an end, but an important end in its own right.

So both workers with material interests and those with post-material interests have reasons to favour the introduction of works councils. But how would these institutions affect the most important existing representatives of workers interests: the unions?

Historically, unions have been wary about the introduction of works councils for fear that they might create an alternative focus of loyalty to the union itself. But, although there are potential dangers, this fear is misconceived. First, works councils provide a legally protected work place base in which unions can operate. Although works councils are typically legally independent of unions, experience in Germany and other countries suggests that they in fact provide unions with an extremely important base for organising at a workplace.[8] In Britain the TUC has recently begun to adopt a more positive attitude to works councils in recognition of this fact.

Secondly, the establishment of works councils could help to re-legitimise unions. Whilst there was more than 50 per cent of the work force in unions, unions could legitimately claim to speak for employees in general. But now with significantly less than 50 per cent membership, those who are hostile to unions can paint the union movement as just another sectional interest. Works councils can help to solve this legitimation problem because we know, from European experience, that it is likely that the vast majority of works councillors will be elected off the union list. In Germany, for example, for most of the post-war period there has been about 35 per cent union membership, but about 80 per cent of works councillors have been elected as unionists. This enables the union movement to speak with an authoritative voice on behalf of the workforce as a whole.

Thirdly, a union initiative on works councils has something to offer people who are now tending not to join unions. By taking up the cause of greater economic democracy, unions could appeal to more 'post-materialist' younger workers and better-off workers in dynamic sectors of the economy. These are both critical groups of potential members: groups which unions are currently failing to attract in sufficient numbers.

It seems then that a Labour government, workers and unions would all have an interest in establishing works councils. Employers may well have a similar interest. But, even if they do not, they are likely to find it difficult to oppose a well-prepared initiative.

One final point is worth noting. The introduction of works councils, or any other initiative to move towards greater economic democracy would resonate with some well entrenched British values. Like other Anglo-Saxon countries, Britain is deeply marked by a liberal tradition: a tradition that claims that what matters most is the protection of individual freedom. The argument that I have set out in this article starts from exactly this claim. It does not rely on any claim for special collective rights. It takes the protection of individual freedom as its starting point and moves on to argue that fundamental changes in the organisation of firms ought to take place. Indeed, in a sense, the promotion of economic democracy can be thought of as a way of taking liberalism back from the neo-liberals. Some have argued that it is only when the Left has been able to mould and control the liberal agenda that it has been able to achieve lasting influence in Britain.[9]

Of course, the establishment of works councils would only be a small step towards full economic democracy. It could be seen as analogous to the first Reform Act which set Britain on the path to political democracy in 1832. Almost another century had to pass before Britain fully achieved political democracy. Nevertheless, like the first Reform Act, the introduction of works councils would represent an important start.

Governments come and go. Some are long remembered, while others are soon forgotten. The Attlee Government will be remembered for the Welfare State, The Thatcher Government for privatisation. If a Blair Government has the courage and vision to initiate a major democratic reform of the economy, it too could come to be remembered as a great British reforming government.

ROBIN ARCHER

Biographical Note

Robin Archer is Fellow in Politics at Corpus Christi College, Oxford. He has done research on labour relations for research institutes or governments in Australia, in Germany and at the United Nations.

Notes

1 Robin Archer, *Economic Democracy: The Politics of Feasible Socialism*, Oxford, Oxford University Press, 1995.
2 Charles Sabel, *Work and Politics: The Division of Labor in Industry*, Cambridge, Cambridge University Press, 1982.
3 Sue Fernie and David Metcalf, 'Participation, Contingent Pay, representation and workplace performance: Evidence from Great Britain', Centre for Economic Performance Discussion Paper 232, London School of Economics, March 1995.
4 Neil Millward, 'The New Industrial Relations?', Policy Studies Institute Research Report 756, London, 1994.
5 Richard Freeman and James Medoff, *What Do Unions Do?*, New York, Basic Books, 1984.
6 Fernie and Metcalf, *op. cit.*
7 Ronald Inglehart, *Culture Shift in Advanced Industrial Society*, Princeton, Princeton University Press, 1990.
8 Kathleen Thelen, *Union of Parts: Labor Politics in Postwar Germany*, Ithaca, Cornell University Press, 1991; and Lowell Turner, *Democracy at Work: Changing World Markets and the Future of Labor Unions*, Ithaca, Cornell University Press, 1991.
9 David Marquand, *The Progressive Dilemma*, London, Heinemann, 1992.

Democracy and Civil Society

PAUL Q. HIRST

DEMOCRACY in modern times has always meant more than just a measure of popular control over the personnel and decisions of the state. A democratic state is widely held to be inconceivable without a democratic society. Hence the major modern political doctrines that have claimed to be democratic have all insisted that democracy involves a definite relationship between the state and the wider society. The doctrines in question—classical liberalism, democratic socialism and corporatism—have seen this relationship in different ways.[1] They have done so in relation to a shared conception of the modern state as a compulsory organisation that claims a monopoly over the right to determine the forms of governance within a definite territory. However, in the late twentieth century both the state and the relationship it has to the wider society are being transformed as a result of profound social changes. This necessitates a radical re-thinking of the role and scope of democratic governance, and the mainstream political doctrines are at best poor guides in this re-thinking, and at worst obsolete.

The Changing Character of the State

The main changes altering the nature and position of the state are twofold. The first concerns its capacity to legitimate its powers of compulsion, to make claims on the lives and property of its members. In the era of total wars and savage internal social struggles these claims were supported because threats to political survival and social stability were very real. Citizens feared invading enemies and domestic attempts to seize power. With the collapse of the Soviet Bloc as an external adversary and the disappearance of internal revolutionary movements, most advanced Western societies no longer face serious enemies that require large-scale political and economic mobilisation to counter them. Hence the territorial integrity of states in itself matters less to citizens and claims to state compulsion can no longer be founded on such genuine and shared fears.

The second main change concerns the growing dispersion of the capacities of governance to agencies 'above' and 'below' the nation state. The internationalisation of economic and social relations has lessened the ability of the state to impose distinct 'national' economic programmes.[2] For at least some of the 'haves' this is a valuable form of liberty. Companies and citizens can use the international financial markets as a sanction, voting with their capital and their savings against state policies they see as imposing excessive costs. States have lost some of the economic coercive power over citizens they had in the

Published by Blackwell Publishers, 108 Cowley Road, Oxford OX4 1JF, UK and 238 Main Street, Cambridge, MA 02142, USA

era of punitive import duties and exchange controls. At the same time as some of the powers of national governments have claimed to possess over the economy have weakened, so many regional governments have become effective sources of economic regulation. Major cities and industrial districts are increasingly becoming social and political entities in their own right and national governments are, willingly or not, ceding powers to them. States are losing their monopoly over who governs in their territories; nation states are becoming just one (albeit vital) part of a division of labour in governance and the nature of that division is no longer under their exclusive control.

Classical Liberalism and Civil Society

Given the eclipse of state socialism and the current generalised acceptance of markets as the main means of economic distribution, it follows that most practical politicians are in fact liberals of one variety or another. Thus, it is necessary to begin our account of the contemporary relationship between state and civil society with classical liberalism. Central to liberalism is the distinction between the public and the private spheres. The public sphere is based on representative government and the rule of law; its purpose is both to govern and to protect the private sphere. The state's primary tasks are to protect private property and individual rights. Laws should be general norms, applicable to all citizens irrespective of status. The state is the public and political sphere, limited in its scope and functions. The private sphere is that of individual action, contract, and market exchange, protected by and yet independent of the state. Lawful association in civil society is a 'private' matter.

Thus, since its inception liberal political theory has regarded its main objective as the preservation of an extensive sphere of private action independent of the state, and has seen this as essential complement to and support of the formal political institutions of representative government. Modern pluralist theory, developing classical liberalism, argues that a society comprised of a wide variety of active 'secondary associations' provides the basis for that diversity of interests and opinions that makes multi-party democracy sustainable in the primary association, the state. In recent years, adding to and developing classical liberalism, the concept of 'civil society' has been redefined and become fashionable both in Eastern and Western Europe. It is seen as a source of authentically democratic social movements separate from and oppositional to the totalitarian or the bureaucratic business-oriented state.[3]

What all these positions have in common is a conception of the private sphere or civil society as a spontaneous order independent of and separate from the state. Modern libertarian radicals and the free-market right have a major common objective, that is, to protect civil society from encroachment by the state and hierarchical bureaucratic administration. They fear that either the spontaneous order of social life or the free market is being displaced. The right fear big government, and libertarian radicals fear both state bureaucracy and big business. Economic liberals like Hayek and post-Marxist radicals like Habermas seem unlikely bedfellows, but they share the belief that civil society is a spontaneous order. Hayek feared not just a state socialist command economy as a threat to freedom, but the steady process of bureaucratic encroachment on the market in the interests of welfare and regulation in a formally democratic society. The market can only function adequately if it is autonomous, and, therefore, spontaneous. The task of government is to guard it against excessive governance. Likewise, Habermas, for all his long and sophisticated reflection on the public and private spheres in modern society, fears that spontaneous substantively oriented interaction, the life world, is threatened by the domination of the formal bureaucratic rationality of the system.[4]

The problem with such views is not that excessive bureaucratic control over individuals by political and social institutions does not pose a threat to liberty. Rather, it is that this classical liberal legacy of conceiving civil society as a spontaneous order separate from government actually undermines the devising of effective remedies to the growth of unaccountable hierarchical power in both the public and the private spheres. The issue is no longer usefully posed in terms of either the autonomy of civil society from government or the restriction of the scope of public governance. In fact both state and civil society are made up of large complex organisations, and the boundary between the two is not all that clear. Seeking to preserve individual freedoms in and through civil society treats it as if it could be purely a realm of individual choice, contract, and voluntary association. The issue is better conceived as the freedom of individuals within institutions and the autonomy of institutions within their legitimate sphere, how to achieve effective democratic governance of both public and private institutions.

If civil society is conceived *non-politically*, as spontaneous, private and prior to politics, then it will become an ever more marginal sphere. It will be those aspects of social action that are left over, that large public and private institutions do not organise. It would be what remains when the corporate economy, bureaucratically organised public services, and compulsory state regulation are subtracted. The answer is, of course, not much. The nation state may be losing certain capacities and some legitimacy, but this does not mean that the scale and scope of compulsory authority and top-down control are lessening in modern societies. Indeed, the relative weakening of the control of the state over certain domains, like national economic policy, may lessen its ability to check other organisations, like major companies, in the interests of democratic accountability and individual liberty.

Economic liberals have favoured de-regulation and privatisation as a means of reducing the role of the state, thereby restoring the power of markets. If anything this has worsened the crisis in the relationship between state and civil society. In privatisation and deregulation, control and social power are not ceded to markets based on equal competing individuals, but to large hierarchically-controlled organisations: to privatised utilities, to quangos and to private companies contracting out services. These bodies are not in the main voluntary associations, and in respect of them the citizen as employee or consumer mostly has little choice and less control. Typically such organisations are bureaucracies, which means that they subject their employees to imperative control and compulsion and they deal with the recipients of their services through standardised procedures. The lower ranks in such institutions obey orders from above and have no countervailing powers; they are subordinates. The recipients of services or customers depend for what they receive on administrative decisions beyond their control; the best they can hope for, if they are lucky, is that they can switch to buying from another unaccountable body that offers a better deal.

Confronting the Organisational Society

It is difficult to see how a political democracy can survive if individuals' 'private' lives are so controlled by undemocratic authority. The scope of democracy becomes limited and citizens have little experience of it. They become subordinate or consumers, and even their leisure time is dependent on the offerings of large business corporations. States may no longer have such well-founded grounds for the more draconian forms of coercion, but, in the absence of a new democratic political settlement, this does not alter the prosaic, day to day powers of most major social institutions, public or private. We have become habituated to a thousand minor but very real restrictions of our liberty, each trivial but as a whole making most of us less than fully free. Most people have little choice but to work for large organisations and to accept services and to buy products from them. We take the power of such institutions for granted, whether it be a private company telling its employees how to dress or how often they may go to the lavatory, or a Job Club determining how many letters an unemployed person must write in a week, or some blatant piece of insolence that undermines the dignity of the consumer and is justified as 'company policy'.

That such institutions may be notionally accountable, to their shareholders or to Parliament, does not alter the compulsory and coercive character of their day-to-day workings in respect of individuals. On the contrary, such attenuated accountability merely legitimises such powers without giving those directly subject to them any control. Top-down hierarchical administration is at best a necessary evil in a free society. In a society that truly valued individual autonomy it would be justified only when there was no option, that no other or less coercive form of organisation was available or sufficiently efficient for the activity in question. In a society where state coercion and compulsion have fewer objective justifications, the powers of major institutions proliferate. To re-state the paradox with which Rousseau begins *The Social Contract* in a form appropriate to modern times: 'citizens are told that they are participants in a free and democratic society, yet at every turn they are subject to the constraints of hierarchical administration without significant opportunities for control and consent.[5]

Rousseau asked, having posed his paradox, what could make it legitimate? The contemporary answers as to how to overcome our paradox are not encouraging. Positions derived from classical liberalism are inadequate to deal with these more complex issues of accountability because liberalism was designed to protect society *from* the state, rather than deal with the problems of liberty in a state and civil society dominated by large hierarchical institutions. In a period when statist and socialist solutions have become ineffective and politically unviable, we are left with a rhetoric of individual rights in politics and the advocacy of market principles in society. Trying to return to an idealised nineteenth century relationship between state and civil society, as the most extreme economic liberals do, is evidently impossible—we cannot re-create a society of perfectly competing small traders and manufacturers in open markets. To recognise this is not just an issue of the economics of competition, it is also a problem for governance. The hegemony of liberalism means that most attempts to counter or meliorate weak economic regulation and social accountability are half-hearted or ineffective. Hence the weakness of communitarian rhetoric as a substitute for liberalism, its failure to confront the reform of institutions and its urging of consensus on deeply divided societies with plural and competing values.

If core activities of central concern to the life of the citizen like welfare, public services, and economic production are not to remain dominated by top-down administration and if policy is not to become the prerogative of a managerial elite, then the whole of society and not just the state needs to be viewed politically, as a complex of institutions that require a substantial measure of public and popular control over their leading personnel and major decisions. That is, civil society must no longer be viewed as a 'private' sphere, it needs to take on elements of 'publicity' in the original sense of the term. We require a constitution for society as much as we do for the state. Once one recognises that society is dominated by large-scale quasi-public and private institutions possessed of powers that dwarf those of many pre-modern states, then the issue of their accountable governance becomes inescapable. We currently have an 'uncivil' society: that is, one dominated by managerial elites, not one controlled by constitutionally-ordered associations. The existing forms of governance have become threadbare—accountability to Parliament for public services and to shareholders for the actions of managers in private firms. These forms of liberal accountability fail in the face not just of big government but also of an organisational society. Thus the major 'private' institutions—for example, firms, media networks, major charities—need to be made accountable in some direct way to the major constituencies involved in or affected by them. Public or quasi-public institutions—for example, hospitals, schools, universities—need to give voice and choice both to service providers and to recipients. This is not an easy matter, especially when some of the most powerful private institutions are multi-national, but a political discourse circumscribed by classical liberalism has no space in which to begin to pose this issue constructively.

Norberto Bobbio, seeking to advance democracy beyond the limits of classical liberalism but without compromising individual liberty, argued that the main issue for modern democracy was not just 'who votes' but 'where' they can vote.[6] Yet this issue has become ever more difficult. The idea of a 'where' where one votes depends on there being readily identifiable and coherent constituencies of interest. But modern societies do not make it easy to enhance democracy by adding a supplementary franchise to existing non-political institutions; divisions of labour and institutional patterns are complex and rapidly changing. This has also undermined the conventional supplements to liberal democratic representation: corporatist interest group representation, and industrial democracy—giving the 'workers' a say in firms through workers' councils or seats on the board. Corporatism is threatened by the decomposition of relatively homogeneous interest groups and workers' representation in companies, by both changing employment patterns that reduce the number of long-service and full-time workers and the recognition that it is no longer credible to claim that producer interests could stand for those of all other currently excluded stakeholders.

Institutional Freedoms and Particular Liberties

Classical liberals have feared any crossing of the boundary between the state and civil society as leading to the inevitable authoritarian politicisation of the private sphere. Thus they will resist any attempt to politicise civil society and pluralise political accountability within the public sector. The very idea of a 'constitution' for civil society smacks of totalitarianism. In the past this concern was legitimate, since the main threats to the autonomy of civil society in this century have been totalitarian mass parties. Yet totalitarian political mobilisation from above is hardly a serious threat now, rather the main danger to liberty is the piecemeal authoritarianism of unchecked managerial elites. Equally, the old liberal bugbear of the 'tyranny of the majority' is hardly credible in demotic societies that lack coherent leadership and are fragmented into a plurality of minorities with different values.

The problem is that old fears are still powerful and that both left and right now define freedom overwhelmingly in terms of individual rights. Modern societies are demotic, if not adequately democratic. Thus they believe that citizens should be formally equal, and that all individuals should have the same liberties. But if institutions are to be adequately governed, and if their autonomy is to be preserved both against the central state and the market, then we also need *particular liberties*, both for institutions and for their participants. The idea of particular liberties, that is grants of distinctive powers and rights to specific institutions and their members, was easily understood in the Medieval *Standestaat*. Cities, guilds, and religious corporations enjoyed privileges, specific and differential grants of power.[7] Medieval constitutionalism was based on such powers, on rights linked to status and privilege. Modern liberalism sought to sweep such privileges away, to destroy status differences and to replace them with equal individual rights. It sought to solve the problem of liberty by making the state accountable through representative governments and society free through equal access to contract and the market.

The competitive society that classical liberalism envisaged as the basis for freedom, one in which equal individual rights would suffice to protect the autonomy of social actors, was no sooner mooted than it was threatened as a political ideal by collectivism. Liberalism overcame absolutist government and a society of privilege. It was then challenged by socialism and meliorated by reformist collectivism. In a society in which the state could be seen as the dominant source of governance, in which people were satisfied with simple uniform collective services like basic social insurance and elementary schools, and in which large-scale standardised mass production could be nationalised or regulated by the state, then liberal collectivism and democratic socialism could be seen as effective means to overcome the limits of classical liberalism and to modify the economics of *laissez faire*.

The recent decline of liberal collectivism and social democracy as alternatives to classical liberalism and the free market is not just a matter of political fashion. It is due to three main reasons: national states can no longer be seen as having a monopoly of public governance functions; public services have become diverse and complex—no longer simply governed and locally replicable basic entitlements; and manufacturing and commercial services have diversified in ways that make uniform central control or standardised regulations less effective. Much of this change is gain. But it also means that markets are more difficult to govern and services more diverse and thus less equally accessible. Moreover, even though states can less credibly claim a monopoly of governance, their powers of intervention in society and the scale and scope of their activities are formidable. Paradoxically, the contemporary state is seen as less effective and as less capable of solving problems, and yet typically it spends a higher proportion of GDP, regulates more extensively, and offers more public services than in the era when collectivism was seen as the solution to the major economic and social problems. The modern state is a power that regulates and intervenes whilst speaking the fashionable languages of the new *laissez faire*.

Herein lies its main danger to freedom and democracy. The language of political choice has been replaced by that of management. Politicians see themselves as managers of a state to be devolved to managers, using financial controls and supervisory auditing to control lesser officials and contractors. Further, they support the corporatisation and contractualisation of public services, running them like private businesses, and they use public power to support the private sector's 'power to manage' in a market economy. This is no longer an 'Anglo-Saxon' peculiarity, as other countries are beginning to follow the lead of the USA, UK and New Zealand.

In a highly centralised state like the UK, without the protection offered by a written constitution, such practices represent a serious threat to the autonomy of a wide variety of social institutions. The danger is that we are witnessing the creation of a bureaucratic monoculture spanning the public and private domains. This will proliferate unless there is both some countervailing power and coherent alternative ideas for the direction of institutions. A managerial stratum is being created, relatively homogeneous in attitudes, working methods and aspirations. Its members are able to move between the public and the private sectors, and as they do so the interests and expectations of this stratum begin to interlock.

Such a new elite is as threatening to liberty in its own way as were, for example, the centralising royal officials of the absolutist monarchy in France to the particular liberties of the *ancien régime*. Tocqueville argued for the autonomy of secondary associations from the state precisely because he saw the consequences of the centralising tendencies of those who had inherited and implemented the programme of the bureaucratic reformers under the monarchy, the officials of the Revolution and the Empire. Montesquieu had earlier also seen that liberty depended on the autonomy of social institutions from the central state. But he argued that such autonomy must be based on specific institutions enjoying constitutionally protected privileges and not just on individual rights or freedom from state interference.[8] Montesquieu was of course defending privileges, the rights and powers of nobles, lawyers, and office holders. His point, however, was that such particular liberties contributed to the defence of liberty in general. That was because they limited the power of the state, its capacity to re-define the powers of and re-make other social institutions at will. We need to return to early modern theorists of liberty like Montesquieu, because political thought since then has been predominantly a struggle between classical liberals seeking to restrict the scope of state power and collectivists seeking to extend it. The danger now is that the language of individual rights and equality between individuals can all too easily be turned against the defence of particular liberties of specific institutions, like the professions, or the BBC, that are necessary to wider freedoms.

The Threat of a Bureaucratic Monoculture

Our problem is that the representatives of the new bureaucratic monoculture effortlessly speak the language of equality. Everyone is to be equally subject to common styles of managerial control, and resistance is stigmatised as representing privileged producer interests, or as the elitist defence of professional prerogatives, or as the attempt to avoid accountability and transparency. Indeed, in an egalitarian and demotic culture (although not one that cares much about equality of income and wealth) it is easy to mount such charges and difficult to resist them. The common people are enlisted by the new managers against claims to exceptional rights or powers.

This difficulty to resist managerial centralisation is further compounded by the fact that we find it difficult to think of preserving the *autonomy* of institutions, that freedom for individuals depends in considerable measure on giving institutions constitutionally protected powers and the members of those institutions specific forms of political voice. The idea of a society consisting of constitutionally ordered self-governing civil associations is ill-developed, not least because state socialism, the main form of opposition to liberal individualism, saw democracy as being enhanced by the control of collective bureaucracies imposing the goals of the people. Liberals saw the dangers of socialist and collectivist centralisation, of totalitarian control, but in the main they have been ineffective in opposing corporate and managerial power. The problem is that threats to liberty come in many forms and not just ideologically motivated state dictatorship or totalitarian mass movements imposing their will by the club and the jackboot.

Freedom is not threatened just by gross oppression; some of the most serious threats are insidious and almost invisible and thus difficult to resist. The most dangerous is the redefinition of freedom and liberty, away from the spheres of the political and governance. The danger is that citizens cease to identify with politics and come to see 'freedom' as what they could do outside of formal organisations, in the spheres of private life and leisure. Freedom at work and in relation to social and public services comes to appear as cranky, uninteresting and irrelevant. Better leave it to the professionals—to managers—to run things. This is just what the growing bureaucratic monoculture thrives on and is an attitude it seeks to cultivate. The managerial stratum has been remarkably successful at redefining accountability from a political category to an accounting one and of redefining legitimate authority in terms of the prerogatives of management. Both of these redefinitions are glossed over by the apologetics of 'efficiency', the claim that this is the most effective and least expensive way to do things. To tax-averse electorates who are distrustful of politicians such appeals are not entirely unattractive. To politicians who can lessen their unpopularity by redefining politics in managerial terms and, indeed, ceding most of the day-to-day responsibility for services (and therefore blame) to managers, this is not unattractive too. The fact is that it represents a very real threat to liberty and needs to be resisted by an articulate language of political ideas.

Bridging State and Civil Society

Accept for the purposes of argument the notion that we can arrive at a 'social constitution', a definition of those institutions that require a definite sphere of guaranteed autonomy and the form of democratic self-governance they should enjoy. Indeed, accept that such a constitution is essential, since neither top-down collectivism nor managerial control has the legitimacy to impose the public will in an increasingly complex, differentiated and divided society. We shall need specific institutions to perform many of the governance functions that those who have favoured more than *laissez faire* in social arrangements have hitherto assigned to the state. This pluralism and con-stitutionalisation of social governance has become ever more necessary, not least because the advocacy of *laissez faire* has now become the defence of corporate privilege and the power to manage. We need to develop a complex division of labour in democratic governance, bridging state and civil society, in order to cope with the complexity of an organisational society that tends to blur the two spheres.

We need to create a new balance between authority and accountability, decentralising governance within the state and increasing the political responsiveness of private institutions to those who work in them or are affected by them. A complex public service state and an organisational society have placed the central lawmaking and supervisory functions of representa-tive government under ever greater strain. Unless democratic governance is redistributed and extended in something like the ways suggested above, then the formal institutions of representative government will be undermined because they will be too over-stretched adequately to superintend social affairs or to protect citizens from harms.

Throughout the Western world our democratic institutions remain those devised by classical liberalism for small government and a *laissez faire* society. Modern democracy has added universal suffrage to these institutions: the rule of law, parliamentary supervision of government, and governmental regula-tion of social affairs. Previous critics of liberal democracy have sought to sweep it away, to replace it with another and allegedly superior form of democracy, such as direct democracy. This is no part of the case being made here: the institutions of representative government remain necessary, but they are inadequate if they remain trapped within the existing liberal conception of the relation of state and civil society. An extended and devolved system of democratic governance crossing the two spheres will need existing state democratic institutions in order to ensure ultimate legal accountability, to provide legitimacy for fiscal settlements, and to act as final arbitrator when conflicts arise in and between self-governing social institutions. Thus the institutions of liberal democracy will not be destroyed or replaced, rather they will be enhanced and preserved by being supplemented by other democratic practices within and between social institutions.

Many analysts and political reformers recognise some of the limitations of our existing democratic institutions, but few of them are willing to accept that these limitations are structural, a product of the increasingly problematic division between the public and private spheres. Communitarians, like Amitai Etzioni, seek to restore ailing institutions by changing people's values, and thus their attitudes and behaviour, thereby rendering major structural reforms less necessary.[9] Other critics see the problem as a demo-cratic deficit, as too little influence by the majority or representative citizens over public decisions. Thus greater use of referenda, electronic democracy, citizens juries, deliberative forums, and so on, will bring the people back into politics. There is nothing wrong with many of those ideas as such. The question is whether they are adequate responses to the crisis of modern democracy. Decisions are only half of the problem; the other part is the institutions that implement or administer those decisions. Even if the scale and scope of popular decision-making were extended it would still be necessary to change the ways in which rules are enforced and services delivered, for these too affect the liberty of the citizen.

One cannot feed democratic decisions into the top of authoritarian structures and expect to get democratic outcomes. One must radically circumscribe the 'power to manage', that is the whole point of trying to create a social constitution. Democratising both public and private governments, state and civil society, requires a double protection of autonomy that can only be achieved by major institutional reforms. First, the constituencies that organisations serve need to have their interests protected by being given an appropriate voice within the governing councils of such bodies, and also they need, where possible, to have the option of exit, that is, some choice between alternative providers of the service in question. As far as is practicable, both public and private services need to be voluntarily subscribed to by their consumers, not compulsory or unavoidable. Secondly, the organisations themselves need to be guaranteed a definite degree of autonomy, a freedom from interference which is consistent with their members having the power to make democratic decisions within their own sphere of operation. Thus organisations need to have their autonomy protected not just against central state encroachment, but also against the kinds of top-down management by external funding agencies and internal bureaucratic elites that enable those bodies' purposes and working methods to be re-defined virtually without check. The latter requirement should be evident in the UK, where we have become accustomed to the closure of 800-year old hospitals and long-established schools by the *fiat* of ministers and bureaucrats.

The key problem is how to define, to assert and to ensure such specific liberties for and within institutions. To advance the case for radical reform we need to combat the fact that politics has been defined into such a narrow sphere. Democracy throughout the Western world has been so reduced in form and meaning that it has become little more than a plebiscite; thus elections empower and legitimate rulers who govern in essentially undemocratic (top-down) ways. Even in those countries where there are relatively decentralised forms of government, where politicians do make a serious attempt to consult the people about major decisions, and where they do not have the degree of exclusive control of power and of contempt for the electorate that they have in the UK, democracy still remains restricted in scope to periodic elections for national and subsidiary governments, to choosing the top personnel at each level. Those personnel, even when they are democrats by inclination, have at best a restricted capacity to control and superintend the mass of decisions and administrative actions made by governmental organs, let alone to check the big organisations that actually control 'civil' society. In a classical liberal society those weaknesses inherent in plebscitarian democracy would matter less, since the scale and scope of government would be limited. However, viewed from a strictly classical liberal standpoint, we are now living in a 'post-liberal' society.

Liberty and Freedom in a Post-Liberal Society

A post-liberal society needs new kinds of defences for liberty and freedom. We cannot hope to return to a night-watchman state or a society in which private individuals could sustain production and exchange. That *is* utopian; the now illiberal dream of a strand of the New Right. At the heart of such new defences must be the recognition that the institutions that deliver services, whether public or private, are not just neutral administrative machines but are forms of governance. Therefore, we must be concerned not just with *what* services are provided and at what cost, but *how* they are provided and how much control recipients have over the provision. Hence the issue of governance needs to be at the heart of the debate on the pattern of public and commercial services we receive, how they should be regulated, and what kind and what scale of institutions should deliver them.

This is a debate that the Conservatives and, indeed, most members of the political class and the policy elite have avoided. The sole issue in Britain today is how to deliver a bare minimum of public services as cheaply and efficiently as possible. Governance is either a complete non-issue or it is equated with the power to manage. Thus political decisions have been made as if they were technical matters, questions of administrative efficiency of concern to a small circle of experts and managers. Under the regime of a political party formally committed to liberalism, a practice of social organisation and service provision has developed that pushes us even further in a 'post-liberal' direction. Far-ranging political changes have taken place whilst leaving the apparent dominance of classical liberal theory unchallenged. The result is a vast transfer of political power and an effective denial that this power is political.

Thus what amounts to a political revolution has taken place in the UK, and unlike most such changes it has been accomplished without an explicit theory.[10] The Conservative governments have permitted a widespread practice of the administration of services to develop that destroys the very idea that the providing organisations could be matters of public concern, let alone that they might and should be constitutionally-ordered civil associations. Authority has been redefined as 'management', a generic skill and a domain of technical competence. Efficiency has been defined in a way that puts it apparently beyond political debate and choice. Management is not the proper concern of citizens; they should be satisfied in their capacity as consumers, by the services provided for them. Producers have no properly political place at all within the organisations in which they work; their task is to be directed to their duties and monitored from above in their performance of them. Thus the Conservatives, often unwittingly, for some are genuine libertarians, have allowed a new post-collectivist and post-liberal model of the public services to develop.

This new redefinition of the nature and role of the public service state is the key point at which a much wider struggle for freedom in a post-liberal society must begin to be fought. The capacity to resist encroachments in the public sphere, to define alternative and more democratic forms of service provision, will decide whether an ongoing struggle for greater democratisation can be sustained. Until public services can be rescued from the managerial model, there is little hope that managerial prerogatives in the private sector can be publicly challenged and new more accountable forms of corporate governance made widespread. Certainly, there is little scope for radical state legislation.

This does not mean that the job of re-building firms as more democratic organisations is impossible, merely that it is very difficult. However, the need for greater openness and accountability is real, and perhaps more credible in a world where the spectre of 'workers' control' can no longer be used to terrify publics into indifference to issues of corporate reform. Actually firms not merely need reform, many would actively benefit from it. Quality manufactured goods and marketed services depend not only on highly committed and skilled workers, they are bought by increasingly knowledgeable and sophisticated consumers. Many of these firms are multi-national, but this does not mean that they are beyond governance or control, or that they will profit from an absence of political superintendence of the company. Careless companies that make short-term narrowly 'commercial' decisions may suffer the wrath of consumers. Thus an oil company that wrecks an environmentally sensitive area on the other side of the globe may find that articulate consumers in, say, Germany, are boycotting its products.

Companies can act to remedy the deficiencies of nationally-based and shareholder-oriented governance. Imagine that the company in question had created a corporate senate, a body of honourable persons representing a wide range of views and affected interests, and deliberative and advisory in its powers.[11] Then perhaps it would have been saved much grief if it honestly put the project in question to such a senate and accepted its majority veto. Obviously, deliberately distorted data presented to stooge senators will reduce the whole thing to a PR exercise. The company must *mean* it. Companies, if they are responsible and have far-sighted leaders, rather than just managers, can begin to build their own governance. If they need a push to start, then the churches, NGOs, and the trustees of major share-holding pension funds can help them to see the costs of pretending that top-down decisions from the boardroom are infallible.

Such changes will be slow in the company sector, but in the case of public services most of their 'consumers' have no such power of boycott, and changes rely on explicit political decisions. The probable outcome is that until public services are reformed, most citizens will be unable to affect them by the power of exit, by saying 'I quit'. Many public services are compulsory:

some rightly so, one would not be happy if shops could choose their own environmental health officer; others less happily so, as when contributors to basic state pensions find the real value of the asset being devalued by government policy. Other services are discretionary, but are given to those in need or who make a case at the discretion of public officials. In other cases services are available as of right and optional in form, but for the majority of their consumers they might as well be compulsory. Thus parents having paid their taxes do not in the main have the option of foregoing state education and paying for a private school on top, and most parents find it difficult to do more than send their kids to the local school or accept the one that is assigned to them.

A New Welfare State

The dissatisfaction of consumers with the compulsory nature of many public services and the desire for choice has been used as an argument against public provision, and in favour of marketisation and privatisation. That is not the point being made here. In some cases only large-scale public provision and collective consumption will suffice: for example, where needs and risks are pooled in social insurance schemes against unemployment, old age and illness. Private provision will never suffice for the majority of the population in such areas. But it does not follow that compulsory consumption through one monopoly supplier, the state, is the only way to realise these advantages of the large-scale sharing of risks. Public and state are not identical; it is possible to have publicly-funded services that give consumers a large measure of choice and control. Services can be organised so as to reap the benefits of collective funding and yet allow citizens choice over the particular fund or service provider, and, having made a choice, the option of a measure of active voice in the control of its affairs.

Compulsory collective consumption organised from above is what has given public services a bad reputation. This failure has legitimised the marketisation and fragmentation of provision and entitlements, thereby destroying one of the supposed key advantages of public provision, common rights to a certain standard of service. The privatisation of services, in combination with chronic under-funding of those that remain public, has not given consumers a better deal or greater control, in fact bureaucrats remain firmly in charge. This reinforces tax-aversion, people feel they are getting less from the public realm and must try where possible to meet the higher costs of private provision of pensions, schooling and health for themselves and their families.

The problem then is to break the link between collective consumption and compulsion. Who would want to suffer that mixture of neglect and administrative interference that local authority housing departments inflicted on council tenants in the past? The gratitude for basic services—the dole, a council house, payment of the doctor's bill—is long since gone, and those services are no longer perceived as minimally adequate by the moderately successful. People do want to craft their own services—to have possession of their own home, to have definite pension rights, to have the choice to send their children to university. What were once 'middle class' expectations have become normal. The problem is that we have not found satisfactory ways of providing them for the bulk of the population. Private provision will exclude the majority from adequate cover across the whole range of services, and tailoring public provision to cater for the poor and unsuccessful, targeting resources, will alienate the majority from services they pay for but increasingly decline to consume if they have another option. Collective consumption remains essential for the majority, most people will not earn enough to meet all their needs from private markets and private insurance. The requirement is, however, to enable consumers to craft such collective services to their own needs, to have the benefits of common participation without the disadvantages of compulsion and subjection to administrative discretion.

Once we begin to think of collective services shaped by choice and voice then we can begin to bridge the divide between the pubic and private spheres. Public pensions give too much discretion to the state in the UK, but the private insurance and pensions markets offer variations in terms of benefits that are a scandal. Consumers need more protection in both spheres. If public services and private providers were both answerable in diverse ways to their consumers, then the stark divide between the two realms would be reduced. In particular more choice and control over public offerings and facilities would reveal to people how little control they have over private welfare services, how much they are at the mercy of companies, and how little pressure markets alone enable them to assert over areas like pensions, and life and health insurance. Once consumers could craft public services to suit them and had the means to exercise some political control over currently 'private' services, then the difference between the two areas would tend to decline, and with it much of the current obsession with the 'cost' of public services.

If the sphere of 'publicity' were to be extended, creating a broad range of self-governing institutions with consumer representation, spanning the currently separate categories of state and civil society, then much of the current concern among economic liberals with lessening the role of the state would appear less relevant. It only makes sense at present on the assumption that public provision is inherently inefficient, and that it is a net cost to successful taxpayers who do not want the services provided. It also only makes sense if we treat the private sector as based on the disciplines of market forces and competition that promote true efficiency, and that we ignore bureaucracy and hierarchy in the corporate sector. Whereas, of course, most firms are large organisations that plan and administer much as states do. It is only on the basis of such assumptions that an intelligent liberal like Robert Skidelsky can be so concerned to get state spending back to around 30 per cent of GDP.[12] But, if we are less starry-eyed about the virtue of markets and also convinced that we can improve the performance of both public and private organisations, then this begins to look like a fixation with certain conventions of national income accounting. Outside of the belief that the state inevitably and inescapably wastes money in providing services, it begins to look like a preference for our giving our money to one set of managers rather than another.

Crudely put, populations need to spend so much on welfare and services, in which sectors they do so is secondary to the overall level of consumption. Thus if the total of public and private spending on health, education and welfare is aggregated—state and private pensions, spending on public and private education—then most advanced industrial countries tend to converge in their overall levels of spending. In aggregate the society spends so much on a given class of services, and the mix between public and private is secondary to that total spend. Whether it is the state or an insurance company that provides your pension, you cannot spend the premiums on other things. The balance of the sectors can only be the primary concern if public services must offer less value *per se*.

That proposition can hardly be sustained. It would be difficult to claim that the predominantly public Swedish health system delivers less care, lower life expectancy, and higher infant mortality rates than does the mixed US system dominated by private producer interests, or that it does so at a higher per capita cost. Compulsory state services may be less attractive, but they are not the only option for publicly funded services. The target of doctrinaire economic liberals is all forms of collective and public welfare consumption.

In a post-liberal society, this rigid thinking in terms of categories of national expenditure and rigidly differentiated social sectors, in which all spending on public goods has to be justified, and private expenditure is inherently preferable, no longer makes much sense. We can then no longer oppose the rigid state to the free market. If civil society is organised rather than spontaneous, then it too is a domain of government and some of its private powers are bigger than many states. One cannot, therefore, contrast 'government' to 'society', and treat either sector as if they had distinct and homogeneous attributes—as if being 'private' could be inherently beneficial. The economic liberals can sustain their case only by pretending we live in another kind of society from the one we do. Even sophisticated thinkers like Skidelsky are using a classical liberal architecture to describe a post-liberal society.

If that is the case and if modern societies spend on aggregate a great deal on welfare, then we need to start another argument, one about how welfare is to be provided *across* society, in both state and non-state but publicly governed institutions. Such a set of social arrangements would not only be post-liberal, but also post-socialist. In such a publicity-governed mixed order the very notions of nationalisation and privatisation would lose much of their meaning. Questions of provision would turn on the precise mix of collective and private consumption, but the majority of organisations that provided services would resemble political societies, in that they would be answerable to the interests they affected.[13] Such a system would tend to evolve in a non-profit direction, consumers with voice would tend to constrain the revenue that managers of services could draw from their operations. Pension funds and insurance companies would be pressured towards lower levels of profit-taking and many firms would change into mutual institutions.

Principles of Associative Democracy

It will be obvious that it is impossible in the compass of a short article to even outline how consumers could participate in the governance of services and how public provision can be combined with consumer choice. I have sketched out what such institutions might look like elsewhere.[14] Reform of this kind faces serious practical difficulties. The point is that people have first to see that there is a problem, that the present state of affairs should be of concern to democrats. Then they may be willing to explore seriously the question of alternatives to bureaucratic control and the ways in which public services may be re-invigorated by active consumer choice, thereby encouraging citizens to support their costs.

Of course it is difficult to find ways of representing some of the interests affected by organisations and, of course, it is a fact that many consumers will be reluctant to become citizens in relation to services, actively to take up the option of voice. A society in which the majority are active democratic participants is highly unlikely. That should give us enough cynicism to face the problem of devising a democracy for the moderately lazy, but not so much as to believe it to be insoluble. To have real powers over organisations, people do not have to attend frequent meetings. Given the option to craft services for themselves by choosing between providers (funds following the customer) then most people will try to make well-informed choices. If they find a service is actually grossly unsatisfactory, or is evolving in a direction they dislike, then they can exercise their right of exit and move to another competing provider. It is also probably the case that enough consumers will be willing to vote for the activists willing to serve on governing bodies to give these representatives sufficient legitimacy in relation to the permanent officials. Choice, competition, and formal democratic accountability to consumers can be built into publicly-funded collective services. The question is whether we care enough to want to have greater freedom in relation to the organisations that constrain and control us whilst purporting to serve us.

The conception of a pluralised state and a democratised society hinted at here is not novel. It was advanced long before the social changes that might now make it possible by such thinkers as P.-J. Proudhon, G. D. H. Cole and H. J. Laski, between the 1840s and the 1920s.[15] This doctrine, called associationalism, enjoyed some popularity because it appeared to offer a third way between capitalism and socialism. It was marginalised by the great wars and intense social conflicts of the middle decades of this century, that reinforced the powers of central authority in the nation state. Yet as we have seen, the threat of such wars and class conflicts has declined dramatically in the advanced countries, and the nation state has lost some of its monopoly hold on governance. We now have an economic and social system that has clearly outgrown the remedies of classical liberalism, but to which the ideas of nationalised ownership and compulsory state services no longer offer an attractive or credible alternative.

We also live in a world that has become, rightly and unsurprisingly, tired of utopias. Change needs to be effective, but also piecemeal and supplemental in form if it is to get started. People are tired of social and institutional turbulence, not least of that caused by the grandiose and failed promises of the New Right. People may recognise the defects of traditional forms of democracy and be convinced that conventional state authority is less effective at solving problems, but they need to be convinced that changes will be for the better. The great advantage of attempts to democratise organisations is that they can proceed piecemeal, institution by institution and sector by sector. Indeed, it would be almost impossible to introduce such changes in a 'big bang' reform, since it would involve forcing consumers to choose, in effect compelling them to enter into voluntary associations. A radical alternative in the relation between state and civil society will only be accepted if it makes sense locally, in relation to particular strategies of institutional reform.

The danger is at present that the political and managerial elites are becoming so homogeneous that citizens have almost no choice with the existing system, and no alternative options. Political power then tends to become illegitimate. The plebs having no choice, elections signify little and fail to strengthen those who win office even if they have larger paper majorities. The implicit and anti-political but very compelling doctrine of government and management we outlined above has bitten deep into the political class. In New Zealand, for example, both major parties accepted this managerialist view of the role of the state, and the public found itself with no choice at all. There is some danger that this might happen in the UK, that the Labour Party may become the vehicle for the younger more sophisticated sections of the managerialist elite. In the end hierarchy becomes compelling for those who find themselves at or close to the top of the pile, whether in government, public services or firms. Labour seems to have conceded to the corporate sector that it will do little to disturb the power to manage. It may also see its task as running public services more efficiently, offering a slightly more open style of post-collectivist public management.

In part Labour's caution is well justified: ill-considered radicalism could lead to electoral defeat. Competent government by a party that is not actively hostile to public services would be a distinct benefit. But this caution is also because it has lost the capacity to imagine that there are effective alternative ideas. It has embraced managerialist conceptions of government because it sees them as competence and practicality. It is encouraged in this by many of its members who are themselves managers. The battle for the soul of Labour is no longer that between socialists and pragmatists, but that between those

114

who are managerialists and those who believe we can provide better services through greater democracy.

Biographical Note

Paul Hirst is Professor of Social Theory, Birkbeck College, University of London. Author of *Representative Democracy and its Limits* (1990), *Associative Democracy* (1994) and *The Pluralist Theory of the State—Selected Writings of J. N. Figgis, G. D. H. Cole and H. J. Laski*. Member of *The Political Quarterly* editorial board; deputy chair of Executive of Charter 88.

Notes

1 Of course, some variants of corporatism saw representative government as inadequate and sought to replace it by chambers based on corporate groups. The democratic variety presented itself as a supplement to representative institutions, as a pragmatic means to link state and civil society in order to achieve economic coordination by promoting the cooperation of the major organised interests. See Alan Cawson, *Corporatism and Political Theory*, Oxford, Blackwell, 1986.

2 This is not the same as 'globalisation', a process that is supposed by many commentators to have dissolved distinct and national economies, placed all societies at the mercy of international market forces, and undermined any possibility of effective public governance in the world system. For a critique see P. Hirst and G. Thompson, *Globalisation in Question*, Cambridge, Polity, 1996.

3 See J. Cohen and A. Arato, *Civil Society and Political Theory*, Cambridge MA, MIT Press, 1992.

4 For Hayek see *The Road to Serfdom*, Routledge and Kegan Paul, London, 1944, and the perceptive comments of Andrew Gamble in this volume. For Habermas see his *The Theory of Communicative Action* (2 vols), Cambridge, Polity, 1984 and 1987—especially Volume 2.

5 Jean-Jacques Rousseau, *The Social Contract and Discourses*, ed. G. D. H. Cole, London, Dent (Everyman), 1913. The passage in question is 'Man is born free; and everywhere he is in chains' (p. 3).

6 N. Bobbio, *The Future of Democracy*, Cambridge, Polity, 1987, p. 56.

7 See Anthony Black, *Guilds and Civil Society in European Thought from the Twelfth Century to the Present*, London, Methuen, 1984, especially Ch. 1–7.

8 Actually despite its Marxist *parti pris*, Louis Althusser's *Montesquieu: Politics and History*, London, NLB, 1972, brings out Montesquieu's role as an aristocratic opponent of absolutism and a defender of particular liberties very well.

9 A. Etzioni, *The Spirit of Community*, London, Fontana, 1995.

10 See P. Hirst, 'Quangos and Democratic Government' in *Parliamentary Affairs*, Vol. 48, No. 2, 1995, and the article by Stuart Weir in this volume.

11 See Shan Turnball, 'Reinventing Corporations' in *Human Systems Management* 10, 1991, pp. 169–86.

12 R. Skidelsky, *The World After Communism*, London, Macmillan, 1995 and 'Welfare without the State' in *Prospect*, January 1996, pp. 38–43.

13 I am grateful to Luke Martell for emphasising the importance of involving *affected* interests and not just those within the organisation.
14 Paul Hirst, *Associative Democracy*, Cambridge, Polity, 1994.
15 See D. Nicholls, *The Pluralist State* (2nd ed), London, Macmillan, 1995.

The Limits of Democracy

ANDREW GAMBLE

A KEY contrast which has helped form political discourse in the twentieth century has been that between the market and democracy. It has been the dominant way in which the economic and the political and the relationship between them have been understood. It has frequently been presented as an opposition, a conflict between two opposing principles of social organisation, an ideological battle between Left and Right. The world-historical struggle between capitalism and socialism was in time replaced by the less heroic but still fiercely contested rivalry between the ideas of a governed market economy and a market-led democracy. The Left became associated with attempts to govern the market by imposing political limits on how it operated, while the Right sought to restrict the scope of democracy by insisting that the market imposed limits on the scope of government action which had to be respected.

This debate has shaped political and emotional allegiances and intellectual alignments. Over time there has been some convergence in positions. Almost everyone now claims to believe in democracy and in markets. The Right gradually lost its fear of democracy and came to accept it as the least bad means of organising government, while the Left came to appreciate that markets were often necessary as a means of coordinating economies and ensuring efficient allocation of resources. Both sides accepted that democracy and markets were the two key institutional structures of a modern socio-economic system. Where they differed was over which should be predominant. Should politics be in command, controlling and steering the market and compensating for its shortcomings? Or should politics be subordinated to economics, confined to supporting the institutional rules required for markets and removing obstacles to their functioning?

At the heart of this argument is the interpretation of the doctrine of popular sovereignty. Are there and should there be limits to democracy? Should all other principles of social organisation be overridden if that is what the people decide? Or is democracy only successful where it recognises and operates within the constraints set by other social structures? In the course of the twentieth century the argument has swayed back and forth. In the first few decades arguments for the supremacy of democracy over markets steadily gained ascendancy and provided the justification for extending the scope and scale of government. In the last thirty years however there has been a pronounced reaction against collectivist ideas, and a strong revival of economic liberalism. The idea of a social democracy—a market governed by democracy—has been supplanted by the alternative vision of a market democracy—a democracy limited by markets.

© The Political Quarterly Publishing Co. Ltd. 1996
Published by Blackwell Publishers, 108 Cowley Road, Oxford OX4 1JF, UK and 238 Main Street, Cambridge, MA 02142, USA

Any serious project for renewing democracy has to assess the arguments for placing limits on democracy advanced by the New Right. Some accept that the idea of a market democracy is now in the ascendancy, but believe that the project of a governed market can and must be resuscitated. They expect that just as the dominance of market liberalism in the nineteenth century was followed by a reaction which saw the imposition of political control over the market, so the new ascendancy will in its turn be followed in due course by renewed demands for political control of the market.

There is a different way of approaching the problem however. Why should we treat the conflict between market and democracy as everlasting? Reclaiming the radical potential for liberty and equality in the tradition from which both liberalism and socialism derive means freeing ourselves from the intellectual and emotional mind-set which has formed generations of social democrats and economic liberals; that democracy and the market are intrinsically opposite principles and that one must dominate the other. To recognise that in any historical instance this has in fact been so is different from arguing that it must necessarily be so.

The political consequences of markets

There is not a single unified discourse on markets and a single unified discourse on democracy. Both discourses are naturally internally highly varied. There are for example many different strands of the New Right—for example neo-liberal, neo-conservative and libertarian. No attempt is made here to cover all these differences. Instead the focus will be on some of the general arguments and basic assumptions which characterise the two sides of the dispute.

One of the most influential explanations of the ascendancy of democracy over the market in the twentieth century is Karl Polanyi's account in *The Great Transformation*.[1] Polanyi's argument rests on two key assumptions; firstly that the market economy far from being the natural phenomenon portrayed by the political economists was a highly artificial political creation, the result of the pursuit of a definite policy; and secondly that once established the market economy became a self-regulating system with its own momentum, outside anyone's control, and no longer embedded in wider social and political institutions. The consequences of this for human welfare were so extreme that it generated political movements which demanded change, and led eventually to the successful imposition of regulation and control. Society organised itself to contain the monster which had been allowed off the leash.

Polanyi's account focuses on the costs of a market economy and explains the growth of government regulation as a response to a series of market outcomes—poverty, unemployment, and waste—which required remedy. Economists analysed these outcomes with the concept of market failure. In mainstream neo-classical economics this concept implied that if markets were working properly these outcomes could not occur. Resources would be allocated in response to the price signals which reflected the preferences of individual economic agents. If markets are fully competitive then the outcomes will ensure that all resources are fully employed and no-one can be made better off without making someone else worse off.

Polanyi argued, however, that market failures were not accidental but necessary features of an actual market system. He adapted the Marxist argument that left to itself a market economy would lead to a polarisation of wealth, reflecting the initial starting point of substantial inequality in power and resources of the agents involved in market exchange. These unequal relationships of power could not be addressed through markets themselves but only through external political involvement. The society organised politically had to be called in to redress the imbalances created by the way the society was organised economically.

There were many possibilities in the type of reform that could be undertaken, from complete suppression of markets and the introduction of command systems, to certain types of regulation and government intervention to modify and correct the way in which markets worked. The issue was whether markets should be replaced or whether they should be reformed and supplemented. But there was no dispute from this kind of perspective that the market system needed to be brought back under political control, as Polanyi argued it had always been before the advent of capitalism and the special circumstances of the nineteenth century. Writing in the middle of the twentieth century Polanyi described the steady advance of collectivism and the retreat of the market. The nineteenth century appeared an aberrant phase in human history, a time when politics had briefly ceased to be in command and had been subordinated to the requirements of the market.

The political consequences therefore of a free and unfettered market economy were the development of pressures for reining in the market, which with the advent of universal suffrage became irresistible. The demand for greater security against the risks of market exchange was translated into programmes for universal benefits to cover health, education, old age, sickness, accident and unemployment, as well as fiscal regimes which were redistributive, and policy regimes which sanctioned a wide range of government interventions to promote general economic welfare.

This tendency was noted by the critics of collectivism as well as its friends. F. A. Hayek, for example, in his polemics against the erosion of the principles of the market order blamed it principally on intellectual error, but also saw the difficulty of arguing the free market case in modern democracies where a majority of the voters no longer had direct experience of risk taking and property holding.[2] Employees, he argued, would always be disposed to vote for programmes of collective security. In this sense Hayek confirmed Polanyi's analysis. The political consequences of extending the suffrage beyond property owners was that the task of defending the market order became much more difficult.

Hayek thought that the doctrine of popular sovereignty especially when allied with democracy made invasion of the market by the state much easier to effect. The modern state acquired a legitimacy from these doctrines which made its agents able to override all opposition to their plans to centralise power. The institutions of the market order were highly vulnerable to attempts to ensure social justice through redistribution or greater security through new rules which reduced or prohibited competition or invaded property rights. Hayek thought all these invasions to be calamitous for both the moral and material health of western society. Democracy was one of the main mechanisms by which it was being pushed forward. The legitimacy which democratic governments could claim made their piecemeal gradual erosion of the market order more dangerous in the long run than the authoritarian oligarchic socialism of the Soviet Union. The latter lacked legitimacy, and was easier to discredit. But it was much harder to challenge the move to establish social democracies in Europe when these enjoyed the support of large well-organised popular movements and were articulated through doctrines which had gained the ascendancy in public debate.

Hayek's pessimistic conclusion about the impact of democracy on the institutions of the market order thus paralleled the optimistic conclusion of Polanyi. One of the main reasons for this difference in perception was the way in which they conceived the market. For Hayek it was a neutral mechanism of exchange from which all agents despite their different starting points and endowments could benefit, whereas for Polanyi it was a mechanism biased from the outset by the relationships of power between the different agents. For Polanyi the market is a political creation which systematically privileges certain interests over others. For Hayek the market is a spontaneous order which arises from exchanges which individuals find to be mutually beneficial. It requires protection by political and legal means but it is not brought into existence by them.

The political economy of labour

The argument from the Left against the market assumed that the market was not a neutral technique of resource allocation but a set of power relationships. The wider changes which the Left wished to see to improve the welfare of the majority required a change in the balance of power between classes. The policy of full employment to which all Left parties became committed could only be realised if a shift in power occurred. Otherwise the doctrines of sound finance and reliance on the disciplines of bankruptcy and unemployment could be expected to continue. Many socialists came to support Keynesian economic ideas but following Michael Kalecki[3] and later John Strachey argued that the political conditions for implementing Keynesian ideas had first to be created. They would only be adopted if the relative strength of the two key interests, labour and capital, was first addressed. In effecting that change the agency of the state was crucial.

In this tradition the growth of democracy and the organisation of the labour movement and mass political parties of the left became the agencies through which the power of capital is confronted and eventually curbed. The free market which operates according to its own laws becomes a governed market which is operated in terms of objectives set through the political process. This does not mean the end of capitalism. Many of the strongest supporters of these changes argued that this was precisely the way to safeguard capitalism and restore its legitimacy. A new partnership between public and private sectors would herald the setting of limits to the freedom of capital but not the abolition of capital.

This project has sometimes been called the mixed economy, but that term suggests two alternative economic systems existing side by side. It is more accurate to refer to this system as a governed market economy, as Charles Lindblom does,[4] in which the public sphere is enlarged to correct particular deficiencies and shortcomings in the market. The main areas of enlargement have been full employment and economic management; welfare and social security; economic growth and urban planning; and redistributive taxation. In all of these the state has proceeded by asserting a higher public interest over private interest as the rationale for intervening in the market economy.

It took different forms in different countries. In Anglo-America Keynesianism was a particularly important doctrine. In the 1950s John Strachey declared that Keynesianism was the democratic solution to the crisis of capitalism about which he had written so eloquently in the 1930s.[5] In other parts of Europe much more thoroughgoing forms of corporatism became established. But the general principle was the same. The market was governed. The tendency of a capitalist market economy to produce greater inequality and polarisation was checked. Democracy set limits to the market, and forced property to make significant concessions as the price for retaining basic rights of control.

The Economic Consequences of Democracy

The hegemony of the idea of the governed market however did not endure. It came under strong attack from a revived economic liberalism in the 1970s and 1980s. The heart of this critique of social democracy was the argument that the market needed to be recognised as an institutional structure which should be inviolable and protected from political interference. The market should set limits to democracy. It had its own legitimacy which government should respect.

The revival of economic liberalism was the work of many different intellectuals and policy entrepreneurs working sometimes alone, sometimes through thinktanks and political parties. In certain respects it was a revival of an older style of discourse which collectivists like Polanyi thought had been buried for ever. But there was also something novel and different about it.

All the economic liberals accepted democracy, but it was always a qualified acceptance. They always gave greater priority to the market. The market was a set of institutions which had evolved over a very long period and had existed long before modern forms of democracy were instituted. Democracy was therefore considered useful but not necessary for the existence of a market, and under certain conditions it could be harmful. Most economic liberals accepted that even though the market had not been planned or designed by any single mind or agency it was still a political creation in the sense that the rules on which it depended had ultimately to be enforced and guaranteed by political decision. If this public power could be conducted under democratic rules so much the better. But it did not need to be. Although there were obvious dangers to economic freedom from authoritarian government, the dangers from democratic government were even greater, particularly because democratic governments were armed with the doctrine of popular sovereignty which gave them a confidence and a legitimacy to impose their will.

Economic liberals chose to attack this hubris of the modern democratic state by focusing on the economic consequences of allowing economic policy to be influenced through a debate in which nothing potentially was out of bounds. This would only be tolerable they argued if government solutions to economic problems were consistently superior to market solutions. The advocates of the governed market had always made much of the presence of market failures which justified state intervention. But this presumed that government possessed the knowledge and the skill to remedy market failures. Economic liberals suggested that on the contrary government solutions were always likely to be inferior to market solutions in any situation where market solutions were possible. Governments were falsely portrayed as omniscient and omnipotent, able to diagnose rationally what was wrong and apply the correct remedy. The reality according to the economic liberals was very different. Government failure was much more prevalent in the modern world than market failure. Where governments had tried to do without markets or replace them they had produced results which in welfare and efficiency terms were far worse than the situations they were seeking to improve.

Compared to markets governments are both ignorant and incompetent, according to the economic liberal critique. If they cannot be better than markets it is essential that that fact be recognised, and that governments restrict themselves to supporting markets and helping them to work better rather than seeking to supplant them by some other mechanism which is grossly inferior, and leads to outcomes which are increasingly damaging.

The economic liberal critique of democracy draws in particular on public choice arguments about demand and supply failures which are inherent in political and democratic methods of decision-making. The analogy is always with an economic market. In the political market the translation of preferences first into party programmes, then into policies and laws, and finally into outcomes is extremely complex. Interests are aggregated in ways which makes it impossible to determine whether voters' interests are actually being represented in the policy process. Voters have to choose between packages of personalities and measures and are unable to be as discriminating as they can be in ordinary consumer purchases, for example by taking goods from different suppliers. A party manifesto offers a wide range of policies and commitments but voters are not free to register support or opposition for particular items. They must either accept the whole or reject it.

The electoral process confers legitimacy on political parties to act as agents of the central state by forming governments. They claim a mandate from the people, but the process is not transparent enough to be sure exactly what mandate the people have conferred. Different electoral rules mean also that governments can be formed with much less than fifty per cent of the vote, or as a coalition from parties which competed against one another. From a public choice perspective the lines of accountability between party programmes and voter preferences are hopelessly blurred. Voters also are only able to cast their vote infrequently. Consumers are able to switch much more readily, except in some very large purchases such as a house. But even here there is a difference. Consumers are locked into the consequences of particular choices like buying a house, but they remain their choices. Voters are locked into the choice the majority makes. Parties and governments gain considerable autonomy and flexibility from this fact.

If aggregating preferences is difficult, even greater problems occur on the supply side. According to standard public choice analysis, government bureaus do not face the kind of disciplines which firms face in a competitive market. There is therefore no means by which outcomes which conform with the preferences of the electorate, or even with the preferences of the political parties elected to represent the people can be guaranteed. Instead those who control the bureaus are able to pursue their own agendas such as maximising the size of their budgets so that they can expand their influence. Government therefore has an inexorable tendency to expand, and very few spending programmes are ever axed. They acquire a momentum of their own, and erode the long-term capacity of the economy to sustain them.[6]

Public choice theorists therefore turn the criticism of market failure back on to the collectivists. The real problem of the modern economy they argue is not market failure but government failure. The problems created by the separation of ownership and control in publicly quoted companies are serious enough in establishing the accountability of the managers who control the assets, but they are as nothing compared with the problems of controlling the actions of politicians and bureaucrats in contemporary democracies. The executives of modern states have become adept at reducing their accountability under a smokescreen of serving the public interest and carrying out the will of the people.

The Limits of Knowledge

This public choice questioning of what the public interest actually means when an attempt is made to disaggregate it into the interests of individual voters is only one part however of the economic liberal critique. A second powerful argument stresses that governments lack sufficient knowledge to be able to plan effectively or to intervene in markets in ways that would lead to improved outcomes, except by chance. On this view, knowledge is dispersed throughout society across a multitude of different sites and locations, reflecting its diversity and complexity. It would be impossible for this knowledge to be centralised; only a decentralised mechanism such as a market which rests on a multitude of exchanges between individuals can hope to make use, and then only partial use, of all the local information which individuals possess, in coordinating economic activity and promoting cooperation.

It follows that if governments, however democratic a mandate they claim, seek to act as if the decentralised nature of knowledge in a modern economy does not exist, they are likely to make fairly large errors, which will lead to waste and inefficiency, and will be compounded because there is no mechanism for correcting the errors quickly. On the contrary the structure of the policy regime can become rigid because the process becomes infested at all levels by special interests who seek to maintain the programmes in being due to the benefits they receive from them.

The conclusion of the economic liberal critique is that governments elected under modern universal suffrage may claim to be acting in the public interest and to be carrying out a popular mandate, but in reality there is no way of determining what the public interest is, and even if it could be determined, no way of ensuring that governments will act in accordance with it. Even if governments wished to act in the public interest how would they know what it was?

The force of this critique depends on reducing everything to the level of the individual, and asking how the preferences of each individual are to be realised economically and politically. There are other discourses about how the public interest can be identified. But the critique in policy terms was a powerful one because it coincided with widespread disillusion in many countries with the perceived outcomes of the programmes of the extended state, which had originally been introduced to deal with the problems of the extended market. If governments had become overloaded and over-extended in seeking to meet the demands and expectations of voters, special interests, and the government machine itself, the correct path seemed to be a drastic scaling down of the scope and scale of government, and the recognition of the limits to its competence, in particular the need to respect the integrity of institutional orders like the market. These should become the practical limits to democracy. By recognising the wisdom and knowledge contained in these institutions which governments could not replicate, democracies would in effect surrender their right to determine large areas of policy.

One of the difficulties with the economic liberals' critique is that despite their strong hostility to the state and government and political processes in general, they still recognise that political processes are essential to sustain the kind of social and economic order of which they approve. James Buchanan for example distinguishes between the protective and the productive state.[7] The protective state ensures the conditions which make an extended market possible, such as the rule of law, the enforcement of contracts, and the protection of property, and is both necessary and desirable from an economic liberal perspective. The productive state on the other hand becomes involved in the direct allocation of resources and instead of sustaining begins to supplant the market order.

Constitutional Safeguards

This economic liberal analysis of the superiority of the economic market to the political market, leads to proposals to rein in democracy and subordinate it as a process to the needs of the market. Suspicion of government and of those who hold power is not confined to economic liberals. It is a strong strain in all forms of liberalism and in many strands of socialism also. The desire to base the legitimacy of the government on its accountability to the wishes and preferences of those who elect it is the fundamental driving force. The difference between economic liberals and liberal collectivists is that the former believes that the best guarantee of that accountability is the protection of the institutional order of the market, while the latter place their faith in the institutional order of democratic government.

The contrast can be observed for example in the different recommendations of Keynes in comparison with Hayek and Buchanan. Keynes recognised the danger of the abuse of power under a democracy, but he put his trust in elites. So long as elites were minded to act rightly, then they could be entrusted with the great powers which modern democracies conferred on them. Keynes' faith in elites has been much mocked by economic liberals, who have denigrated the public service ethos of public sector workers, arguing that it simply conceals their efforts to advance their personal interests. But the economic liberals have found it difficult to find a convincing alternative. One of their favourite solutions is the design of constitutions which will prevent governments from taking decisions or pursuing policies that harm the market order. Rules on balancing the budget, or maximum levels of taxation, are the kind of measures they have in mind. These would place very specific limits on what a democracy could do. Such a constitution however would only be viable if there was a very strong and permanent consensus behind it. Otherwise the doctrine of popular sovereignty would be invoked to tear it up.

The constitutionalist devices proposed by Buchanan and the Virginia school to set limits to democracy seek to restore the original safeguards of the US Constitution which have been weakened in this view by the advent of democratic politics. The problem is the classic liberal one of how to keep the power of government limited. In his review of the different constitutionalist devices which have been used—the English balance of powers, the American division of powers, the German rule of law—Hayek noted the deficiencies of all of them in the face of the pressures of democratic collectivism, and recommended instead an elaborate model polity which contained elements of all three. He proposed two separate assemblies, a government assembly concerned with the routine business of government, and the other with the general rules governing social and economic life, and in particular what sort of government actions are just and what unjust. The government assembly and the government which it appointed would have to work within the framework of rules established by the legislative assembly. This second chamber would be chosen by each age cohort when it reached 45 from among its own members, excluding those who had already served in the government assembly or who had worked for party organisations. Representatives would hold office for fifteen years, and one-fifteenth would therefore be elected every year. They would be excused other work and would act as a permanent constitutional court, which would set strict limits to what the lower assembly could decide to do.[8]

If however the world is as economic liberals and public choice theorists describe it there is no good reason why governments should seek to divest themselves of their existing powers and no means by which they can be forced to do so. The drive to reduce the scope and scale of government seems therefore to require a change in hearts and minds, a conversion to the principles of economic liberalism on the part of elites and voters sufficient to override the desire to maximise their self interest. The cutting edge of public choice analysis in unmasking how elites behave is the assumption that agents are not only instrumentally rational but that what they seek to maximise is their own power and wealth. Persuading elites to establish an institutional order which reduces their power by setting limits on what democracies can decide requires them to behave altruistically in the public interest.

The Hollowing Out of Democracy

The ascendancy of economic liberal ideas in public discourse in the last twenty years has been marked, particularly in Britain and the United States and some other English-speaking countries such as Australia and New Zealand. The hegemony of social democratic ideas has been successfully challenged. Changes in the institutions and practices of the extended state have been more elusive but still significant. Nothing approaching the new constitutional order favoured by Buchanan or Hayek is in sight but the defenders of the extended state and the governed market are pessimistic about the chances of resisting the economic liberal tide.

The reason for this is that although democracy has never been more widely established in the world as a system of government it is increasingly seen as subordinate to and invaded by the market, to such an extent that its distinctive character as an institutional order separate from the market is being lost. Democracy is being hollowed out. This process is not new, but is seen to have acquired a fresh momentum in the last twenty years. It is becoming increasingly difficult to sustain the notion of a public interest and a public space, defined in ways which are separate from market relationships.

The decline of the public sphere is associated with the decline of the mass political party. Despite their tendency towards oligarchy, mass parties were still regarded as one of the most important avenues for public debate and participation in the formation of the public interest. The involvement of party members has weakened, at the same time that party leaderships have increasingly come to regard electoral politics as a marketing operation, and are prepared to adjust programmes and image in whatever ways will maximise short-term votes. The emphasis comes to be placed on current ratings rather than building long-term allegiance and identity.

The political market has become increasingly structured as Schumpeter predicted by the competition between rival teams of leaders. Parties become oligopolies seeking to control and manipulate the behaviour of voters. The terms of their competition are increasingly set by modern media, whose general influence has been towards trivialisation and personalisation of politics, as well as setting the agenda of debate by defining what counts as sound policy. The ignorance of the electorate about most public policy matters is reinforced by the media and little countervailing pressure is now exerted either by civic education in schools or by alternative education programmes in the community.

The ideal of self-governing democracies has also been undermined by the encouragement to voters to think increasingly in terms of pocket-book voting, the direct material benefit to themselves and their families to be expected from particular policies and the programmes of different parties. The effect of this has been to elevate the question of taxation to a crucial position and has made it extremely difficult in the Anglo-Saxon democracies to advocate an increase in taxation without paying a penalty in lost votes.

All these trends are related to perhaps the greatest threat of all to self-governing democracies—the declining capacity of states to manage national economies in the face of the growth of new forms of economic and cultural interdependence and transnational networks. The re-emergence of a global political economy as the dominant institutional order after seventy years in which the state system had taken priority raised questions in every state about the ability of national governments to make effective policy choices, and how far therefore democracy was now constrained by the global market and its key institutions such as the financial markets.

One of the effects of the discourse on globalisation has been to reinforce the argument for making democracy subordinate to the market. If states now found themselves once more in a truly global political economy pursuit of national strategies was a vain delusion. The correct course was to align national policy with the policies which were favoured by the international financial markets. Any other course risked a painful collision from which the loser would most likely be the credibility and reputation of the national government. In terms of Kalecki's analysis this new global political economy represented the reassertion of the power of capital over labour at the global level, the reimposing of the disciplines of bankruptcy and unemployment for those sectors which failed to maintain their profitability, and the steady rolling back of the concessions on welfare and union rights which had been won during the high tide of social democracy and national economic management. The ransom once demanded by labour no longer had to be paid. Any country which continued to pay it risked placing burdens on its industries and making itself less competitive in the global market.

In this way the critique of social democracy by the economic liberals arguing that democracy should be subordinated to the market was buttressed by the claim that economic and political realities of the world economy after the collapse of Bretton Woods made national Keynesianism impossible and exposed the potential burden of universal welfare. The economic liberals argued that the essential need was to recognise the market order as an independent institutional order whose boundaries democracies must not interfere with. This market order was now openly understood as an international order. The solidarities, communities, civic traditions, and national sovereignties which sustained democratic politics had to be made compatible with the more fundamental reality of the market order.

Rethinking Democracy

As noted above one response to the tide of economic liberalism is to argue that its ascendancy will be short-lived and that it will in its turn be succeeded by a new wave of collectivism. The more triumphant economic liberalism is on a global scale the more the effects of unrestrained free market will trigger the kind of consequences which produced the social movements and collectivist doctrines at the end of the nineteenth century from both right and left demanding control of the market. The impact of unregulated capitalism on the environment will it is suggested in time create pressure to establish a new regime of regulation and intervention.

Such a regime, however, will be flawed if it resembles the regulatory regime of the past and repeats their errors. What needs to be explored are new ways of achieving the traditional objectives of the Left. The argument that ideological discourse is at an end because current forms of democracy and the market cannot be improved upon overlooks the chasm that still exists between the goals which both liberalism and socialism proclaimed and the reality of inequality and lack of freedom in so many contemporary societies.

The ritual opposition between market and democracy has become increasingly disabling and sterile for radical thought and action. It prevents new

128

ways of thinking about how long-term institutional change can best be promoted. The strength of the democratic critique of the market was its exposure of the power relationships which established markets and biased their outcomes. The strength of the market critique of democracy was its exposure of the elitist relationship which defined the public interest in terms of private agendas. Both market and democracy are imperfect systems. What is mistaken is to treat the market as though it were a spontaneous order which emerges solely through the unplanned interactions of individual agents, and to treat democracy as though it were a planned order which involves the extension of conscious control over blind and unconscious processes. It is more useful to think of both market and democracy as particular institutional orders which are both the product of spontaneous interaction, in the sense that many things happen within them in an unplanned way as the result of individuals adjusting to each others plans and behaviour, and also the product of deliberation and decision, in the sense that the conditions for this interaction are only sustained through political will and commitment.

If democracy is to be renewed, those acting in its name have to learn to utilise the market rather than supplant it. Appropriate exit and voice mechanisms need to be established for all organisations as part of their systems of governance. If there is a problem with 'the market' it lies with the forms of governance of the organisations that operate in particular markets. The idea that 'the market' is corrosive of the extra-market rules, attitudes, and beliefs on which it depends needs to be broken down into specific arguments about the effects of particular markets which arise from the way in which they are constituted.

One of the greatest difficulties for designing appropriate systems of governance is the problem of knowledge. What is the basis of the knowledge which governments can claim for the changes they seek to introduce? Democracy in the twentieth century tended to become increasingly centralised, and this has made it extremely vulnerable to the economic liberal critique. The possibility exists however for a much more decentralised democracy, an institutionalised order which enables interactions between individuals to take place and can draw together the dispersed and fragmented knowledge which they possess.[9] Such a democracy is not antagonistic to the market but complementary to it. They interpenetrate one another in the sense that forms of associative democracy are necessary to establish many of the conditions such as interpersonal trust which markets need in order to function effectively. The unequal power and property relationships which so often define markets can be challenged not by suppressing markets but by proposing new forms of governance to reform property rights which currently exclude the majority of citizens.

None of these changes would be easy or painless or conflict-free. By reaffirming the goals of securing equality and liberty for all human beings, the attempt to bring markets and democracy together are likely to raise expectations and increase radicalism by highlighting the gap between promise and achievement which still exists in all capitalist societies. Decentralised forms of democracy and civic association does not mean that other levels of democracy—national and international—become unimportant. Just as the extended market embraces these levels, so must the extended state. The problem is rather that to build any kind of effective democracy at these levels, there have to be solid foundations at local and regional level.

The process is not just one way. Institutional orders which encourage mutual adjustment and the solving of problems by incremental means still require a public power which can enable them to come into existence and then sustain them. Difficult problems remain as to how such a state should be organised and how it can be kept responsive. The key point in any perspective for reform however is that such a state needs to recognise and respect the institutional orders of both the market and democracy, without seeking to dominate either. Such a state policy would need to be experimental encouraging the development of a learning society, seeking to discover those institutions that actually work in finding solutions to problems and improving welfare.[10]

Renewing democracy in this perspective is about recognising the limits to democracy but also the limits to markets, and no longer supposing that political virtue consists in a triumph of the one over the other. There would still be conflict and frictions. Both institutional orders are imperfect, and there will always be scope for reform and adjustment. But what has to be found is the confidence once again to propose and facilitate institutional changes aimed at regaining a sense of a public purpose and the importance of a public sphere without demonising the market as an institutional order which is only fit to be tamed and corralled, or demonising democracy as a system which always tends to incontinence and excess. The institutional orders of democracy and the market have a critical part to play in providing the frameworks within which new ideas can be tried and new solutions to social problems can emerge. Decentralised markets joined with associative democracy offer mechanisms of exit and voice which are both egalitarian and libertarian. The renewal of democracy requires a release of social energy and social imagination, a synergy which new forms of governance and new kinds of markets might provide. There are many obstacles in the way but also the promise of renewing the search for the institutional conditions which will best promise justice, equality and freedom.

Biographical Note

Andrew Gamble is Professor of Politics at the University of Sheffield, and author of *Hayek: The Iron Cage of Liberty*, Cambridge, Polity, 1996.

Notes

1 Karl Polanyi, *The Great Transformation*, Boston, Beacon, 1957.
2 F. A. Hayek, *The Constitution of Liberty*, London, Routledge, 1960.
3 Michael Kalecki, 'Political Aspects of Full Employment', *Political Quarterly*, 1943, pp. 322–31.
4 Charles Lindblom, *Politics and Markets*, New York, Basic Books, 1977.
5 John Strachey, *Contemporary Capitalism*, London, Gollancz, 1956.
6 For a critique of this position see Patrick Dunleavy, *Democracy, Bureaucracy and Public Choice*, Brighton, Harvester, 1990.
7 James Buchanan, *The Limits of Liberty: Between Liberty and Leviathan*, Chicago, University of Chicago Press, 1975.
8 F. A. Hayek, *Law, Legislation and Liberty, Vol. 3: The Political Order of a Free People*, London, Routledge, 1979, ch. 17.
9 Paul Hirst, *Associative Democracy*, Cambridge, Polity, 1994.
10 Two applications of these ideas are Gavin Kelly, Andrew Gamble, Mike Dietrich, & Randall Germain, 'Regional Finance and Corporate Governance: Do We Need Regional Development Banks?', *New Economy*, 1995, pp. 251–61; and Andrew Gamble & Gavin Kelly, 'One Nation Socialism and Stakeholder Capitalism', *Renewal*, 1996, pp. 23–31.

Democracy and the European Union

IAN HARDEN

The democratic deficit

THE institutions of the European Union exercise authority over individuals and over the governments of member states that those individuals elect. States and companies can be fined for breaches of Community law. If there is conflict between Community law and national law, the former takes precedence—even in national courts. Furthermore, some of the money that national governments collect from their citizens in taxes must be transferred to the Community budget to be spent. What is the legitimate constitutional basis for these powers? It is not sufficient to reply that they are contained in the Union Treaties, or derive from Community law. Making laws and spending money raised through taxes are public powers that normally require legitimation through democratically elected institutions.

The Union does have some electoral credentials. They are partly direct and partly indirect. The former element is provided by the European Parliament, which has been directly elected since 1979. Its powers have been progressively extended, first by the budgetary Treaties of the 1970s, then by the Single European Act of 1986 and most recently by the Maastricht Treaty on European Union. Even so, its constitutional role remains peripheral. Most Community legislation is made in the name of the Council (usually referred to as the Council of Ministers) or by the Commission. Although the Council and the Parliament jointly constitute the Community budgetary authority, the Council has the final say over the majority of spending. In any event, the really vital budgetary decisions—on the maximum level of Community spending and the distribution between states of the burden of financing it—are determined by heads of state and government in the European Council.

The indirect electoral credentials apply to the Council. The Council as a whole—as a Community institution—is accountable to no-one. However, it consists of individual representatives of the member states, usually from the executive branch of central government, who are accountable within the national constitutional frameworks. Such indirect democratic legitimation has proved only a partial success. Provided that it has the necessary constitutional powers, a national Parliament can influence the positions taken by its state's representatives in the Council and call them to account. The Danish Parliament is often cited as an example. As long as the Council must act by unanimity, it is even possible in principle for national Parliaments to exercise the right of veto. In practice, opportunities for national Parliaments to call ministers to account for what is done in the Council are limited. The main problem is that the Council and its infrastructure—the Committee of Permanent Representatives (COREPER) and the Monetary Committee—operate largely in secret.

The Commission carries out a variety of administrative and quasi-judicial functions, but also has a key political role in setting the legislative and budgetary agendas of the Community. Commissioners are appointed by the Council. The European Parliament must approve the appointment of the Commission as a whole and can subsequently dismiss it by a two-thirds majority vote. Under the constitutional framework established by the Union Treaties, however, the legitimacy of the Commission is primarily based on its independence—both of national governments and of other Union bodies—not on accountability to the Parliament or Council.[1]

The problem of democracy at the level of the European institutions thus has three interlocking aspects: the limited constitutional role of the Parliament; the imperfect operation of the indirect democratic accountability of the Council; and the free-standing political role of the Commission. Two proposed methods to tackle the problem have been much discussed. They go in quite opposite directions.

The first is to create a democratic European federal state, with a parliamentary or presidential form of government at the federal level. In this scenario, the Parliament would become the principal law-making body, with the Council acting as a kind of senate. The Commission would become a European government. It, or its President, could be directly elected. Alternatively they could be appointed by the Parliament. This is the federalist solution. The second and opposite course is to renounce any further transfer of powers from member states to the Union. Existing competences would ideally be returned to the states and hence to the possibility of democratic control at national level. If this were not possible, they would at least be kept firmly subject to national rights of veto in the Council. Neither of these methods of tackling the democratic deficit is satisfactory. We need to find a different approach to the question of democracy in Europe. To explain why and how, let us begin by examining the idea of democracy itself a little more closely.

Critical and affirmative democracy

Democracy is founded on the idea of popular sovereignty, to which many written constitutions make explicit reference. The Italian constitution, for example, says that sovereignty belongs to the people. There is a similar provision in the French constitution about 'national sovereignty'. The German Basic Law says that state power (*Staatsgewalt*) comes from the people.[2] Even in the UK, one of the many overlapping shades of meaning of the 'sovereignty of Parliament' is popular sovereignty. Popular sovereignty has two fundamental dimensions, to which I shall attach the labels '*critical* democracy' and '*affirmative* democracy'. These are not competing ideas about what democracy is. Rather, they denote different aspects of the same basic principle of popular sovereignty.

Critical democracy questions, limits and constrains public power. It does so for two reasons. The first reason is that, for most purposes and for most of the time, modern societies must rely on representation rather than direct decisions by the people. Critical democracy is doubtful about the extent to which governments really give effect to the wishes of the people, because of the inherent flaws of representation. Elections are a poor method of discovering citizens' views about matters of public policy, because all the issues are bundled together. They are more about selecting which party or leader is to have power. Furthermore, politicians and public officials may use the decision-making space which power gives them to pursue private or factional agendas, rather than the public interest. So although winning elections is essential to claim legitimate authority to govern, critical democracy is sceptical about just how much authority winning an election should confer.[3] Critical democracy is also suspicious of referendums. Within the overall context of representative democracy, it fears their likely manipulation by governments or factions.

The second reason why critical democracy constrains public power is because individuals have rights that cannot legitimately be taken away. Political theorists often treat individual rights and democracy as different and potentially conflicting ideas. However, the most persuasive basis for democracy is an individual right to political equality.[4] Approaching the question from the opposite direction, political rights (such as freedom of expression and assembly) are an essential part of democracy itself. Without them, there is no democracy.[5] Many other rights, including some social and economic rights, can be seen as preconditions for an effective opportunity to participate in democracy and thus as corollaries of the basic democratic principle of political equality. From this perspective, individual rights are a necessary component of democracy itself.

The problematic nature of representation and the need to protect rights lead critical democracy to emphasise issues of constitutional design and devices such as Bills of Rights and judicial review of legislation. It favours checks and balances between different institutions and the separation of powers. Critical democracy also lays stress on the need for effective processes of accountability between elections. Democratic legitimacy is not something to be acquired like a chain of office. It requires constant scrutiny and debate of the conduct of those exercising public power. This in turn requires 'transparency'. That is to say, the process of making decisions should be understandable and open and the decisions themselves should be reasoned and based on information that is publicly available.

The purpose of critical democracy is not to constrain popular sovereignty, but to give effect to it by constraining and channelling the conduct of governments. Affirmative democracy, on the other hand, emphasises that popular sovereignty is the positive source of legitimacy of public power and of collective choices about goals and purposes. This has of course nothing necessarily to do with collectivist politics. Even if we begin by thinking about government in terms of a contract between individuals who are all trying to promote their own self-interest, it is clear that there is more to the business of government than delivering a set of express contractual promises. No contract can decide everything in advance, which means that there must always be a delegation of authority. Within the scope of that delegated authority, individuals must be bound by rules and decisions with which they may disagree. The affirmative aspect of democracy is that popular sovereignty is the source of government's authority to create and enforce such obligations.

The state

The phenomenon of rules and decisions that are binding on individuals who disagree with them is not confined to the public sphere. In the business corporation, for example, decisions are made by directors and managers, not by shareholders. But the relationship between government and the governed is different. For most citizens, exit from the jurisdiction of a government is a last and desperate resort, not a response to marginal calculations of shifting advantage like selling shares on a stock exchange. More fundamentally, the institution of government is more than just an agent for defined and limited purposes. The authority delegated to it includes authority to determine the scope of its own authority.[6] Critical democracy suggests that this dynamic aspect of authority should be subject to the most stringent checks, limits, conditions and safeguards. However, even when constrained to the maximum extent possible, the authority to determine its own competence remains the most distinctive aspect of public power and so most in need of legitimation by affirmative democracy.

The relationship between citizens and government must therefore be constituted in a way that can cope with conflicts of interest and opinion. What is more it must be open-ended, both as regards its duration and in terms of the potential scope of public power and the purposes for which it may be used. To make such a relationship viable requires a larger framework of trust and of shared beliefs and assumptions on which that trust is based. That is to say, it requires there to be a political community, with a shared political identity.

In modern Europe, political community and political identity are focused on the state. The states that exist are an arbitrary product of history rather than the result of acts of democratic will. War, marriage and bribery all played a part in their formation. These unpleasant facts are covered up by historical myths that are an important part of what is called 'national identity'. If we found ourselves in the position of negotiating a social contract, we would not necessarily design the states in Europe that we now have. Perhaps we would not design the so-called 'nation state' at all. However, states do exist and they are the principal forums for both the critical and affirmative dimensions of democracy. The importance of the role played by states means that, contingent and contestable as it may be, there exists a strong connection between political identity and national identity. It would be preferable to ground political identity in rational allegiance to constitutional principles. But it must be recognised, without celebrating the fact, that the actual situation is different. Existing political identities, based on states, have a large non-rational component.

The successful democratic European state is, however, relatively new. At the end of the Second World War, most European states looked back on a recent history of abject failure. They had failed to prevent the rise of fascism and most of them had been invaded and defeated militarily at some stage of the war. The success of the state in post-war Europe is in large part due to the success of the European Community in promoting peace and prosperity. Peace and prosperity cannot be guaranteed by any individual state, but only through effective co-operation. For this reason, as Alan Milward has argued, European integration cannot be put into reverse without threatening the 'nation state' itself.[7]

The European Union

So far in its history, the European Union has been based on a contract between its member states. The scope of the contract is confined to specific areas of policy. Many details are laid down in express terms, so as to limit the delegation of authority to EU institutions. National vetoes have been retained over the use of authority that has been delegated. European integration has thus resembled a low-trust business arrangement rather than a political community with which individuals identify. The rhetoric of European integration has been just the opposite. It has appealed to the language of political community. Indeed, until the Maastricht Treaty introduced the concept of the Union, the word 'community' was a fundamental symbol. The central legitimating idea was that the European Community and its institutions are the embryo of a European federal state. An important element of national identity is a mythical past. The point about a myth is not that it is necessarily false, but that the question of its historical truth is irrelevant to its social role in interpreting and legitimating the present. In this sense, Europe has been based on a myth of the future.

The provisions of the Maastricht Treaty—in particular monetary union and a common foreign and security policy—made the idea of a European federal state seem more like a potential reality. At which point, many Europeans took fright. It became clear that there is not a sufficient degree of shared political identity between the peoples of Europe to envisage a federal state as the main framework for democratic politics within the territory of the European Union.

Reversing European integration and moving to a federal state are thus equally unacceptable as solutions to the problem of the democratic deficit. However, the *status quo* is not an option either, for two main reasons. First, the exercise of public power by European institutions in the present can no longer be legitimated effectively by the myth of the future European federal state. On the contrary, efforts to equip the Union with the trappings of statehood may serve to exacerbate conflict, by appearing to compete with states for the primary allegiance of citizens.

The second reason why the *status quo* cannot be maintained is the prospect of further enlargement of the Union. Membership for the Central and Eastern European states cannot be long delayed, because Germany perceives it as a fundamental German national interest. Furthermore, what good reason is there for refusing to admit such states to the Union? To exclude them would be to reproduce the arbitrariness and injustice which characterised the process of state formation in Europe and to run serious risks of provoking instability.

Enlargement will make it necessary for there to be greater delegation of authority to the Union institutions. That is to say, it must become easier to make new rules and decisions and to change old ones. Getting unanimous agreement is becoming unmanageable with a Union of 15. It would clearly be even more difficult with a Union of 25–30 member states. To deal with the problem, it will increasingly be necessary to use majority voting in the Council. This risks making the democratic deficit worse, because the practical influence which national Parliaments could hope to achieve will be diluted. Furthermore, they will no longer have even the theoretical possibility of mandating their ministers to veto certain possible outcomes.

Towards greater democracy?[8]

European integration cannot be safely put into reverse, but there is not enough shared identity amongst European citizens to construct a European state. At the same time, effective co-operation between states increasingly demands willingness to accept decisions that may be opposed by a majority of citizens in any particular state. Where do we go from here? There is a good case for strengthening the role of national Parliaments in making the Council more accountable. However, this is not enough by itself. There must also be more democratic legitimation at the level of the Union institutions themselves. This seems to present an insuperable difficulty. A European state is not possible, because the necessary political identity is lacking. But without a *demos*, there can be no democracy. Seductive as it may appear, this argument is flawed; it fails to distinguish between the critical and affirmative dimensions of democracy.

Affirmative democracy invites the question 'who are "the people"'? Who belongs to the sovereign *demos* and who does not? This rapidly brings discussion to a dead end in the non-rational aspect of political identities based on national identities. In contrast, a focus on critical democracy invites a more constructive constitutional debate. There is broad agreement in Europe about many of the principles of critical democracy. Although there are differences of interpretation, all the Member States of the Union acknowledge the rule of law, the existence of fundamental rights and freedoms and the role of Parliaments in scrutinising and criticising the exercise of public power. Building on that agreement by extending the European dimension of critical democracy is much less threatening to existing national identities than trying to construct affirmative democracy at the European level.[9] This perspective opens up a formidable agenda of reform, with greater transparency at the top of the list.

More transparency in Council decision-making would increase the ability of national Parliaments to call their executive governments to account. At the same time, there must be greater use of majority voting in the Council, which means that national Parliaments lose the possibility of mandating their representatives to veto proposals. This represents a weakening of critical democracy; removal of part of the system of checks and balances to which the Council is subject. From this perspective, it makes sense to strengthen the role of the European Parliament. The so-called 'co-decision' procedure, through which only a small part of Community legislation passes at present, is really a right of veto for the European Parliament.[10] If this procedure became the normal route for legislation, one potential veto power would be replaced by another. There are other aspects of the European Parliament's role in critical democracy that could also usefully be strengthened: for example, the Budgetary Control Committee's scrutiny of the value for money achieved by Community expenditure.

More transparency is also needed elsewhere. In particular, the multi-dimensional role of the Commission presents a structural problem. In some areas, such as mergers and state subsidies, the Commission's regulatory and political roles tend to become confused. Even within the regulatory role, the Commission makes rules, investigates, prosecutes and adjudicates. Hiving-off some of these functions to independent agencies, with clearly defined responsibilities, would make the regulatory process more transparent and enhance accountability.

Greater transparency in decision making may offer encouragement to cross-border interests to develop and participate in the administrative process. Since this would be a bottom up process of self-definition, there is no need to agonise over the 'right' level of aggregation of interests from a top down perspective. At the political level, it would similarly be possible to facilitate the formation of cross-border coalitions by giving each voter two votes in elections to the European Parliament; one for a local constituency and the other in a pan-European proportional ballot. This does not presuppose the existence of a European *demos*. It merely requires a European political identity that is additional, or subsidiary, to national identities. There need be no conflict between such a limited European political identity and national identities provided that individual states can remain the focus of affirmative democracy.

Flexible Integration

For this to be possible, the essential requirement is that the Union institutions should not have the authority to determine the scope of their own authority. The competence of the Union must remain a matter for the member states to determine, through the explicit process for revision of the Union treaties. This process includes the constitutional requirements of ratification that exist in the different member states. Since money and legitimacy are to some extent fungible, member states should continue to determine the overall level of the Community's resources, in a decision which similarly requires constitutional ratification in the member states.

If states are to remain the focus of affirmative democracy, then it must be recognised that they may differ in their preferences about the scope and depth of European integration. An *Europe à la carte*, however, would probably prove unworkable and eventually disintegrate. To avoid this, the Union needs a 'common base'. This would include the basic principles of Union governance, its institutional structure and fundamental commitments such as democratic government, the rule of law and respect for human rights. There would also need to be areas of policy competence that apply to all member states and which should therefore be part of the common base. What policy areas these should be is ultimately a matter for political choice at the level of the member states themselves. However, the natural starting point is the single market, since this has always been fundamental to the economic purpose of the Union. This means that the common base must at least include the rules and policies needed to ensure the free mobility of goods, services, people and capital. It also needs to contain some transfer programmes that are necessary to make the single market politically viable.

Once the contents of the common base are established, its further extension should require the unanimous agreement of all the member states. Until recently, the myth of the future European state has encouraged the belief that it was legitimate to extend the competences of the European institutions through the ordinary process of legislation by the Council, or by judicial interpretation, rather than through Treaty revisions. To protect against such creeping centralisation, the competences included within the common base need to be clearly listed. Such a list cannot be self-applying and there should also be an impartial institution to decide disputes about whether a proposed action falls within the competence of the Union institutions or not. The 'tribunal of competences' could be the existing European Court of Justice, but it might be better to establish a new judicial institution for the purpose. Separate jurisdictions would emphasise that the task of deciding whether a purported competence exists is different from the task of ensuring that a competence has been lawfully exercised.

The idea that states are the focus of affirmative democracy gives rise naturally to the principle that the policy competences of the common base can be extended only with the unanimous consent of the member states, ratified through their own constitutional mechanisms. There is, however, a further implication; sub-groups of member states should be able to pursue further integration between themselves, even if other member states are unwilling to participate. It should be a principle of Union governance that there must be no arbitrary exclusion from such an 'open partnership'. Equally, however, membership would be voluntary. A state could decide not to join a particular partnership without thereby prejudicing its membership of the Union, or of other partnerships to which it might belong.

In some cases, proposals to create open partnerships might cause conflict between member states. To minimise this risk, non-members should have a say in their formation and operation. The internal organisation of open partnerships would be largely a matter for the participating states to determine, but where necessary, the common base must contain rules about the relationship between a partnership and the other members of the Union. Policy outputs (for example, from a foreign policy partnership) would be the responsibility of the members of the partnership and would not be identified with the Union as a whole.

The combination of common base and open partnerships—'flexible integration'[11]—requires a departure from two articles of faith of European integration. The first is that all Member States share a common set of goals. That remains true of the common base, but not necessarily of the open partnerships. The second is that integration is a one-way process; every step taken becomes part of the *acquis communautaire* and must not be reversed. However, an open partnership that was established could, in principle, be dissolved without any implications for the common base or for other partnerships. The conditions under which an individual state might leave a partnership would be determined at the outset and set out in the rules of the partnership.

Flexible integration meets a number of needs. The operation of the common base can involve greater delegation of authority to Union institutions, coupled with an extension of critical democracy at the Union level. The role of states as the primary focus of affirmative democracy is not threatened, because the range of competences included in the common base is clearly delimited and does not give the Union authority to determine its own authority. The open partnerships can accommodate differences in the extent to which majorities in different member states wish to integrate in additional policy areas. Furthermore, open partnerships allow in principle for the reversibility of integration, thus making transfers of authority revocable without calling into question the Union as a whole.

A further advantage of flexible integration is that the Community legal order could be made more transparent and better suited to more effective governance of the common base. The content of a Union Treaty could be limited to the fundamental principles of Union governance, including the general rules for setting up and changing open partnerships and the list of competences in the common base. Most of the substantive policies made in the exercise of these competences could be incorporated in a lower tier of the law. This would have two advantages. First, it would make it easier to amend the substantive policies, whilst offering more constitutional protection against any extension of the competences. Second, the Union constitution would be contained in a document that was much easier to read and understand than the current Treaties.

Within the common base, however, it must be acknowledged that majority voting in the Council allows the wishes of a government in a particular state to be overridden by decisions at Union level. Although there could be compensatory extension of the European Parliament's role in critical democracy, affirmative democracy at national level is restricted by membership of the Union. Some at least of these restrictions, however, are themselves justified by critical democracy. For example, the 'four freedoms' can be understood as individual rights, guaranteed by an economic constitution.

Similarly the institutional arrangements for monetary policy in the third stage of economic and monetary union, in particular the independence of the future European Central Bank are not 'undemocratic', any more than the role of the German Bundesbank is undemocratic. They are best understood in terms of critical democracy. Governments have strong incentives to abandon, privately and for short-term reasons, their publicly pronounced commitments to price stability. The opportunity to punish such a government in subsequent elections is one mechanism of critical democracy, but it is less effective than insulating the objectives and conduct of monetary policy from secret manipulation.

There are, however, two features of the arrangement for the ECB which are problematic. The first is that the mandate to pursue 'price stability' as its primary objective is too vague to make the Bank adequately accountable. It should announce a more specific inflation target. The second problem is that the Bank's independence is constitutionally entrenched *vis-à-vis* the member states. It is one thing to set up arrangements to ensure that governments elected on a promise of low inflation cannot resile from that promise in secret. But what if a majority in a state votes for a government that explicitly promises to retain the power to direct monetary policy to whatever goals it chooses? They may be unwise to do so. However, except in its rights dimension, critical democracy is not about preventing majorities from making choices, but about making sure that government does not subvert those choices.[12] This suggests that monetary union should be organised as an open partnership, rather than as part of the common base. Although there might be a high economic price to pay, it would be possible for a state to leave the monetary union without leaving the Union. Similarly, if the stability of the single currency was threatened by fiscal indiscipline (despite the Treaty mechanisms that exist to prevent this from happening) a state committed to low inflation might decide not to participate in the monetary union.

The distinction between the common base and the open partnerships offers two possibilities for the role of the Commission. The first is that it could be restricted to the task of administering the common base, with an agenda-setting and gate-keeping role only in relation to the competences included in the common base. Alternatively, it could continue to have a broader mandate of promoting further European integration. The natural source of democratic legitimation for such a mandate would be the European Parliament. The Parliament already has power to dismiss the Commission by a two-thirds majority vote. Democratic accountability of the Commission to the Parliament would be enhanced by allowing a 'constructive vote of no confidence', by simple majority. That is to say, the Parliament could sack the Commission provided it could first agree on a replacement.

Can it happen?

These proposals are offered more as a basis for constructive debate about the question of democracy in the European Union than as the blueprint of an answer. Conflict between those who wish to promote further European integration and those who oppose it is real and unavoidable. Power and interests as well as identities are at stake. Such conflicts cannot be wished away. However, we cannot go backward, we cannot stand still and the idea of a European federal state has lost its power to convince. If democratic principles are to play any part in shaping events they have to be detached, in some measure at least, from the concept of the state—whether the 'nation state', or a putative European federal state. I hope the suggestions here at least have the merit of addressing the issue of democracy seriously and putting it in the forefront of concern.

The 1996 Inter-Governmental Conference is clearly not going to embrace explicitly an agenda of reform as radical as flexible integration. However, the medium-term development of the Union may nonetheless move in this direction, since elements of its constitutional structure correspond to the demands of significant political forces. In Germany, for example, the Constitutional Court has emphasised both the need to define and enforce the boundaries of the Union's competences and the fact that the Union institutions have no authority to extend their own competences. Furthermore, the Maastricht opt-outs represent an acknowledgement of the need for greater flexibility in the structure of the Union. According to the Maastricht Treaty, all Member States other than the United Kingdom and Denmark are committed to join the monetary union when it begins, or as soon as they meet the convergence criteria thereafter. However, Germany and Sweden have subsequently claimed the right not to join the monetary union without a further favourable vote by their national Parliaments. Why should new member states be required to sign up for the single currency as a condition of joining the Union?

Finally, the idea of 'variable geometry' has been floated by both French and German politicians, not just as a short-term fix for dealing with an uncooperative Conservative Government in Britain, but as a way of coping with a

Union that consists of a much larger and more heterogeneous set of countries. Unlike the various proposals for variable geometry, flexible integration has the advantage that the Union would be identified not with the scope and depth of integration achieved between a 'hard core' of states, but with the principles of the common base in which all member states participate. This is much less divisive than a Union divided into two or more tiers. At the same time, it shares with variable geometry the advantage of allowing those states that want further integration to proceed without being blocked by those who do not want to participate.

Biographical Note

Ian Harden is Professor of public law and carries out research in the Department of Law and the Political Economy Research Centre of Sheffield University. This article is a revised and expanded version of a British Council Science and Society Lecture, given at the University of Mannheim, Germany, on 6 November 1995.

Notes

1 See especially Articles 155 and 157 of the EC Treaty.
2 Article 1 of the Italian Constitution; Article 3 of the French Constitution; Article 20 (2) of the German *Grundgesetz*.
3 Bruce Ackerman, *We the People*, Vol. 1, London, Belknapp Press, 1991.
4 As Ronald Dworkin put it: 'individuals have a right to equal concern and respect in the design and administration of the political institutions that govern them', *Taking Rights Seriously*, London, Duckworth, 1978, p.180.
5 J. H. Ely, *Democracy and Distrust*, Cambridge, MA, Harvard U.P., 1980.
6 In English, the word 'sovereignty' is sometimes used to express this idea. The German term *Kompetenz-Kompetenz* is more precise.
7 Alan S. Milward, *The European Rescue of the Nation State*, London, Routledge, 1992.
8 This and the following section draw heavily on Dewatripont *et al.*, *Flexible Integration: towards a more effective and democratic Europe*, Monitoring European Integration No. 6, London, CEPR, 1995.
9 It must be recognised, however, that national identity may also play a role in willingness to accept the legitimacy of aspects of critical democracy: see J. Gibson and G. Caldeira, 'The legitimacy of transnational legal institutions: compliance support and the European Court of Justice', *American Journal of Political Science*, 39, 1995, pp. 459–89.
10 Article 189b.
11 Dewatripont *et al.*, *op. cit.*
12 I see no merit in attempts to argue that individuals have either a right to price stability, or a right that governments should pursue policies intended to achieve it.

Three Challenges to Reinventing Democracy

BENJAMIN R. BARBER

IT is in the nature of democracy that it is a process, not an end; an ongoing experiment, not a set of fixed doctrines. Its ideals, unless we repossess them generation to generation, fossilise and become little different from any other ideology. The 'Open Society' is a society without closure, a society open to challenge and criticism. When a nation announces 'the work of democracy is finished!' it is usually democracy that is finished. Under these circumstances, anyone—any nation—wishing to reinvent democracy must proceed with caution. To invent it takes patience and wisdom and depends on conditions that change from one country to another and from one era to another.

It must also be remembered that while democracy is many things—it involves popular sovereignty, accountability, equality, participation, and solidarity—it is not everything. If the term is used too broadly, as Anthony Barnett tends to want to do, it loses not only its specificity but its legitimising utility. If, for example, it also is taken to denote constitutionalism, the rule of law and the preservation of rights (constructs better described under the rubric of liberalism or republicanism or constitutionalism), we can no longer distinguish between such obvious antipodean participatory communitarianism and laissez-faire individualism. If it is defined as proscribing all violence, its own birth in violent revolution is paradoxically barred. Even where the localist character of democracy is touched by universalist ideals, universalism cannot be allowed to become conceptual anarchy, the claim that just about everything we care about politically somehow is part of democracy. That would be to do with democracy what Sir Isaiah Berlin worried was often done with liberty: pretend that it denotes all that we cherish.

These general observations aside, at least three specific challenges that grow out of them face the reform-minded democrat pursuing reinvention: the challenge of indigenous struggle, the challenge of civil society and the challenge of global capitalism. These challenges are nearly connected to three myths: the myth of democratic universalism, the myth of formal institutions, and the myth of 'market democracy'.

The Challenge of Indigenous Struggle

Democracy is never a gift of one people to another, but the hard-won fruit of costly local struggle. It is something to be *taken*, not given. Moreover, while there are universal ideals that undergrid the struggle everywhere, demo-

© The Political Quarterly Publishing Co. Ltd. 1996

cracy's forms are as various as the struggles through which they are won. Great care must thus be taken in importing or exporting institutions or in borrowing from one people's experience to reinvigorate another people's politics. In the years before the American Revolution, Puritan Massachusetts developed one constitutional system, progressive Pennsylvania another and the royal charter plantation-slave colonies still others: American regional institutions are marked by these differences even today.

Democracy grows up indigenously and country to country it is always distinctive. The Swiss celebrate communal rights rather than individual rights, *Gemeindefreiheit* not abstract personhood. Great Britain has no separation of powers though we Americans think such a separation is indispensable to the preservation of liberty; Ethopia's new constitution addresses the problem of tribalism; Poland is a deeply Catholic nation and like Ireland has no separation of church and state. Germany is federalist, while France is unitary and centralist. Given this indisputable diversity among the old democracies, why then should the new democracies not find their own appropriate institutions and democratic identities? Surely they too can afford to look to their own histories and cultures for sources of inspiration. Is there some localist promise to be found in the Russian village *mir*? How about Romanian fraternal organisations? After all, Robert Putnam discovered a linkage between North Italian choral societies and later attitudes towards democracy! Even the old Russian idea of the worker's council—the soviet—in its pre-Bolshevik, plural manifestation may hold some promise. To reject communism need not mean throwing away alternative economic strategies that diverge from capitalism: say Employee Stock Ownership Plans (ESOPs) or consumers cooperatives.

In the ancient world, prudent sceptics used to say 'distrust the Greeks, especially when they come bearing gifts'. New democrats might do well to distrust old democrats, especially when they come bearing the gift of advice, and I include THIS advice as a fit subject for scepticism. The only way the unique American experiment in democracy or the ancient English experience of common law can be borrowed or improved upon is to make sure each reform, each experience with renewal, is equally experimental. Proportional representation may have a role to play in a reinvigorated British politics, but the legacy of single member districts needs to be fully understood.

At the same time, though common ideas and old institutions play a role, there must always be a sense of fresh experiment, what Jefferson called a little revolution every nineteen or twenty years. Convention and history condition and mould a nation's institutions, but they can also freeze hierarchies of power and give hegemony (or simple habit) a legitimacy they do not deserve.

BENJAMIN R. BARBER

The Challenge of Civil Society and the Myth of Formal Constitutions

The belief in the universality of democratic forms rests largely on the myth that democracy is no more than certain formal political arrangements that can be plopped down like a tent more or less on any soil anywhere in the world: the myth that it is a used car to be handed over from generation to generation, an old reliable heap that, with a few new parts, a little accommodation to climate and conditions, can be driven anywhere. History suggests, however, that democracy is not an automotive universal, a blueprint to be followed regardless of conditions. It cannot be imposed top down. It grows bottom up, and anyone hoping to design survivable democratic institutions needs first to understand the landscape and topology on which their structures are to be erected.

A constitution cannot create democracy, democracy creates a constitution. Bills of rights do not create rights, they codify rights already defined, fought for and won. America had one hundred and fifty years of experience with local civic culture and civil liberty and municipal freedom before it codified that experience in a federal constitution. Switzerland's nineteenth century constitutions followed on the heels of 600 years of experimentation with confederalism and communal liberty. Britain still has not written down the evolving principles of constitutional liberty by which it has lived for nearly eight hundred years since Magna Carta; and those who today think to do so need to recall that they are engaged as much in codification as regeneration.

They perhaps need to be reminded of what the Federalists insisted upon in their debate over whether to include a Bill of Rights in the constitution of 1787. What is a bill or rights, after all, but a piece of paper? 'Parchment parapets' said James Madison, paper castles from which no defence of real liberty could possibly be waged. For that reason, Madison thought the American Bill of Rights was a poor idea: the constitution and the experience it codified *was* a bill of rights, he declared. Without citizens there can in any case be no rights and no liberties, and without a civic culture and civic education there can be no citizens. The logic of liberty leads from citizenship to rights, not the other way round. The struggle for citizenship *is* the struggle for rights.

'Democracy,' said John Dewey, 'is not a form of government, but a way of life.' It is a set of engrained attitudes, a culture of independent thinking as well as cooperation, of conflict as well as consensus. Such attitudes constitute the essence of citizenship and need to be taught: democratic culture is an acquired trait, not a natural attribute. We may be born free on paper, but in reality we acquire our liberty through a long and arduous apprenticeship— Tocqueville called it the apprenticeship of liberty.

The old Soviet Union had a quite impressive bill of rights, but without the apprenticeship of liberty there could be no true Soviet citizens, and in their absence the Soviet Constitution was a fraud, empty promises and vacant

146

rhetoric that only exposed the hypocrisy of a tyrannical party leadership. Today Russia has many of the formal institutions of democracy (indeed, it had some during the Soviet era), but the struggle there is to give these institutions a foundation in civil society, to root them in the culture of democracy, in an education in liberty and in a civil religion; what Justice Black once called in America 'constitutional faith' and what Jurgen Habermas has labelled '*Verfassungspatriotismus*' or constitutional patriotism. Cultivating the 'habits of the heart' associated with the democratic way of living takes time. Patience is democracy's foremost virtue, yet in the modern world there is less time, and after long decades of frustration ever less patience.

Cultivating citizenship takes not only time but space. But in this era of big governments and big markets, the geography of civil society has been radically compromised. Privatisation has been the dominant public policy since the Thatcher and Reagan Revolutions. Frustrated 'clients' of government wanting to curb the excesses of elephantine and paternalistic public bureaucracy have turned to a radically solipsistic and nearly anarchic private market sector that does little to satisfy their civic and communitarian longings. In this radical polarising of state and individual, of big government and the little consumer, the middle ground has fallen away. The civil society sector most crucial to democracy is omitted. No wonder voters are outraged at politicians.

Once upon a time, between the oppositional poles of government and market, there was a vital middling choice. Though in eclipse today, the powerful imagery of civil society held the key to America's early democratic energy and civic activism. For it was the great virtue of civil society that it shared with government a sense of publicity and a regard for the general good and the common weal, yet (unlike government) made no claims to exercise a monopoly on legitimate coercion. Rather, it was a voluntary and in this sense 'private' realm devoted to public goods. Civil society remains the domain of church, family and voluntary association; the domain whose middling terms can potentially mediate the state and private sectors and offer women and men a space for activity that is both voluntary and public. It unites the virtues of the private sector, liberty and voluntarism, with the virtues of the public sector, a concern for community and the interests of the commonweal. When the only alternative to government is the private sector, individuals feel compelled to withdraw from community and think of themselves as narcissistic consumers.

There is no task more pressing for leaders who understand how deeply many Europeans and Americans now distrust government than the restoration of civil society: the rehabilitation of a non-governmental civic space that citizens can call their own. Without civil society, suspended between big bureaucratic government they no longer trust and private markets they cannot depend on for moral and civic values, citizens are homeless. A free country depends for its liberties first of all neither on democratic government nor on free markets, but on a vibrant civil society. Alex de Tocqueville celebrated the *local* character of American liberty and thought that democracy could be sustained only through vigorous civic activity in America's municipalities and neighbourhoods. He would scarcely recognise America today, where our alternatives are restricted to government gargantuanism and private greed, and where the main consequence of the recent elections seems to be the supplanting of New Deal arrogance by market triumphalism. How ironic that we in Britain and the United States should be recalled to our own founding vision of civil society by dissidents in Eastern Europe employing the idea to resist totalitarianism. In Havel's Czechoslovakia where it helped transform the nation, and in Fan Lizhi's China where it is being cultivated, civil society has proved itself to be an ideal of civic solidarity that serves as a prelude to democracy it has been clear to those who live under tyranny that freedom has first to be won by citizens establishing their own public space; only afterwards can it be secured by constitutions and law.

Where is Civic Society?

At the time of the American Founding, the so-called Committees of Correspondence played a role comparable to that of Civic Forum in Eastern Europe, creating space for civic action in the face of an unresponsive colonial government. Today government in many Western nations has outgrown and finally usurped the space of civil society and the situation cries out for a reclaiming of civic space.

How could so rich a political idea as civil society drawing sustenance from John Locke, James Madison, Thomas Jefferson and Alexis de Tocqueville succumb to the bipolar politics of government and markets, leaving us with an unhappy choice between bureaucratic welfare-statism on the one hand, and privatistic individualism on the other? This constricting choice leaves the politically alienated public homeless: equally uncomfortable with what it understands to be a rapacious and unsympathetic government which in the United States (and increasingly in Western Europe) it confronts as a foreign body to be cut down to size and curtailed with super-majorities, constitutional amendments and term limits; and a fragmented and self-absorbed (but also globalising) private sector, which can satisfy the public's yearning neither for community nor for civic ideals.

Without a civil society to nourish engaged citizens, politicians turn into 'professionals', out of touch with their constituencies, while citizens are reduced to their whining antagonists or turn into ungrateful clients of government services they readily consume without being willing to pay for. There is much talk on the right about family values, self-reliance and social responsibility, but these virtues are best cultivated in the free space of civil society. Character *can* be a source of renewal, but if anyone thinks commercial markets are likely to have any better success in instilling character than government, they have not spent any time with consumption-obsessed

© The Political Quarterly Publishing Co. Ltd. 1996

shoppers cruising Thursday evening suburban malls in America, England or Germany.

What then exactly is civil society? How might it be reconstituted in a fashion that gives citizens and politicians alike a space in which to act which is neither governmental nor commercial? A civic dwelling place that is neither a capitol building nor a shopping mall? Civil society is no abstraction. The best way to move towards a definition is to think about the actual domains Americans occupy as they go about their daily business when they are engaged neither in politics (voting, jury service, paying taxes) nor in commerce (working, producing, shopping, consuming). Such daily business includes going to church or synagogue, doing volunteer work, participating in a voluntary or civic association, supporting a philanthropy, joining a fraternal organisation, contributing to a charity, assuming responsibility in a P.T.A. or neighbourhood watch or a hospital fund-raising society. When we engage in these activities, we occupy civic space and (whether we know it or not) help define citizenship as membership in civil society rather than just as voting.

What we call things counts. We need to understand our civic engagements, not as private activities, but as non-governmental public activities, and to call the spaces we share for purposes other than shopping or voting 'civil society'. For civic society shares with the private sector the gift of liberty: it is voluntary and is constituted by freely associated individuals and groups; but unlike the private sector, it aims at common ground and consensual (that is, integrative and collaborative) modes of action. Civil society is thus public without being coercive, voluntary without being privatised.

It is in this civil domain that traditional civic institutions such as foundations, schools, churches, public interest groups, voluntary associations, civic groups, and social movements belong. Unions, when they are not devalued and counted as one more species of special interest group, can best be understood as civil society associations. And the media too, where they privilege their public responsibilities over their commercial ambitions, are better understood as part of civil society than of the private sector. Only when the free space that is civil society goes unrecognised are we forced to treat all civic activity as private activity no different from commerce. This is how certain traditional liberal constituencies concerned with the public environment, public safety rules, full employment and other social goods lost their status as public interest entities and seemed to reappear as private sector 'special interest groups' indistinguishable from for-profit corporations and private associations with far narrower interests.

The Nineteenth Century

Throughout the nineteenth century, in Tocqueville's 1830s America and afterwards, our society comprised then not two but three sectors: governmental and private, but also a third arena of civil society. In that era when (as

Tocqueville observed) liberty was local and civic activity more prevalent, a modest governmental sphere and an unassuming private sector were over-shadowed by an extensive civil society tied together by school, church, town and voluntary association. The Federalist Constitution and later the Unionist Republican Party, however expansive they looked by the standards of eighteenth century Whig liberals who deeply distrusted *all* government, were by today's benchmark studies in civic humility. Though opponents feared he would be a kind of monarch, George Washington in fact governed with an executive staff which numbered only in the dozens. And the states and the people to whom the Tenth Amendment of the Bill of Rights had left all powers not expressly delegated to the central government by the constitution were the real theatre for civic action throughout much of the century.

In this simpler time, individuals thought of themselves as citizens and their groups as civil associations. Citizens and associations together comprised civil society. Only after the Civil War did they begin to lose ground to burgeoning capitalist corporations with an appetite for expansion and a tendency to monopoly. As such corporations, legitimised as 'legal persons' and limited liability partnerships, supplanted voluntary associations as the primary actors on the non-governmental side, market forces began to press in and encroach on and crush civil society. With markets expanding radically, government responded with an aggressive campaign on behalf of the public weal, but not one directly involving the public. In taking on the powers it needed to confront the corporations, government inadvertently took its own toll on civil society, encroaching on and crushing it from the state side. Squeezed between the warring sectors of the two expanding monopolies, state and corporate, civil society lost its pre-eminent place in American life. Some time during the era marked by the two Roosevelts, it vanished and its civic denizens were compelled to find sanctuary under the feudal tutelage of either big government (their protectors and social servants) or the private sector, where schools, churches and foundations were forced to assume the identity of corporations and aspire to be no more than special interest groups formed for the particularistic ends of their members.

Hence, paradoxically, groups organised in desperate defence of the public interest found themselves cast as mere exemplars of a plundering private interest association pursuing one more private good. Unions, for example, though concerned with fair compensation, full employment and the dignity of work for all became the private sector counterparts of the corporations. When they tried to break the stranglehold of corporations over labour, they were labelled as another special interest group no better than those against whom they struck, and in time they came to act that way, losing their place in populist mythology as authentic representatives of the people. Something similar happened with the British Union movement in the 1970s and 1980s. Environmental groups have undergone the same redefinition more recently. Although pursuing in theory a genuinely public agenda of clean air for all (i.e., including the polluters), the polarisation of society robs them of the middle ground. In place of civic discourse on behalf of civic goods they are seduced into strident polemics focused as much on their own moral self-righteousness as on the common good. Under such conditions, the 'public good' could not and did not survive as a reasonable ideal.

We are left stranded by this melancholy history in an era where civil society is in eclipse and where citizens have neither home for their civic institutions nor voice with which to speak. They are passively serviced (or passively exploited) by the massive, busy-body, bureaucratic state where the word 'citizen' has no resonance and the only relevant civic act is voting (which less than half the eligible electorate engages in); or they sign on to the selfishness and radical individualism of the private sector, where the word 'citizen' has no resonance and the only relevant activity is consuming (which just about everybody engages in). Be a 'citizen', and vote the public scoundrels out of public office and/or be a consumer and exercise your private rights on behalf of your private interests; those are the only remaining obligations of the much diminished office of American citizen.

The Third Domain

It is against this background that we need to resuscitate the idea of civil society as a mediating third domain between the overgrown governmental and the metastasising private sectors, and thus as a seedbed for the cultivation of citizenship. Critics of big government think that the only way to shrink it is to cede power and privilege to the private sector: devolution of power turns out to mean privatisation. By the same token, critics of an overly privatised market sector believe that the only way to regulate and contain corruptions of the private sector and the market economy is to expand government.

In the past three decades, Democrats and Republicans, Labour and Tories, have drawn their battle lines accordingly. Until at least the time of Clinton and Blair, the former have been pledged to defend government, however alienating and inefficient a tool it has become; the Republicans and the Tories on the other hand remain committed to privatisation, even when it means compromising the very moral and civic ideals to which they have traditionally been committed (family values, religious norms, civic liberty). Locked in a zero-sum game in which the government cannot protect justice without diminishing liberty, and the private sector cannot support freedom without diminishing equality, the parties are confronted with a Hobson's choice, a kind of caricatured Big Brother government which enforces justice but in exchange risks becoming tyrannical, and a caricatured run-away free market which secures liberty but in exchange fosters inequality and social injustice.

Citizens are happy with neither choice. For they sense that democracy is precisely that form of government in which not politicians and bureaucrats but an empowered people use legitimate force to put flesh on the bones of their liberties; and in which liberty carries with it the obligations of social responsibility and citizenship as well as the rights of legal persons. It is that form of government in which rights and responsibilities are two sides of a single civic identity that belongs neither to state bureaucrats nor private consumers but to citizens alone.

Civil society is in fact *the* domain of citizens: a mediating domain between private markets and big government. Interposed between the state and the market, it can contain an obtrusive government without ceding public goods to the private sphere, while at the same time it can dissipate the atmosphere of solitariness and greed which surround markets without suffocating in an overly energetic big government's exhaust fumes. For *both* government *and* the private sector can be humbled a little by a growing civil society that absorbs some of the public aspirations of governments, without casting off its liberal character as a non-coercive association of equals engaged in voluntary activity.

Citizens are sick of the partisans who would make them choose between the equally unpalatable alternatives of a far too filling government stout and a much too vapid market 'lite'. What citizens need and want and have a right to get is neither simply private liberty nor simply state-mandated justice, but civil liberty. Because it depends on equal citizenship, civil liberty is consistent with equality. It represents the liberty earned by citizens engaging in self-government, willing neither to turn over their destinies to government proxies, nor to pretend that commercial markets can produce the social goods and public ideals necessary to democratic community life.

The task today in theory no less than in practice is then to reilluminate public space for a civil society in eclipse. Unless a third way can be found between private markets and coercive government, between anarchistic individualism and dogmatic communitarianism, we seem fated to enter a time where America's public voice is replaced by a raucous babble which leaves the nation's civic soul forever mute.

The Challenge of Global Capitalism and the Myth of Democratic Markets

To listen to politicians and policymakers on both sides of what was once called the Iron Curtain, democracy is but a synonym for the marketplace. This is perhaps the most dangerous, because the most compelling and widely held, myth of our time. The freedom to buy a coke or a video of the Lion King is not yet the freedom to determine how we will live and under what kind of regime. Coke and McDonald's and MTV are in undemocratic Singapore and China as well as in semi-democratic Russia and the democratic Czech Republic. Historically, it is not capitalism which produced democracy, but democracy which produced capitalism. Capitalism *needs* democracy but does not know how to create or sustain it, and frequently produces circumstances that may undermine it.

The myth of the market is our most insidious myth because so many believe it, because the market's invisible shackles are so comfortable, and because its velvet despotism feels so good to those under its sway. 'We only serve the expressed wants and needs of the people,' say the purveyors of modern capitalism, as if there were no feedback loop, no connection between popular needs and wants and the merchandising and advertising budgets which are increasingly the most significant item in corporate budgets.

As manufacturing is internationalised and traditional industrial powers cede dominion to new markets with cheaper labour and lower safety and environmental standards, the industrial sector is itself being transformed. Making and selling goods is still the dominant form of economic activity, but the goods are increasingly defined by symbolic interactions which belong to the service sector in its postmodern virtual manifestations. Hard consumer goods are now associated with soft technologies rooted in information, entertainment and life style, a veritable 'infotainment telesector' in which products are emerging which blur the line between goods and services.

It is no longer clear that postmodern capitalism serves real needs at all. In the ancient capitalist economy, products were manufactured and sold for profit to meet the demand of consumers who made their needs known through the market. In the new postmodern capitalist economy, needs are manufactured to meet the supply of producers who make their products marketable through promotion, spin, packaging and advertising. Whereas the old economy, mirroring hard power, dealt in hard goods aimed at the body, the new economy, mirroring 'soft' power, depends on soft services aimed at the mind and spirit, or at undoing the mind and spirit, I have written about this new post-industrial economy in terms of 'McWorld' elsewhere (in *Jihad versus McWorld*, Times Books, 1995). But the point to make here is that there is nothing about McWorld that automatically entails or supports democracy.

It was easy for East Europeans and Russians to believe that the replacement of communism and its command economy with capitalism and its market economy was all there was to securing democracy. For that made it possible for many to prosper and assume that their prosperity was the same thing as democratic equality and justice. However, as the current political condition of Russia and many of its former republics demonstrates, 'wild' capitalism can exist perfectly well not only without democracy but as democracy's nemesis.

Unregulated or Flexible?

There is today, however, a disastrous confusion between the moderate and mostly well-founded claim that flexibly regulated markets remain the most efficient instruments of economic productivity and wealth accumulation, and the zany, overblown claim that naked, wholly unregulated markets are the sole means by which we can produce and distribute everything we care about, from durable goods to spiritual values, from capital development to social justice, from profitability to sustainable environments, from private wealth to the essential commonweal. This second claim has moved some to insist that goods as diverse and obviously public as education, culture, penology, full employment, social welfare and ecological survival be handed over to the profit sector for arbitration and disposal. To solve problems by the logic of this myth means to privatise more or less everything.

Yet markets are simply not designed to do the things democratic polities do. Markets give us private rather than public modes of discourse, allowing us as consumers to speak via our currencies of consumption to producers of material goods, but preventing us from speaking as citizens to one another about the social consequences of our private market choices. Markets advance individualistic rather than social goals, permitting us to say, one by one, 'I want a pair of running shoes' or, 'I need a new VCR' or 'buy Yen and sell dollars!' but not allowing us to say, in a common voice, 'our inner city community needs new athletic facilities' or 'there is too much violence in the movies' or 'we should rein in the world bank!' Markets preclude 'we' thinking and 'we' action of any kind at all, trusting in the power of aggregated individual choices (the invisible hand) to somehow secure the common good. Consumers speak the elementary rhetoric of 'me'. Citizens invent the common language of 'we'.

Markets are also contractual rather than communitarian, which means they stroke our solitary egos but leave unsatisfied our yearning for community, offering durable goods and fleeting dreams but not a common identity or a collective membership. The disastrous consequences that follow from patterning political reforms on macro-economic theory are patently visible in countries from Russia to Latin America and Africa, where according to Guillermo O'Donnell, a leading Latin American political scientist, 'as the private sphere flourishes . . . the public sphere crumbles'. To him, the matter is simple: privatisation is not democratisation. Period.

So not only do we need, beyond our markets, the virtues of democracy; but our markets need democracy too if they are to survive. Nor can they, by themselves, produce it. They are as likely to undermine as to sustain full employment, environmental safety, public health, social safety nets, education, cultural diversity and real competition. Capitalism depends on such public goods for its private functioning, but it does not and cannot produce them.

Indeed, to the extent that global capitalism is rooted in telecommunications and the power of images, it not only fails to produce but often undermines civic values. The true pedagogy of the post-modern era is plied neither in school or family or church, but in television and films. Can an hour of civics once or twice a week rival the twenty-four hour a day mind-whacking of MTV? Can an election campaign attract as much attention as a prime-time soap opera? How are we to teach peace when films celebrate violence so seductively? What are 25,000 NGOs compared to one Walt Disney Company or a Microsoft Corporation or the global McDonald's network? The lessons of Oliver Stone and Bruce Willis and Arnold Schwarzenegger are not civics

lessons. Nor can they be. The aim of Hollywood is as plain and straightforward as the aim of Madison Avenue: a profit on investment. They are not
selling democracy, they are selling tickets. Which is as it should be, as long as
we do not pretend that films can become our civics teachers.

* * *

These three challenges need to be answered and the myths associated with
them repudiated if democracy is to have a chance in a world where borrowed
formal institutions and global markets cannot by themselves secure democracy, whose quality, I believe, depends on the quality of citizens rather than
the quality of leaders. Fascist and communist regimes—dictatorships—need
great leaders to survive. All they have is their leaders. Democracies need
effective citizens. In Bertolt Brecht's play *Galileo*, one character remarks, 'pity
the country that has no heroes'; another retorts, 'no, pity the country that
needs heroes'. Democracy is government without heroes; ordinary women
and men doing extraordinary things on a regular and continuing basis.

Back in the 1890s, the American populist leader Eugene Debs was addressing a particular grim meeting in a particularly dour era where things had
gone badly for the movement. Voices from the crowd echoed through the
room: 'Save us, lead us out of the darkness!' they implored. Debs replied in a
fashion democrats everywhere would do well to heed: 'I will not lead you out
of the darkness, I cannot. And if I could, I would not. For if I could lead you
out, I could lead you back in again.' Charismatic leaders are problematic in a
democracy. Americans, wrote Garry Wills, get in the most trouble under the
leaders they love best. 'Strong leaders,' said Emile Zapata, 'make a weak
people.'

The work of democracy is *our* work—the mundane tasks of civic education
and community organisation and the establishment of a global civil society. In
the words of the old Negro spiritual, 'we are the ones we've been waiting for'.
Civic space is our space, but it exists today mostly in our imagination,
especially in the international sphere. In reality we have malls and shopping
arcades and voting booths and movie houses and bureaucracies but little real
civic space.

I am not sure what kind of future civil society has in England, America or in
the transitional societies where democracy remains, at best, a fragile promise.
It is easy to be pessimistic, in part because the myths described here are so
widely shared. I do know that without a robust civil society and a will to push
it beyond national boundaries, there will be no citizens, only consumers of
goods and subjects of bureaucratic states. And without citizens, there will be
no democracy.

Liberty, wrote J. J. Rousseau, is a food easy to eat but hard to digest. If we
are not careful, in New York and Washington no less than in Prague and
Moscow, we may produce not free civil associations and democratic societies,
but only an enduring civic indigestion.

Benjamin R. Barber

Biographical Note

Benjamin Barber, Walt Whitman Professor of Political Science at Rutgers University and Director of the Walt Whitman Center for the Culture and Policies of Democracy, is the author most recently of *An Aristocracy of Everyone* and *Jihad Versus McWorld*. He is an advisor to President Bill Clinton.

The Creation of Democracy

ANTHONY BARNETT

Lost in the multitude, the individual can almost never perceive the influence he exercises. Never does his will impress itself upon the whole; nothing confirms in his eyes his own cooperation.[1]

For although 'the people' may influence the actions of their rulers by the threat of dismissal, they never rule themselves in any concrete, practical sense.[2]

A phrase

THE phrase 'Reinventing Democracy' is alluring. It follows the title of Osborne and Gaebler's influential *Reinventing Government*. Like the title of that book it implies a practical rather than an idealist approach, suggesting workable solutions. And it draws on a justifiable sense of dissatisfaction with the current state of 'democracy'. The notion presumes, however, that democracy exists in the way that government undoubtedly does.

Debate about modern government, the dangers of bureaucracy and the best forms of administration date back well over a century. In the face of similar problems concerning the need for literacy, public health and elementary welfare, large scale government developed (was invented if you like) in societies with different political systems—monarchical, parliamentary, republican, authoritarian. Government increased hugely in scale during the world wars and extended its domestic reach after them. Now, in the century's last decade, new methods of dealing with large scale organisation are being applied; 'downsizing', customer responsiveness, privatisation, the introduction of information technology. Osborne and Gaebler described the process as 'mission-driven' customer-oriented, entrepreneurial government designed to replace 'rule-driven' bureaucratic government. Their terms may be fashionable, but they also describe a process that *can* be termed 'reinvention'—the reorganisation of large scale publicly-funded national and local administration that has existed in familiar forms across the world.

Democracy does not exist in this fashion. Indeed, the current dissatisfaction with government, that provides part of the justification claimed for their reforms by Osborne and Gaebler, draws upon resentment at the lack of democracy. Far from being too big, fat, inefficient, oppressive or old, democracy is experienced as inadequate, incomplete, biased, or as a ruse to obtain acquiescence.

Whether the reforms now taking place under the rubric of the reinvention of government will further democracy is a moot point. Osborne and Gaebler argue that,

© The Political Quarterly Publishing Co. Ltd. 1996
Published by Blackwell Publishers, 108 Cowley Road, Oxford OX4 1JF, UK and 238 Main Street, Cambridge, MA 02142, USA   157

Democratic governments exist to serve their citizens. Businesses exist to make profits. And yet it is business that searches obsessively for new ways to please the American people . . . this may be the ultimate indictment of bureaucratic government.[3]

Their explanation is entirely financial. 'Why is it this way? Simple. *Most public agencies don't get their funds from their customers.*' Their answer, therefore, is that government needs to simulate the market. The transformation of government they advocate is double-edged. It may help to give expression to different public demands and citizen satisfaction. It is also an attempt to manage demand and target and control state expenditures from the centre. Dawn Oliver has described the British government's considerable efforts in this direction as an attempt to depoliticise citizenship.[4] William Waldegrave explicitly justifies removing functions from local government so as to 'devolve' institutions in local government 'away from party line'.[5] One should always be on one's guard against politicians denouncing politics (it is a tasty bait but something fishy is taking place). In the case of the United Kingdom the re-invention of *government* is an attempt to shield control of the administration from the new demands of democracy.

A Thesis

Yet the 'reinvention of government' tacks to the wind of demand for better and more responsive government. The strength and freshness of this force, for a better say in public affairs, for more direct and honest responses from the arms of the state, for greater accountability and consultation, suggests that, far from being a barnacled institution like government in need of re-invention, democracy is still a new force.

This is the thesis that I want to explore: that democracy is just beginning. The exploration will be tentative, a probe that takes the form of an initial historical and sociological exercise in definition. I will leave aside the economic aspect, the importance of which can hardly be overestimated.

Broadly, there are four sets of meaning attached to the term democracy (sets because the term describes kinds of society, or possible societies, which do not therefore fit into singular categories). The first is the direct rule of the many. This is a chimera, a spectre, a form often imagined that cannot have stable existence but which haunts all discussion of government like the bad conscience of power. As Aristotle noted in his survey, 'It must not be assumed, as some are fond of saying, that democracy is simply that form of government in which the greater number are sovereign'. Describing different kinds of democracy, Aristotle distinguishes between, 'that in which all the citizens who are under no disqualification share in the government, but still the law is supreme', and 'A . . . form of democracy . . . in which not the law but the multitude, have the supreme power, and supersede the law by their decrees'. And he goes on to say immediately about this form, 'This is a state of affairs brought about by demagogues'. That is to say it turns into tyranny and is not democracy at all. 'For the people becomes a monarch, and is many in one.'

The second set of meanings look back to what might be termed Athenian democracy which *is* law based, in which all citizens have 'the power to take part in the deliberative and judicial administration'. Regulated by their constitution, citizens of such a state participate in direct democracy. When, with the rise of nationalism, the modern debate over democracy begins, the limitations of such direct democracy were strongly debated. Constant found the absence of individual rights and liberty 'revolting', while a generation before him, arguing for the indirect representation of federalism, Madison distinguished between democracy and republicanism,

In a democracy the people meet and exercise the government in person; in a republic they assemble and administer it by their representatives and agents. A democracy, consequently, must be confined to a small spot. A republic may be extended over a large region.[6]

To these early objections to direct democracy we would now add the exclusion of women and the presence of slavery. A community in which all persons participate equally in power may sound wonderful, but it meant smallness, exclusion, no basic rights.

Madison's republicanism also opposed calls for the 'mirror principle' and survived attacks that he was seeking to transfer power 'from the many to the few'. Similarly, John Adams clashed with Tom Paine in an argument vividly described in John Keane's biography of Paine, drawing upon Adams' *Thoughts on Government*. Adams strongly criticised Paine's tendency to pre-serve the monarchic assumption that power ultimately rests in a single, sovereign body. In effect Adams accused Paine of treating the nation or the people as a substitute for the sovereign monarch. In so doing, Paine had overlooked the fact that the people and popular assemblies, like monarchs, are avaricious and fickle, 'products of hasty results and absurd judgments'. The organisation of government, wrote Adams, 'ought to be more complex'.[7]

The creators of representative democracy thus sought to avoid all the dangers of 'King Mob', of the rule of the many, and did so in part by dismissing any calls to reproduce direct democracy as impractical in terms of size as well as inappropriate in terms of individual rights. They were right to feel that what they were doing was quite different sociologically and economically from City-state experiments in Greece.

The third kind of democracy they developed is representative democracy. From its origins this was not a means of indirect reproduction of majority decisions. It was an attempt to secure government *from* any simple majority. This could be done in Burkeian terms, by insisting that the representative had to be answerable to his conscience rather than loyal to his constituents. Or it could be done through institutional measures that entrenched checks and balances, as in the United States. Either way, a new form of democracy was created. Robert Dahl observes that the union of representation and democracy sometimes seemed a marvellous and epochal invention, James Mill calling it 'the grand discovery of modern times' that held out 'the solution of all difficulties'.

Democracy could now be extended to large states and embrace people in unprecedented numbers, people who had no prospect of common or direct decision making. Representative democracy was concerned with excluding 'the people' from direct influence on national power. At the same time it was concerned to ensure that they gave their consent, if not to the extent of their exclusion, then at least to the legitimacy of the government and regarded the state as their own, giving it loyalty and obedience. Representative democracy was a form of anti-democracy, but one recognised and even supported as such, as the franchise grew, by a popular majority. For people can identify with and feel themselves to be represented by those who also exclude them from direct influence.

It seems that we are now witnessing the end of what might be termed the epoch of representative democracy and the beginning of new forms of democracy that are more direct, reflexive or dialogic. For the first time, perhaps, it is possible to imagine modern large-scale societies whose citizens regard democracy as a possibility. Direct democracy in large-scale societies cannot be re-invented, having never existed. Rather, a process is underway that could lead to the actual 'invention' of large-scale democracy. But unlike government, which is a machine for administration, democracy is a relationship. So I prefer to cal it the possible *creation* of democracy.

A Definition

How should we define this fourth kind of democracy? For simplicity and attractiveness it is hard to beat Lincoln's at Gettysberg: government of the people, by the people, for the people. It was formulated, literally, on the decisive battleground of representative democracy yet it suggested something greater, hence its appeal. I want to look at its history and context because it is vital that discussion of how democracy might develop is filled with recognition of the huge effort and human price involved in changing political relationships.

Fourscore and seven years ago our fathers brought forth on this continent, a new nation, conceived in Liberty, and dedicated to the proposition that all men are created equal.

Now we are engaged in a great civil war, testing whether that nation or any nation so conceived and so dedicated, can long endure . . . It is for us the living . . . to be here dedicated to the great task remaining before us . . . that this nation, under God, shall have a new birth of freedom—and that government of the people, by the people, for the people, shall not perish from the earth.

Government of, by and for the people. An aspiration that draws on theory and belief and is fought out in the sometimes terrible battlefields of human interests. The definition is based upon a 'proposition' that all are equal. But it emerges from a nation at war with itself. Coercion is needed to create a space in which men and women can contest for power free from coercion. When you hear the word democracy you should smell the cordite that makes it possible.

Government of the people. This seems clear enough. Who else but the people are governed? *Government by the people.* This too is clear. It does not exist. It is the aspiration of democracy, the inspiring ideal that provides its motive force. It is this, I suggest, which is only now being created. *Government for the people.* Thanks to its simple repetition, *the people* is assumed as a known constant in the Gettysberg address, a typical device of such rhetoric. Yet a strange distance is established by phrases that seem at first to fit so naturally side by side.

Why bother to distinguish *for* the people alongside *by* the people? Not just because to govern *for* them is to do so on behalf of their best interests, which they might not know. When a politician tells us that he or she is doing something 'for the people' one asks 'which people?'. The cynical side of the question suggests that the only 'people' likely to benefit are the politicians and their friends and backers. The healthy side of the scepticism is born of the simple observation that people are divided and have no shared, uniformly common interest. 'The people' is a complex term. It is essential to establish at the outset an important principle in the definition of democracy. It does not mean simple 'majority rule', or government by most of the people. It is not majoritarian dictatorship. It is also, ideally, government for *the* people, for *all* people despite their manifest differences—a description that extends beyond a simple majority. How this may be achieved, if it can, is the question facing the creators of democracy.

Nationalism

Who are the people? Any definition of democracy involves a delineation of the citizenry who enjoy and exercise it. It is not 'Government of any old people, by any lot of people, for whatever people happen to stay around'. *The* people. Rarely do three letters carry such disguised force. It appears to be an inclusive category. But others are not part of 'the people'. It is not an open description but a closed one. *The* people are the nation.

Nationalism is intrinsic to representative democracy, to its birth in the late eighteenth and nineteenth century as an aspiration and to its exercise today. Democratic theory and debate often ignores this, or sidelines the observation. Just as much of the current study of nationalism, its sentiments, origins and drives, ignores the connection between nationalism and democracy, so the sociology of democratic theory striving for ahistorical plausibility puts parentheses around nationalism. Yet it is the mass feeling of shared identity that makes it possible for *a* people to want to choose *their* government. Nationalism lays the basis for democracy. It brings the masses into consciousness of themselves as historic actors, to steal a phrase, without which democracy is inconceivable. The ideals of democracy and nationalism came into existence together, replacing the twin authority of monarchy and religion as publicly defining forces. Nationalism and democracy are twin suns. At first the former shone the greater, and generated 'representative democracy' as the best way to handle the need for consent unleashed by nationalism. Today, as the deference necessary for consent wears away, in part thanks to the role of the mass media, the people are consuming their representatives. Perhaps now democracy may come to shine brighter than nationalism, taming it with international and constitutional norms.

Lincoln Again

All too often democracy is presented as a Hellenistic universal, developed by the Greeks, renewed by the Renaissance and now embraced by all. It is enjoyable, intellectually and imaginatively, to draw upon the debate pioneered in Greece about democracy. Historically, it is not our starting point at all. Democracy is something that we are still approaching; sliding towards, demanding and resisting. I want to emphasise again its recent and vulnerable character, its novelty, especially its relationship to nation-formation. A good illustration is the history of Lincoln's battlefield definition of 1863, which I draw from Gary Will's account.[8]

Lincoln learnt the definition from its repeated use by the polymath, transcendentalist and ardent anti-slavery campaigner, Theodore Parker. Here are two examples from Parker's writings from 1855 and 1856 respectively, both (unlike Lincoln's) explicit definitions of democracy:

- a democracy—a government of all, for all, and by all . . .
- By Democracy, I mean government over all the people, by all the people, and for the sake of all.

Lincoln and Parker shared a common source. The arguments against slavery and for retaining Union emphasised the Declaration of Independence as a more fundamental document to the founding of America than the Constitution. Lincoln's declaration that 'Fourscore and seven years ago our fathers brought forth on this continent, a new nation, conceived in Liberty, and dedicated to the proposition that all men are created equal', was promptly attacked within the North. The Chicago *Times* said that the Constitution makes no reference to equality and tolerates slavery:

It was to uphold this constitution and the Union created by it that our officers and soldiers gave their lives at Gettysberg. How dare he, then, standing on their graves, misstate the cause for which they died, and libel the statesmen who founded the government? They were men possessing too much self-respect to declare that Negroes were their equals, or were entitled to equal privileges.

Lincoln was familiar with this argument. For him, the Declaration—which does emphatically open with a claim to equality—established the norms inadequately developed by the Constitution. He said this about the Declaration:

> I think the authors of that notable instrument intended to include *all* men, but they did not intend to declare all men equal *in all respects*. They did not mean to say all were equal in colour, size, intellect, moral development, or social capacity. They defined, with tolerable distinctness, in what respects they did consider all men created equal— equal in 'certain inalienable rights, among which are life, liberty and the pursuit of happiness.' This they said and this they meant.

Thus, Lincoln, despite his willingness to tolerate slavery in the South, argued that the Declaration was a pledge 'to people of all colours everywhere'.

The argument for the priority of the Declaration also established the legal basis for the priority of the Union against state's rights. Lincoln's guiding interpretation was Webster's *Reply to Hayne*. Lincoln apparently consulted it on key occasions and it had deeply influenced him as he was beginning his career in 1830. Webster declaimed against both slavery and the threat of separation, 'Liberty *and* Union, now and forever, one and inseparable'. He argued that Americans came together to form a Confederation in the first congress, that accordingly the Declaration was made by them jointly. Hence the Constitution was not made by a league of prior existing states. The bond of union *pre-existed* the adoption of the Constitution, an argument Lincoln was to repeat in his Presidential inaugural. For Webster it was the people who, in their Declaration of Independence, had brought America into existence, not the governments of the separate states: 'It is the people's Constitution, the people's government, made for the people, made by the people, and answerable to the people.'

Here we see the form of words that were later picked up by Parker as a definition of democracy, before being echoed by Lincoln. But they are not being used here as a definition of democracy but as a description of the formation of a nation state. It is not government *by the people*, that Webster claims was laid down, but a government *made by the people*, that he wishes to assert. Two quite different things. Many a populist dictatorship could claim with some accuracy that it was 'made by the people'. Webster's purpose was to insist upon the prior existence of the people as a nation, so as to undermine the claim that state governments could secede. A form of words used to describe the creation of the first modern republic, that was hardly a democracy, became the source for the term's boldest definition. We can thus see in the history of its definition the link between democracy, nationalism and state formation; the simultaneous emergence of people, state, and nation, in recognisably contemporary relationships within a market economy.

Representative Democracy

I also want to emphasise Lincoln's definition because of the hope that it holds out. In a tradition that goes back to Marx's early writings, critics on the left have exposed and pilloried bourgeois democracy for its false promise, for its hypocrisy, for its inability to deliver on its fine words. But while speaking in the name of working people much of this tradition is also more naive than working people. They don't believe in words, but nor do they simply believe in deeds. The first is the prerogative of intellectuals and the second the privilege of criminals. Those who toil by their hand and their brain are neither.

The weak are realists and the promise of more influence and representation may be a poor deal but is better than none. They embraced it and their pressure helped to ensure it happened. More than their strikes and demonstrations, however, it was the collaboration of the working classes in war and the confirmation of their patriotism that won them the vote. They pressed for their inclusion but broadly they were not its architects. Representative democracy was created from above. In Europe, too, the hope implicit in Lincoln's words was linked to acceptance of the lesser offer of representative democracy. Yet this was never a finite deal. The gradual widening of the franchise established democracy as something that was being achieved. Direct democracy was absent from its representative incarnation, the individual might never perceive his influence, yet the possibility of its arrival in the future could not be ruled out. It was never a promise, therefore never a false promise, and therefore never accepted in false-consciousness. Perhaps it was a wager. And perhaps now, much to all parties' surprise, the wager is about to come good.

I have noted that representative democracy is the creation of power rather than the achievement of the powerless. Second, that it is not a given, but holds out the possibility of its own improvement as people become literate, more trustworthy, experienced and, also, are able to express effective demand. This internal process, the democratisation of representative democracy, was and is always contested. Both within the elite, as those who express their vested interest are opposed by those who want to further secure popular consent; and amongst those at the 'bottom', between those who want to be included and those who perceive dangers of subordination. One way of understanding the dynamics of this contest at the elite level is to see it as being between liberals and democrats, as described by Norberto Bobbio in a wonderful passage,

Liberalism and democracy differ in the way they understand the relation of the individual to society. Liberalism amputates the individual from the organic body . . . Democracy joins him together once more with others like himself so that society can be built up again from their union, no longer as an organic whole but as an association of free individuals . . . For liberalism, the individual is the author of every kind of action performed outside the confines of the state; for democracy, he is the protagonist of a different kind of state . . . liberalism is concerned with that which is inward-looking, democracy with that which is outward looking.

For Bobbio, both liberalism and democracy contest organicist models of society but the first wants to 'reduce public power to a minimum' while the second 'seeks to reconstitute it'.[9] It is worth emphasising the contest between the two poles, because 'liberal democracy' is currently being debated as a natural unity, for example by Fukuyama. He observes that 'liberalism preceded democracy' in 'the strongest contemporary liberal democracies—for example, those of Britain or the United States' (not the examples I would have chosen). He then describes the way democracy unfolds naturally. The sequence allowed 'liberal democratic practice' to become 'engrained' and then reinforced with patriotism as a preparation for full democracy.[10] This is an implausibly benevolent interpretation, understanding both the achievement of representative democracy and its vulnerability—for in the major powers the central state remains under the influence of those for whom democracy is a problem, not a solution or a way of life.

In addition to the, always dangerous, mobilisation of hope and the internally contested nature of representative democracy, it is also historically novel, as Robert Dahl demonstrated.[11] His carefully defined 'polyarchies', whose seven conditions would lead most people to describe them as full representative democracies with accountable officials, are historically recent, being mostly mid to late twentieth century phenomena. Representative democracy may thus be seen as a form of indirect rule organised primarily from above to integrate the explosive forces of national sentiment and organise consent to a state form that remains centralised. It is a process and it is recent.

Some Achievements of Representative Democracy

As Dahl points out, representation was not invented by democrats but developed instead as a medieval institution of monarchical and aristocratic government. One of the most extraordinary historical achievements of this form of government is the way it has transformed itself. Its elasticity, its capacity for some degree of 'openness', its adaptability to extension of franchise and the democratisation of style and culture, has encouraged the development of consumer capitalism and allowed commercial democracy to be imposed back on ruling institutions.

Within the framework of representative democracy there has been an exponential expansion of education—providing today a possible social base for the beginning of unqualified democracy—and the development of the rule of law in terms of a framework of basic rights and the security of common norms. No one could be complacent about the state of education or of justice in the major democracies. But looked at from a twentieth century perspective the relative achievement in both areas is formidable. Alongside these achievements, representative democracy saw the routinisation of peaceful changes of government. It is striking that, writing in wartime, at the conclusion of his Report, Beveridge thought that the essence of democracy is the effective means of changing the government without shooting.

A similar observation was developed by Popper. What seems to us almost normal was, barely more than a generation ago, still regarded as quite exceptional. It is here, perhaps, that the achievement of the Anglo-Saxon states, both British and American, has been exceptional for world powers. For all the limitation of their democratic character, they witnessed genuine, contested yet peaceful changes of government. This dates back to well before the modern franchise. Which is why the development of 'bourgeois democracy' should not be minimised, as it tends to be if it is just measured in terms of franchise qualifications. I don't want to underestimate the importance of the vote. But it is also important not to see it as the be all and end all—the single measure—of democracy. Millions of the women who gained the vote in the early part of this century did not believe that they were living in a dictatorship beforehand. If it is a fact that public administration is honest and that governments change when they become unpopular, and that, however restricted, the opinions of those who have the franchise are affected by larger currents of public opinion, then those without a vote can still identify strongly with the nation-state and hold it to be far more democratic for them than competing regimes that are monarchies or have few effective representative institutions.

Some Limitations of Representative Democracy

Peaceful change was achieved at home in the UK because Empire was so successfully established overseas, where the non-violent change of government was not on offer to the natives. Representative democracy was the creation of states mobilised for war and expansion thanks to the competitive opportunities of industrialisation. This was not a 'limitation' while military success was the order of the day. But it has become so now, especially in the representative democracies of the United States, Britain and France, that inherited a nuclear reach. The lack of democracy in the inner workings of the 'national security states' that were organised during the Cold War was justified on the grounds that it was needed to defend democracy against those without the scruples of democracy. Today the lifting of external threat has still not been worked through internally. This is especially so for the post-war British State which needed the Cold War more than any other. But these three representative democracies will find peace difficult. Their size, and the experience of their populations, means that pressure will grow on governments to be open, accountable, in short, rule-bound. At the same time the validation of closure on grounds of security becomes increasingly lame.

This internal process is intensified by the development of 'cosmopolitan democracy'. We have suggested that the political elites organised representative democracy through their control of the central state, thus enabling them all the better to mobilise their populations against hostile regimes. Internal democratisation was also patriotic unification in a system of states whose competition was premised on 'non-interference' in each other's internal affairs. The presumption of international sovereignty can be dated back to the 1648 Treaty of Westphalia.[12] One of its effects was that each state reinforced the domestic domination of its competitors. This mutual respect may have been frequently observed in its breach, but it came to a formal end with the Helsinki Agreement of 1977, which established international norms of human rights and legitimised domestic appeal to international authority, undermining the exclusive political authority of the nation state.

Whether federal or centralised, the nation state concentrates authority, and representative democracy is a political form that extends legitimacy while reinforcing its concentration. This is why it is compatible with both republican and monarchical regimes. But as cross-national lines of authority and appeal are established, the political space organised by national representation is punctured. Shared sovereignty means over-lapping forms of authority, hence new possibilities for pluralism and different kinds of democracy, which in turn reinforce perceptions of the hollowness and inadequacy of the exclusively representative norm.

International comparison and internal pluralism lead people to look upon the way they are represented in a broader perspective. The sociologically unrepresentative character of elected personnel becomes more obvious and an object of contention even while it diminishes in degree. Especially important is the representation of women. Hugely lop-sided male predominance is seen as undermining the legitimacy of the ruling assemblies or parliaments. As a result two consequences are now visible that extend much further than arguments over specific incidents of discrimination. First, the debate over the 'politics of presence' is accelerating the reassessment of the limits of representative democracy. The feminisation of politics will mean more than substituting women for half the men who have virtually monopolised the main national assemblies. Women are proportionately more active 'lower down' in local and community politics. Their kind of politics, less adversarial, more problem solving, is advancing in authority and eroding the old tram-lines of public life.[13]

Secondly, as the question of the literally representative (or mirror) character of legislators is posed by the politics of presence, so the politics of selection is brought into question and with it the party system, on the grounds that people are beginning to ask, 'who chooses our choice?'. Originally, the party system both ensured the penetration of representative democracy into the broad population and allowed the excluded classes to penetrate the legislature, thus binding them into loyalty organised from above. The party also become the chief means whereby representatives from the lower classes could enter national political life. But today, the hyper-development of well funded party organisations has led to a paradox fiercely expressed by Ulrich Beck in his 1992 book, *Risk Society*:

Ultimately the monopolisation of the right to democratically constituted decision-making is founded on the contradictory image of a *democratic monarchy*. The rules of democracy are limited to the choice of political representatives and to participation in political programmes. Once in office, it is not only the 'monarch for a term' who develops dictatorial leadership qualities and enforces his decisions in an authoritarian fashion from the top down; the agencies, interest groups and citizen's groups affected by the decisions also forget their rights and become 'democratic subjects' who accept without question the state's claims to dominance. (p. 191)

It seems that we are back to Aristotle's warning. Or rather, representative democracy was created to protect the elites from King Mob and succeeded, with the exception of fascism. But while it stopped the mob from becoming king, it has not rid the exercise of sovereignty of royal form. In Britain especially, that form has been protected with considerable energy. Today, the remaining royal character, the top-down, 'leadercratic' character of representative power as organised by its party system and the timing of the electoral system, is becoming exposed in a culture familiar with different sorts of power outside the party political sphere.

The Undermining of Representative Democracy

In its fully developed form, this part of the argument would be dedicated to examining in detail the structural flaws, weaknesses and inequalities that scar the major societies that call themselves democracies today, but are often engines of domination. Here, we can simply consider some raw aspects of contemporary America. Abstention rates are now approaching 50 per cent in presidential contests, and are well above this in mid-term elections for the legislature. Some communities are so disconnected as to be effectively disenfranchised. A staggering million people languish behind bars. Much of the population is armed and live in a mental state of siege. Meanwhile, $1,058,503,284 was spent in 1992 on the House, Senate, Presidential and primary elections, according to the Federal Election Commission. This does not include the estimated $70 million of personal money spent by Ross Perot. It was the first billion dollar election, with a total expenditure well over that benchmark.[14]

If people vote less as levels of expenditure rise, and if the reason for this is that large numbers of citizens are 'turned off' by the observation that politics is a rich man's game, it surely follows that a function of the expenditure of money is to narrow the size of the active electorate while seeking predominance within what remains. Were we to look back to some earlier 'society than our own and note the massive expenditure of gold, the prevalence of fear, and a voting participation of less than 50 per cent, would we call it 'a democracy' even if it did have a strong culture of rights?

The role of money and media has served to empty the American electoral system of much of its support. There is room for at least three studies here. *First*, on the role of money, especially bankers as policy makers. There is a blatant aspect to this, the negotiation of NAFTA and the Mexican bail-out being two recent examples in the US. Politically, it can stimulate a populist response, which in the States, may be either Democratic or Republican (as in the 1996 campaign with Buchanan). The almost inevitable frustration of such 'protest' through the massive deployment of fear as well as intelligence by the dominant interests, further alienates citizens from active engagement. *Secondly*, on the specific role of media conglomerates—of media-money—that are dependent on licensing, are prejudiced against regulation and have an interest in as wide and as atomised a market as possible. *Thirdly*, on the role of television as a medium transforming the relationships of representative democracy.

This last aspect warrants much more consideration, because it presents itself as one of the means for establishing new democratic forms and has clearly played a role in dissolving the legitimacy of representative rule. Since Alvin Toffler published *Future Shock* in 1970, with its breathless advocacy (or prophecy) of electronic town-hall meetings, it has been easy to emphasise the positive potential of inter-active electronic communication in developing new forms of direct democracy and to contemplate the re-organisation of the media into decentralising forms. The arrival of the inter-net may have enhanced the possibility. Against this Robert Putnam is now publishing research that shows that television is a prime contributor to what he terms the 'disappearance of social capital' from American life. The term was developed in his study of civil traditions in modern Italy, in which he argues that it is the prior existence of networks of social life that determine how effectively democratic institutions succeed and whether a region will put external investment to good use. In his attempt to study the effects of American television, Putnam suggests that heavy television viewing as well as massively diminishing social participation increases distrust and scepticism. If so, television is the first 'religion' to spread disbelief. Cynicism appears to be part of its charisma, as it induces its couch potatoes to believe that they are sentient beings—by convincing them that they know best. Ironically, then, those who are most glued are least persuaded of what they see. A pervasive disenchantment is spread by the medium. It convinces viewers that the scepticism it radiates as part of its edgy entertainment is an acknowledgement of their own good judgment, whereas it reduces them even further into positive passivity. Direct human inter-action is essential for the success of democracy.

Television may be a factor in Trevor Smith's observation of post-election *loss* of legitimacy that has made itself felt since the end of the Cold War. The only exception seems to be Chancellor Kohl, who regained the Chancellorship because of what he achieved with unification rather than what he promised. But from Yeltsin in Russia to Berlusconi in Italy, Major in Britain (at one point the most popular British Prime Minister of all time), Clinton in the United States, and now Chirac in France, plummeting support—plunging through poll records—has followed election victories. This does not prevent them from carrying on in office legally. Nor is the hostility towards them sufficiently strong to inspire young people to take to the streets demanding a revolution. But when the main elected leaders almost everywhere are regarded with sullen contempt, or derision, then we can say the representative democracy everywhere is in disrepute. While each circumstance might seem the response to a peculiarly national problem, the ubiquity of the phenomenon suggests that each collapse is also a national variant of an international crisis of legitimacy in traditional politics everywhere.

Challenging the Legitimacy

I want to discuss two forces that are challenging the legitimacy of representative democracy, the first highly focused and the second more general. Pressure groups are now seen as a danger to the practice of government, by those in government. Michael Portillo, for example, denounced the 'enemy within' in the form of 'pressure groups' responsible for the 'self-doubt and cynicism' that 'gnaws away at the sinews of our institutions and weakens the nation' and that now represents 'one of the greatest threats that have ever confronted the British nation'.[15]

The concern is exaggerated, but its fantastical expression may be evidence that something real has discomforted those used to exercising power behind the scenes of representative democracy. New forms of representation have forced themselves into the political marketplace, as interest groups have organised and then created constituencies of interest that focus their concerns on elected politicians. It is useful to look at this process from the point of view of the citizen. He or she, or even they as a family unit, can consider in what 'portfolio' of public concerns they should invest a given proportion of their incomes in each year. The effectiveness of this compared to voting is very great. The relationship the 'pressure-citizen' has to the pressure group is direct. Effectiveness can be rewarded and sloth punished. Influence can be witnessed. The politics is action oriented and honest. It is a way of claiming priorities and giving expression to life interests that is, in some ways, much more effective than the big stick of party politics and quinquennial voting.

Issue campaigning is not a substitute for voting, because government is needed to balance priorities. But whereas lobbying used to be a privilege of the powerful, it is now also available to the otherwise powerless. Relatively small numbers, a donor base of, say, 50,000, can have a great impact, especially if they can demonstrate much wider public concern through opinion polls. The impact on the environment is evident: it was a world wide campaign that saved the Antarctic from development. An extraordinary achievement of late twentieth century democracy but *not* one achieved by representative democracy.

The second pressure concerns the way that decisions are taken, especially in the more adversarial parliamentary systems. Albert Hirschman has written a characteristically witty and erudite essay on the recurring discovery that conflicts help to secure democratic societies and expressing doubt about calls for 'community spirit'. He suggests,

What is actually required to make progress with the novel problems a society encounters on its road is political entrepreneurship, imagination, patience here, impatience there.[16]

This process, however, needs an openness of mind and a relaxed political culture in which ideas can be argued through. We are beginning to see experiments in deliberative democracy that are introducing these notions to wider audiences. Yet party debate appears to suffer from a narrowing of flexibility. Television creates a heady demand for strong leadership now so exposed it loses face if it changes its views. Yet it must be in the nature of democratic politics that views can be altered as new arguments and new information call for re-assessment. As Hirschman puts it, rather nicely, 'opinions should not be fully formed in advance of the process of deliberation' and he continues,

The traditional strong emphasis of Western culture on the virtue of strong opinions turns out to be curiously wrongheaded. The suspicion arises that this emphasis is rooted in a long aristocratic tradition, and has not been suitably modified by the subsequent, still rather young, democratic age. As is well known, ideological relics of this sort have considerable potential for mischief. (*op. cit.*)

Public disenchantment with electoral democracy may stem in part from a widespread if inarticulate understanding of the limited intelligence deployed by public, democratic debate. Here, it may be that, however television driven, scepticism is justified and voters are ahead of the politicians who are supposed to 'lead' them in opinion forming.

Replacing Representative Democracy

I have selected two examples of what, following Ulrich Beck, could be called the beginning of reflexive democracy. Beck has provided a highly suggestive analysis of what he calls the 'unbinding of politics'. We are seeing, he argues, limits to action within the political system thanks to the advance of rights and other technical and juridical forms of authority, and at the same time we are seeing demand growing for political participation outside the traditional political sphere including, for example, the appointment of judges. 'The political becomes non-political and the non-political political.' The phrase may sound superficial to Anglo-Saxon empiricists, but the evidence for his argument is compelling. 'Business and techno-scientific action acquires a *new political and moral dimension*' as it pushes into a series of uncharted areas— such as the beginning and end of life and the sustainability of the environment. Beck's larger argument is that modern development means that the main problems that humankind now faces are the problems posed by its own decisions. Hence the new role of 'risk'. We are less concerned with growing enough food, or producing enough houses, than with the effect of modern agri-business and the consequence of urbanisation. The new modernity of his 'risk society' is reflexive: our modern past is now the inheritance for our future. Humans have left the cycle of fate and entered a world whose parameters are now man-made.

The party politics of representative democracy was constructed to deal with a non-reflexive epoch. One in which there were ideologies which spelt out how mankind was to deal with the world, and power was needed to organise and ensure ideological supremacy. The combination of manifesto and orga-nisation that finds its roots in medieval religion is reproduced in the party—especially the two-party—forms of representative democracy. This form of politics now seems to be sliding into desuetude.

In an approach developed alongside that of Beck, Tony Giddens argues that 'Democratisation combats power, seeking to turn it into negotiated relationships, whether these be between equals or are relations of differ-ential authority'. Drawing on David Held's assertion that 'The principle of autonomy' is 'at the core of the democratic project',[17] Giddens describes what he calls 'dialogic democracy'. By this he means not the proliferation of rights or the representation of interests, or a focus on the state although it 'refracts' back on the state in important ways, but rather a democracy that emerges from cultural cosmopolitanism and personal autonomy. A dia-logic that leads to both the democratisation of personal life—the negotia-tion of partnerships based on respect and autonomy—and of the indivi-dual's relationship to the world—a world that millions regard as their own in a way that is quite new.

This is an attractive perspective that describes the politicisation of the non-political. Almost by definition it leaves to one side the actual, old political processes that still have a lot of life and toughness in them. Their sustaining beliefs cannot simply be consigned to archaic fundamentalism. Taking a different approach that also has some parallels, in his sustained, pioneering essay on Associative Democracy,[18] Paul Hirst has argued for strong, volun-tary, free communities, providing the means of delivering a decentralised welfare state and regenerating regional economies. In his view the state should withdraw to becoming a 'secondary, but vitally necessary, public power' (providing accountability, transparency and scrutiny) while 'self-governing civil society becomes the primary feature of society'. Like 'civil society' arguments that are growing in influence, these approaches predict a growing future for the institutional organisation and expression of society outside the normal lines of state power.

The striking absence from the scholarly literature of any sustained, credible defence of the existing organisation of politics as a means of confronting and administering the demands of the current world also suggests that we are witnessing an end of an epoch. The hegemony of representative democracy is on the wane. High on consent and sovereignty, low on democracy and decentralisation; monolithic rather than pluralist; a machine for protecting rather than revealing the administration of state power; a product of inter-national war and rivalry rather than co-operative economic contest; the expression of big nationalism now wilting before constitutionism and the autonomous, 'reflexive' individual; perhaps much the best that can be said about representative democracy today is that it is a system within which new forms of democracy are growing. This is not a small achievement. Within its incubus it has given birth to government 'for' the people and the stirrings of government 'by' them. *For* the people because it has allowed the formation of constitutional structures that might protect all from the arbitrary power of a simple majority. *By* them because constitutional democracy and constitutional nationalism that have developed amongst the representative democracies point towards shared sovereignties in which varieties of direct and free associations may be created.

How does the British state look from this perspective? More representative than democratic, the British state has long marshalled the twin aspects of consent and acquiescence. Most legislation and government is accepted by most people with acquiescence. Most people have presumed the probity of the civil service and the general competence of Ministers as a class. Even if policies are wrong, at least they are presumed to be honest and carried out with sufficient support to be regarded as legitimate, while important, contested decisions gained positive support and consent. Today acquiescence has been undermined, not least by government attitudes themselves. First politicians began to regard acquiescence *as* consent, confusing passive acceptance for positive and legitimating endorsement. Since the fag end of Thatcher's premiership, they seem to regard passive resignation at their 'getting away with it' as consent. Thus decisions which remove democracy from local government are justified on the grounds that voters cannot stop it. In a remarkably short period of time the belief in the legitimacy of the system has been eroded.

But it would be another form of short-sightedness to see this process as simply a function of the decline of Britain's narrow, sovereignty-obsessed and absolutist political system. Genuine attempts have been made to modernise the old centralism. If these have made matters worse in terms of democracy and even consent it is not because the system is archaic. On the contrary, the British system has always combined energetic dedication to flexibility and moving with the times, concerned only to retain monopoly of final authority in 'the Crown'. The British state should not be looked on as peculiarly backward, but as a peculiar version of a number of forward looking regimes caught in problems of legitimacy and consent that beset representative democracies everywhere.

Among these problems are:

1. An unprecedented extension of legislation and regulation into areas of life, personal and environmental, commercial and workplace, local and international.
2. A completely new form of access, apparently direct and instantaneous, to the people involved in supreme power via television.

The first means that traditional assumptions of acquiescence are ceasing to be effective because people are more directly touched by government in a reciprocal, rule-based fashion and 'know' more issues than representative government allows for. The second reinforces disenchantment with the presumption behind traditional acquiescence. Together these processes are dissolving the inherited structures of sovereignty internally, which further disables its ability to handle the external dissolution of traditional sovereignty created by international cooperation.

These problems are not going to be resolved through by-passing the state. A distribution of government away from the state and new forms of deliberative and direct democracy are needed. The rise in the number of referendums may be a signal of this. But popular representation will still be required at the national level. Direct and deliberative forms can supplement but not supplant the joint processes of choosing representatives who exercise national power. The nature of the power that they exercise, however, the *way* they represent nations, will alter and this will alter the form of state administration profoundly. Perhaps the heart of this is the *sharing* of sovereignty. State power will need to negotiate, relinquishing much of the power it is used to enjoying. For such negotiations to be trusted, rules of constitutional authority will themselves need negotiating. This may seem close to the familiar trope that the nation state is too small for the big questions and too big for the small, but the likelihood is quite the opposite. For sovereignty to be shared there have to be partners to carry out the sharing. For sovereignty to be negotiated, there must be authorities capable of conducting and policing negotiations. A different kind of nation state is emerging to replace the Westphalian model (dates: 1648 to 1977). In it, consent and acquiescence will be replaced by democracy and consent.

Why do we want democracy? Because it is an adventure. We don't want it in the way that we desire an improved economic life. We want it because we do not want to proceed without it. We want it because we do not want someone else to tell us where to go or how to live or what to think. We want our say in whatever it is that is to come. For better or worse, through good and bad, through illness and health. Democracy is a form of marriage to ourselves. We want to make the choice and not have it arranged, even if, as some evidence suggests, skilfully arranged marriages may on the whole be longer lasting.

Biographical Note

Anthony Barnett is a Senior Fellow of Birkbeck College, London, and Strategy Adviser to Charter 88.

Notes

1 Benjamin Constant, 'The liberty of the Ancients Compared to that of the Moderns', in Biancamaria Fontana (ed.), *Benjamin Constant Political Writings*, Cambridge, C.U.P., 1988, p. 316.
2 Karl Popper, *The Open Society and its Enemies*, London, Routledge, 1945, Vol. 1, p. 125.
3 D. Osborne and T. Gaebler, *Reinventing Government*, Reading, Mass., Addison-Wesley, 1992, pp. 166–67.
4 Dawn Oliver, 'Citizenship in the 1990s', *Politics Review*, Vol. 3, No. 1, 1993.
5 William Waldegrave, *Recruiting to the Little Platoons*, Social Market Foundation, 1994, p. 19.
6 The Federalist papers No. XIV, Isaac Kramnick (ed.), James Madison et al., *The Federalist Papers*, Harmondsworth, Penguin, 1987, p. 141.
7 John Keane, *Tom Paine, a political life*, London, Bloomsbury, 1995, p. 125.
8 Gary Wills, *Lincoln at Gettysberg—the words that remade America*, New York, Simon & Schuster, 1992.
9 Norberto Bobbio, *Liberalism and Democracy*, London, Verso, 1988, pp. 42–4.
10 Francis Fukuyama, *The End of History and the Last Man*, London, Hamish Hamilton, 1992, p. 219.
11 Robert A. Dahl, *Democracy and its Critics*, New Haven, Yale University Press, 1989, pp. 233–40.
12 For a discussion in this context see David Held, *Democracy and the Global Order*, Cambridge, Polity, 1995, pp. 77–80.
13 Anne Phillips, *Engendering Democracy*, Cambridge, Polity, 1993 and *The Politics of Presence*, Oxford, O.U.P., 1995.
14 Martin Walker, *The Guardian*, 9 December 1995.
15 See my, 'The Empire State' in Anthony Barnett (ed.), *Power and the Throne*, London, Vintage, 1994, p. 18.
16 Albert Hirschman, *A propensity to self-subversion*, Cambridge, Mass., 1995, p. 248.
17 David Held, *op. cit.*, p. 146.
18 Paul Hirst, *Associative Democracy, new forms of economic and social governance*, Cambridge, Polity, 1994, p. 26.

Index

accountability 4, 5, 59–60, 125;
   accounting and 3–4; authority
   and 106–7; of European
   Parliament 132–3; of institutions 101–
   2, 109; of public services 22–3; of
   quasi-government 24–34
accounting 3–4, 61–6
acquiescence 173–4
Adams, John 159
advisory quangos 30–1, 36
affirmative democracy 134–5, 137, 140,
   141
Aristotle 158
associationalism 14–15, 87, 113–15, 172
authority 87, 135, 167; and
   accountabilty 106–7

Bains Report, 1972 42
Barings Bank 82
Beck, Ulrich 167–8, 171
Beear, Samuel 12
Benefits Agency 79
Beniger, J. 71–2
Beveridge, William 165
bill of rights 146–7
Blair, Tony 23, 81
Bobbio, N. 102, 164–5
British Broadcasting Corporation
   (BBC) 35
British Telecom (BT) 81
Buhlman, E. 47
bureaucratic monoculture 104–5
Burnham, David 72
Burnheim, John 50

capitalism, 14, 121; global 152–5
CCTA (Government Centre for
   Information Systems) 73, 82
Central Veterinary Laboratory 76
centralisation 2, 104, 129
choice, public services and 111–13
citizen's charter 17
citizens' initiative 53
citizens' juries 18, 50–1

citizenship 146–7, 151, 152, 155
CITU 73–4, 75, 82
civic space 148–52, 155
civil service 3, 70, 74; computerisation of
   70–1, 75
civil society 147–52; democracy and 97–
   114; future of 155
Coase, Ronald 64
collectivism 10, 103, 119, 128
Commission for Local Democracy 46, 54
companies 4, 14, 109; computer 76–7;
   and economic democracy 85, 89, 92–3
compulsory collective consumption 110–
   11
Computer Sciences Corporation 77, 78
computers, government use of 70–83
Conservative governments 2; and local
   government 43; and public services 8,
   108–9
Constant, Benjamin 159
constitutions 125–6, 146–8
contracting out, of information
   technology 76–8, 82
control state 71–2, 73, 80
corporation 88–9, 102
costing 61–2; activity-based 62–3
Council of Ministers 132, 138
councillors, number of 44–5
critical democracy 133–4, 135–6;
   European Union and 137–8, 140, 141
Cronin, Thomas 53
Crosby, Ned 50
Curry, David 43

Dahl, Robert 20, 159, 165
Dean, Joel 64
Debs, Eugene 155
Declaration of Independence 162–3
deliberation 48–9, 51
democracy 127–8; creation of 160–1;
   economic consequences of 121–3;
   meanings of 158–9, 161–2; reduction
   of 107–8
democratic deficit 22, 106, 132–3

© The Political Quarterly Publishing Co. Ltd. 1996
Published by Blackwell Publishers, 108 Cowley Road, Oxford OX4 1JF, UK and 238 Main Street, Cambridge, MA 02142, USA

Denmark 36
Dewey, John 146
dialogic democracy 172
Dienel, Peter 50
direct democracy 48, 71, 106, 159, 160
discounting techniques 63–5
disenchantment, with electoral
    democracy 169, 171, 174
DVOT 78

economic democracy 14–15, 85–95
economic liberalism 121–3, 125–6, 128
Edwards, Ronald 63, 64
elections 3, 22, 134; voters and 123, 127
electoral reform 17
Electronic Data Systems 77, 78, 79, 82
employers, and works councils 92–3
environmental groups 150–1
Ethiopia 145
Etzioni, A. 106
Europe, local government in 41–2
European Central Bank 141
European Commission 133, 138, 142
European Parliament 132–3, 138, 142
European Union 136–7; member states
    and 132, 139–43

Fishkin, James 49, 51
flexible integraiton, into European
    Union 139–43
Fordism 90–1; responses to 91–5
France 145
freedom 105, 108–10; individual 86–9,
    95, 99, 102–3, 105; institutional 102–4,
    105, 107
Freedom of Information Act 32

Gaebler, T. 8, 157–8
Germany 137, 142; works councils in 89,
    95
Giddens, A. 172
globalisation 127–8, 152–4
government 122, 124; citizens and 135,
    151–2; and the people 160–2, 163, 173;
    reinvention of 8, 157–8; use of
    computers in 70–83
Government Centre for Information
    Systems (CCTA) 73, 82

Grove, J. W. 33
guardianship 20–1, 22

Habermas, J. 99, 147
Halsey, A. H. 9
Hayek, F. von 99, 119–20, 126
Helsinki Agreement, 1977 167
Hirschman, Albert 170–1
Hirst, Paul 172
Hogwood, Brian 21, 23
Home Office 71, 80
Horticultural Development Council 29
Housing Corporation 28–9, 36

IBM 78, 80
individual rights 134, 146–7
informatioon, access to 25–7, 28–9, 36
information technology 4, 54;
    government use of 70–83
Inland Revenue 75, 78, 82
institutions, accountability of 101–2, 109
investment appraisal 63–6
Ireland 145

Johnson, H. T. 61

Kaplan, R. S. 61
Keynes, J. M. 125
knowledge 129; limits of 124–5
Kohl, Helmut 169

labour, political economy of 120–1
Labour Party 8–10, 114; and information
    technology 74, 80–1; and local
    government 42–3, 54; and works
    councils 92–3
Leeson, Nick 82
Left: markets and 4, 117, 120; public
    services and 8–10
legitimacy 120, 169, 170–1; of political
    parties 3, 123
liberalism 95, and civil society 98–100,
    101, 102–4; and democracy 11, 164–5;
    economic 121–3, 125–6, 128
Lincoln, Abraham 160, 162–3
Lindblom, Charles 121
local government 16–17, 32–3, 36;
    democracy and 39–55; destruction
    of 2; representative base of 43–7

Maastricht Treaty 137, 142
Mackenzie W. J. M. 33
Madison, James 146, 159
management 3–4, 103–4, 105, 108–9, 114
markets 5, 13, 60, 103, 121; democracy
    and 4, 117–18, 128–30, 152–5; political
    consequences of 118–20
mayors, elections for 46–7
mediation groups 52–3
Mill, James 160
Mill, John Stuart 39
Miller, David 49
Mitchell, W. C. 22
monetary union 141, 142
Montesquieu, Charles de Secondat 104
Montreal City Council 52

nation states 5, 135–6, 167
National Audit Office 73, 75, 82
National Performance Review 80
nationalism 161–3
neighbourhood forums 51–2
Next Steps programme 78–9
NHS performance guide 57

O'Donnell, G. 154
Office of Public Services (OPS) 74, 81
Oliver, Dawn 158
Ombudsman 27
open partnerships 140–2
organisational society 100–5
Osborne, D. 8, 157–8
Oslo 47

Page, E. 47
Paine, Thomas 159
Parker, Theodore 162, 163
Parliament 16, 30
participation, in local government 39–40,
    48–9, 50–5
particular liberties 102–4
performance indicators 3, 57, 59–60, 66
Plant Commission 17, 45
Plato 20
Poland 145
Polanyi, Karl 118–19
political parties 2–3, 123, 127
political reform 10–11, 13, 34
Popper, Karl 165–6

popular sovereignty 117, 120, 133–5
post-liberal society 108–10, 112
power 114, 134–5; of government 126; of
    organisations 100–1
pressure groups 170
Prior Options 78
Private Finance Unit 74
private sector 60, 147; civil society
    and 98–100, 102–3, 151, 152; and
    computerisation of government 76–9;
    and welfare state 110
proportional representation 45–6
public services 8–10, 108–10;
    accountability of 22–3; and new
    welfare state 110–14
Putnam, Robert 169

quangos 20–1, 23; accountability of 24–
    33; reform of 33–7

referendum 18, 134; local 53–4
representative democracy 1, 159–60, 161,
    163–5; achievements of 165–6;
    limitations of 166–7; in local
    government 43–9; undermining
    of 167–71
responsible society 13–16
restaurant guides 57–8
Right 118; democracy and 8, 117
risk society 171–2
Roland, Stanley 64
Rousseau, Jean-Jacques 100–1
Russia 147

Salisbury, Lord 11
Sartori, Giovanni 22
Schumpeter, E. 40
SEMA 77–8
Simmons, R. T. 22
Single Regeneration Budget 43
Smith, Chris 80–1
Smith, Trevor 169
social constitution 105–6
state 5, 103, 135–6; changing character
    of 97–8; civil society and 9, 99, 100–2,
    105–8
statutory instruments 21
Stone, M. 72
Strachey, John 121

Switzerland 48, 53, 145, 146
systems integrators 76–7

technological complexity 75–6
teledemocracy 54
television, role of in loss of
  legitimacy 169
time value of money 63–4, 65
Tocqueville, Alexis de 104, 147–8
trade unions 150; and work councils 94–
  5
Treaty of Westphalia 1648 167
turnout, in local elections 40–1, 43–4, 50

United Kingdom 145, 146, 166, 173–4
United States of America 48, 146, 148;
  citizens' initiative in 53–4;

Constitution 125–6, 162–3; 19th
  century civil society 149–51;
  representative democracy 168–9
user groups 171–8
USSR 146–7

voluntarism 14–15, 147, 149, 172

Waldegrave, William 17, 22–3, 76, 158
Warner, M. 72
Washington, George 150
Weber, Max 70
Webster, Daniel 163
welfare state 10, 111–13
workers, and work councils 93–4
works councils 14, 89, 92–5